"A MASTERPIECE. A powerful study, remarkable both for the scope of Dr. Langer's understanding and the depth of his research." —*The New Republic*

"FASCINATING. Langer outlines Hitler's various manias (wolves, severed heads, pornography), phobias (horses, germs, moonlight, syphilis), and contradictions." —*Newsweek*

"AN ABSORBING, FAR-REACHING BOOK." —*Chicago Tribune Book World*

"FASCINATING READING. Stands the test of time remarkably well." —*Los Angeles Times*

"COMPELLING, FASCINATING, AND UTTERLY READABLE." —*Publishers Weekly*

WALTER C. LANGER, an eminent Cambridge (Mass.) psychiatrist, was asked by Colonel William ("Wild Bill") Donovan, head of the Office of Strategic Services, to compile this secret profile of Hitler as part of the war effort.

The Mind of Adolf Hitler

THE SECRET WARTIME REPORT

BY
WALTER C. LANGER

A MERIDIAN BOOK

NEW AMERICAN LIBRARY

NEW YORK AND SCARBOROUGH, ONTARIO

MERIDIAN TRADEMARK REG. U.S. PAT. OFF. AND FOREIGN COUNTRIES
REG. TRADEMARK—MARCA REGISTRADA
HECHO EN HARRISONBURG, VA., U.S.A.

SIGNET, SIGNET CLASSIC, MENTOR, PLUME, MERIDIAN
and NAL BOOKS are published *in the United States* by
New American Library, 1633 Broadway, New York,
New York 10019, *in Canada* by The New American Library of
Canada Limited, 81 Mack Avenue, Scarborough, Ontario M1L 1M8

First Meridian Printing, April, 1985

1 2 3 4 5 6 7 8 9

PRINTED IN THE UNITED STATES OF AMERICA

CONTENTS

FOREWORD

by *William L. Langer*

In his introduction to this psychological analysis of Adolf
Hitler, my brother Walter gives a vivid account of the unusual progression of events leading up to his involvement
with the Office of Strategic Services and of the circumstances under which his essay was written. These matters
had gradually faded from my memory, and I was therefore
glad to be reminded of them, if only because they brought
into high relief the character of the moving spirit: "Wild"
Bill Donovan. My brother's introduction pays an implicit
tribute to that extraordinary character, but a full appreciation of Walter's role and assignments calls for a more ex-
plicit portrayal of the man who inspired them. Having myself worked closely with Donovan throughout the war
period I can testify to the brilliance of his mind, the range
of his imagination, the independence of his judgment, and
the foresightedness of his thinking.

"Wild Bill" was decidedly an activist: restless, daring,
and utterly fearless. At the same time, he was a man
widely read and traveled, constantly preoccupied by domestic and international issues, and ever groping for new
solutions to old problems. While he was not academic by
nature or training, he had an enormous respect for schol-
arship and was always ready to listen to those who had
specialized knowledge. In my earliest contacts with him,
he frequently expressed impatience with the crude, inane,
and generally immoral propaganda characteristic of the
First World War and expressed the hope that something
better could be devised for the conflict that impended. Under these circumstances my brother's initial letter, written
from a hospital bed, could not have fallen on more recep-
tive ears. Still, I marvel at Donovan's readiness to accept
psychoanalysis as a potential contributor to the solution of
current problems. After all, psychoanalysis did not at that
time enjoy the wide acceptance it has now attained. Dono-

van's initial idea of studying domestic morale by mobilizing the talents of psychoanalysts across the country was, to my mind, a truly bold venture into unexplored territory.

Donovan had an ingrained interest in problems of human motivation and reaction, presumably a reflection of his distinguished career as a lawyer and later as a military leader. In any event, his prime objective was always to learn as much as possible about his adversary, to study his tactics and to evaluate their effectiveness. With his temperament, he undoubtedly chafed under the divergences of opinion among our policy makers concerning Hitler and his relationship to the German people. As an activist, he had but a low tolerance for uncertainty. He never could see why, given our ignorance on this or that point, we could not call in experts from the universities or business and get a professional evaluation on which to base our future course of action. It was this general approach to problems which led him to initiate scholarly research on a large scale, and at the same time to inspire a psychological study of Hitler and his influence on the German people.

I played no part in the preparation of my brother's book and saw it for the first time in printed form. It seemed to me both fascinating and revealing. I was particularly intrigued by my brother's approach, which reflected many discussions I had had with him, especially those after his return from Vienna in 1938. The all but incredible events that were unfolding in Europe left no doubt that the world was threatened by irrational and demonic forces. I more and more came to realize that we historians often indulged in very superficial estimates of men and their motives. In time I became completely converted to the notion that historians should explore and exploit the findings of modern psychology. And, eventually, I became a veritable apostle of the doctrine. At times my brother and I even toyed with the idea of attempting a collaborative study of some historical figure or movement in which psychological insights could be blended with historical data to yield a deeper understanding of its significance. Circumstances never permitted us to carry out this potentially interesting enterprise.

This psychological study of Hitler was a pioneer effort to apply modern psychological findings not to a distant historical figure, but to one who was very much alive and busily engaged in making history. As far as I know, this was the first systematic attempt to deal with a pressing political problem in this way. The final product may have some shortcomings, of which my brother is only too keenly aware. These were inevitable in view of the fragmentary data at his disposal and the wartime difficulties and pressures under which he had to operate. Nevertheless, his effort set the pattern for later investigations of this type. While it is and always has been impossible to psychoanalyze personalities with whom direct and frequent contact is out of the question, it has been demonstrated that a good deal can be done to study their character and make their actions more meaningful by gathering all pertinent data and subjecting them to the dispassionate evaluation of qualified persons who have clinical experience to draw upon.

Within the last decade or two both historians and psychologists have developed a lively interest in joining forces for the solution of specific problems. This has been most notable in the field of biography, where serious students would now hardly embark upon a study without reference to the psychological factors. But impressive work is now being done also in attacking the psychology of historical groups and movements and in analyzing human reactions in times of great stress. It now goes almost without saying that professional, historical, and psychological associations should, at their annual meetings, schedule sessions dealing with this order of problems. Despite the many difficulties, I am convinced that in the years to come notable advances may be expected in historical understanding. Why, after all, should not the psychological aspects of human personalities and problems be taken into account just as religious, economic, or geographical factors have long since been considered? It would be an exaggeration, of course, to suggest that such basic departures stem from the hectic wartime efforts reflected in the present study of Hitler. It must be deeply regretted that government regulations kept this essay secret and so obstructed whatever direct influence it might have had. Yet it can fairly be said that this study retains a long-term significance, that it is, so to speak, a milestone marking new and fruitful directions in historical study.

myccophenolate

— cell sept — 500 my
Tab —

INTRODUCTION

How in the world did a psychoanalyst get mixed up with an outfit like the Office of Strategic Services during wartime? This question has been asked many times over the years. Inasmuch as the circumstances leading up to this involvement were somewhat unusual, it may be of interest to review them briefly, particularly since they may serve to throw some light on the background of the accompanying study. It all started in the latter part of August 1941. Theoretically I was on vacation. In reality I was in the hospital recuperating from a double hernia operation. At that time it was customary to keep the patient in the hospital, immobile, for a period of ten days. I have always hated hospitals and I loathe immobility. To make bad matters worse, the weather in New England was simply superb. Being thoroughly bored, I spent much of my time daydreaming about how nice it would be to be out on the golf course, close to the ocean with its refreshing easterly breeze. In contrast I was in the city, flat on my back, hot and uncomfortable. With each succeeding day my mood blackened.

About the seventh or eighth day of my hospital stay I read in the morning newspaper that a new agency to be known as Coordinator of Information had been created. Colonel William J. Donovan, commonly known as "Wild Bill" as a result of his exploits during World War I, was to be its head. One of the functions of the new agency, in addition to pooling the information gathered by all of our Intelligence Services, was to organize and conduct psychological warfare. It was the psychological warfare part that caught my attention. I had never concerned myself with the problem of psychological warfare, but I had served overseas during World War I and had been far from impressed with our blatant psychological warfare endeavors. Psychological warfare, it seemed to me, should be

13

much more than a constant repetition of fabricated atrocity stories which are designed to prove that the enemy
were all "bad guys" who had to be eliminated so we "good
guys" could live in peace.

Being in a foul mood and having nothing else to do, I
brooded on the problem. The more I thought about the
psychological warfare I had been exposed to during the
previous war, the worse it seemed. There must be better
ways of making use of this potentially powerful weapon, I
thought. But how? I had no answer to this question but
was convinced that, to be effective, a program should be
imaginative, subtle, and daring. Instead of dwelling on superficial aspects, it should seek to exploit the unconscious
and irrational forces which were far more potent. Since
one of the primary functions of psychoanalysis is the exploration of these forces in individual cases, it appeared
logical, to me, that it might be of value in working out an
effective program. I did not know just how this might be
done. Yet I felt that it deserved further investigation.

The unhappy state in which I was living was, I suppose,
largely responsible for my becoming emotionally involved
with the problem. In any event, by the time my wife arrived for her afternoon visit, I had worked myself into
quite an emotional frame of mind. My wife is not a psychologist, and all my ranting about missing the boat when
so much more could be done meant very little to her.
Nevertheless, she listened patiently for a while without
comment. As my tirade continued, however, her tolerance
level became lower. She finally interrupted, saying, "Why
tell me about it? Tell Colonel Donovan!"

This possibility had not occurred to me. I had always
been under the impression that only cranks wrote letters
to government officials expressing their views on any particular subject and I was convinced that such letters were
destined to be filed in a convenient wastepaper basket. In
my state of mind, however, the idea seemed to have some
merit. Not only would it provide me with something to do,
but it might serve as an outlet for the feelings of frustration that had been building up during the previous week.
So, on the spur of the moment, I dictated a letter to Colonel Donovan covering the range of topics I had been mull-
ing over. Then, having disgorged my sentiments on the
subject, I felt that I had done my duty, and the rest was
up to him.

My evaluation of the situation proved to be completely erroneous. Scarcely had I returned to my home and begun to "toddle" when I received a call from Washington informing me that Colonel Donovan was very much interested in my views and inviting me to have breakfast with him a week hence. I was flabbergasted both by the invitation and his interest in what I had written. Taken off guard, I accepted, without stopping to consider my physical condition. When I informed my doctor of what had happened, he insisted that I was in no condition to make the trip and urged a postponement. I was adamant, however. I had inadvertently put myself out on a limb and the least I could do now was to follow through as best I could. With great reluctance, he finally consented to the trip, providing I observed a number of restrictions.

I arrived at the Donovan home at the appointed hour, and, during a delicious breakfast that lasted almost two hours, we discussed many of the points I had raised in my letter. I was pleasantly surprised to find that the colonel was well versed in psychoanalytic theory and much impressed with the possibility of making use of it in a psychological warfare program. This, of course, made it much simpler for me to explain what I had in mind. The discussion, consequently, progressed from generalities to more specific topics and finally to the problem of the morale of our young men. The enthusiasm that preceded our entry into World War I was clearly absent. Across the nation there were more and more rallies and demonstrations condemning the war in general and, more specifically, our possible involvement in it. Many of the sentiments that became so vocal and violent in the late 1960's were smouldering at that time. Why this drastic change in attitude? How would the young men who would be called upon to fight respond if this country was drawn into the war?

"What light could psychoanalysis shed on these pressing problems?" Colonel Donovan asked. "And how would you go about getting it?"

Now I was really on the spot. It is one thing to toy with possibilities, quite another to face up to a concrete problem. After some hesitation, I replied, "I have had several patients, mostly college students, in whom this antiwar attitude was manifest and I am sure that every other analyst in this country has had some experience with cases of this type. Consequently, I would enlist the aid of psychoan-

alysts across the country and try to organize study groups
in the various psychoanalytic centers. Each group could
carry on an independent study by pooling their clinical experiences, discussing their implications, and trying to arrive at a common denominator concerning the psychological factors underlying these attitudes. Each group would
also be asked to venture an opinion concerning the probable response of these young men in case they are called
upon to fight in the war. The findings of the individual
study groups could then be compared to each other in order to determine the degree of agreement across the country."

"That sounds very interesting," replied Colonel Donovan, "but since all of these patients are presumably neurotic, it would throw little light on the psychology of the
normal young men of this age. What we want to know is
how the cross section of young men would react in the
event of a draft."

"I think you will find, Colonel," I answered, "that the
neurotics in any culture at a given time are not different
from the average in kind, but in degree. The cultural pressures have had, for one reason or another, a more telling
effect on them than they have had on the average. If this
is true, the neurotic presents us with a magnified picture
of what is going on in the culture and affords us the opportunity of exploring in detail the underlying factors that
are involved."

"Very good," replied Colonel Donovan. "How soon can
you come to Washington and get the project under way?"

This was a bolt from the blue. In writing the letter I
had only intended to call attention to the possible contributions that psychoanalysis might make to an effective
psychological warfare program. The thought that I might
be called upon to implement them had not occurred to
me. I pointed this out to Colonel Donovan, together with
the fact that I could not come to Washington since I had
a full schedule of patients in Cambridge, Massachusetts, to
whom I had a prime responsibility inasmuch as we were
not at war. However, he was anxious to get the study started, and, after some discussion, I agreed to cut my work
week in Cambridge down to four days and devote the remaining time to organizing and supervising groups designed
to study the problem of morale and any other problems
that might arise. And that is how a psychoanalyst inadver-

tently got mixed up with the Office of Coordinator of Information.

The response of psychoanalysts across the country was admirable. Within a month I was able to set up study groups composed of psychoanalysts who volunteered their time and resources, from all the major centers from coast to coast. I attended the initial meeting of each group and outlined the problem and the proposed mode of procedure. They were free to arrange their own work sessions and attack the problem in whatever way seemed most feasible to them. Periodically, I would meet with each group (either on Saturday afternoon or on Sunday) for a first-hand progress report and direct their future endeavors when necessary. A wealth of significant clinical material was being accumulated and preliminary attempts to digest it were under way when two events interfered with its progress. The first, of course, was the Japanese attack on Pearl Harbor which outraged the country. The response of the young men across the country was such that there was little room for doubt concerning their probable reaction to a draft. Our project, consequently, diminished in importance.

The second event had an even more telling effect. Sometime in 1942 the Office of Coordinator of Information was reorganized into two independent agencies. Colonel Donovan became the head of the newly created Office of Strategic Services, but the problems of domestic morale and overt psychological warfare were no longer in his domain. Since the other agency, the Office of War Information, was not interested in carrying on the project, it was doomed to die in its infancy. It was with deep regret that I witnessed its demise. To me it meant that a golden opportunity to test the value of psychoanalysis in the exploration of the unconscious factors underlying an important social problem had been lost.

Colonel Donovan, however, still had faith in the worth of the psychoanalytic approach. Not long after the creation of the new Office of Strategic Services, he suggested that I set up a Psychoanalytic Field Unit in Cambridge, Massachusetts. This would not only be close to my home, but it could also make full use of the Harvard University Library and draw on the talents of many experienced psychoanalysts. The Unit was to be staffed by fulltime psychoanalytically-oriented assistants, and its function would be the exploration of pertinent problems which could best be carried out away from the hurly-burly atmosphere of wartime Washington. Suitable office space close to the University was found, and an option taken. A number of potential assistants were interviewed, and one was engaged. It looked as though psychoanalysis would have an ideal opportunity to prove its mettle. But it was not to be. Much to my embarrassment, the entire plan miscarried when the Bureau of the Budget refused to finance it on the grounds that two independent psychological units within the same agency were not permissible. So I stayed on as a kind of free-lance psychoanalytic consultant.

It was not long, however, before another opportunity to put psychoanalytic knowledge to a test appeared on the horizon. This test was of quite a different order insofar as it demanded a deep involvement in the psychological mysteries of a single person—namely Adolf Hitler. The accompanying essay is the product of that involvement. Among scholars an undertaking of this type is usually the consummation of a long-standing interest in the individual and a strong desire to comprehend the many facets of his personality. In order to achieve this goal, the scholar frequently devotes years of his life to the task of unearthing all pertinent information, determining its reliability and significance, and painstakingly arranging the evidence to form a well-rounded, meaningful picture of the man as a whole. The end result is usually the publication of a book through which he hopes to share his newly gained understanding with the widest possible audience. If his efforts are crowned with success, he experiences a sense of achievement and is rewarded with a deep feeling of satisfaction.

When working for a government agency, particularly during wartime, one rarely has the opportunity of traveling this primrose path. Assignments are more or less thrust upon an individual, quite apart from his personal preferences or special interests. It was over this more impersonal path that I became enmeshed in the life and legend of Adolf Hitler. This is not to say that I had no interest in the man. On the contrary, I had been studying in Germany and Austria during 1937 and 1938 and was in Vienna at the time of the Anschluss. I had watched Hitler's triumphant entry into the city. I had heard him speak to the multitudes and witnessed their reaction to his words. I had also seen the Nazi machine in action—pogroms, wholesale arrests, regimentation, etc.—and had been exposed to the Nazi propaganda apparatus for a long period of time. As a psychologist, I could not help but be interested in all the things that were happening around me and in the people who were leading this incredible regime. There was not, however, a burning desire to devote years of my life to an exhaustive study of these phenomena. My primary interest carried me in other directions.

It was sometime in the spring of 1943, as nearly as I can now recall, that it happened. I was conferring with General Donovan (who had been promoted in the meantime) about other matters when, seemingly out of nowhere, he asked; "What do you make of Hitler? You were over there and saw him and his outfit operating. You must have some idea about what is going on."

I had to confess that although I had given the subject some serious thought on various occasions, the psychology of Hitler and his hold on the German people were still a complete mystery to me. He assured me that I was not alone in this respect, and I gathered from the subsequent conversation that there was a wide divergence of opinion among our top policy makers concerning Hitler and his relationship to the German people. It was the General's view that we should have something more reliable to guide us than what the German propaganda machine and foreign correspondents were feeding us.

"What we need," the General said, "is a realistic appraisal of the German situation. If Hitler is running the show, what kind of a person is he? What are his ambitions? How does he appear to the German people? What is he like with his associates? What is his background? And most of all, we want to know as much as possible about his psychological make-up—the things that make him tick. In addition, we ought to know what he might do if things begin to go against him. Do you suppose you could come up with something along these lines?"

This was clearly an assignment that could not be taken lightly. To the best of my knowledge no such study had ever been attempted—particularly under the prevailing circumstances. I pointed out that the value of such an undertaking would be highly uncertain since, to a large extent, we would have to glean our information from the literature. The literature, although extensive, was mostly unreliable, and it was difficult, at this time, to know how much pertinent material it would reveal. Furthermore, I pointed out, neither psychological nor psychoanalytic techniques were designed or readily adaptable to such an enterprise. But General Donovan was not one to be deterred by such considerations. "Well, give it a try and see what you can come up with," he said. "Hire what help you need and get it done as soon as possible. Keep it brief and make it readable to the layman." And so I became a psychological bedfellow to Adolf Hitler.

When starting out on a project of this type one rarely has any realistic conception of the magnitude of the task or the length of time it will take to complete it. In the present instance, the study became more exhaustive than the General had originally intended, but in the end—although he chafed at the many delays in receiving it—he was pleased with the result. The delays were unavoidable. Even a preliminary survey of the problem indicated to me that the task would be nothing short of monumental. Hitler, clearly, was more than the crazy paperhanger depicted in popular prints. Up until the age of twenty-five he manifested many of the characteristics that we now associate with the "hippies" of the 1960's. He was shiftless, seemed to lack any sense of identity, appeared to have no real sense of direction or ambition, was content to live in filth and squalor, worked only when he had to and then sporadically, spent most of his time in romantic dreams of being a great artist, was anti-Establishment and vocal on the shortcomings of society, but was short on deeds. Even his war record bears testimony to a certain incompetence. After spending four years in a regiment that had suffered heavy losses, he had never been promoted to a rank above Lance Corporal. Nevertheless, this apparently insignificant and incompetent ne'er-do-well was later able, in the course of a relatively few years, to talk his way into the highest political offices, hoodwink the experienced leaders of the major powers, turn millions of highly civilized people into barbarians, order the extermination of a large segment of the population, build and control the mightiest war machine ever known, and plunge the world into history's most devastating war. How could one, in a short period of time, hope to unravel the psychological mysteries underlying such a transformation?

I suppose that it was this kind of project that General Donovan had in mind when he attempted to set up the Psychoanalytic Field Unit. It would have come in very handy now, when we were confronted with the task of gathering as much background material as possible in a limited period of time. Since no competent assistants were available in Cambridge, I was forced to look for help in New York. Three psychoanalytically-trained research workers were finally found. Their job was to comb the literature on file in the New York Public Library and excerpt or abstract those sections that they believed might be pertinent to our project. In addition to my own reading on the subject, I scoured the United States and Canada in search of persons who had had more than a passing contact with Hitler at some period of his life. A number were found. I personally interviewed each of these individuals at length in the hope that first-hand information significant to our study might be uncovered.

By and large, these interviews proved to be interesting and instructive. They were not of the "question and answer" type. Instead, every attempt was made to keep the atmosphere as informal as possible. I simply told the informant that I had learned that he had known Hitler personally and asked what he could tell me about him. Since many of the informants were confined in American detention camps due to their earlier Nazi affiliations, it was to be expected that they would use the occasion to disavow any sympathy for Hitler or the actions of the Nazi Party. When it became clear to them that I was not there to gather further evidence to justify their incarceration, they were gradually able to talk more freely. The individual was then encouraged to recall specific incidents rather than to dwell on generalities or personal conclusions. When incidents were recalled that held promise, the informant was urged to supply additional details. "What exactly did Hitler say?" "What else did he do on that occasion?" "How did he act?" "What was his attitude?" "Was there anything unusual in his manner?" "Were there other occasions when he behaved in this way?" This type of interview is more time-consuming, but it is usually more fruitful insofar as it tends to minimize the influence of the informant's personal prejudices and convictions. It also reduces the temptation, on the part of the informant, to limit his answers to the things he believes we want to hear. For

the most part the interviews went smoothly and produced
considerable first-hand information that was not generally
available at the time.

Sometimes, however, they resulted in unexpected consequences. For example, when I interviewed Princess von
Hohenlohe in a detention camp far out on a Texas prairie
on a very hot summer day, she not only took the time to
disavow all sympathy for the Nazis but also used the occasion to roundly condemn the FBI and all its agents for the
"unjust" charges brought against her and the degrading
treatment to which she was being subjected. The fact of
the matter was, she claimed, that she had done her utmost
to dissuade Hitler from pursuing his aggressive course because she was convinced that it would ultimately lead to a
war. Having been warned in advance that she had the reputation of being a slippery individual who could not always be trusted, I listened patiently while she ranted, in
the hope that as soon as she got this off her chest we
could get down to the real purpose of my visit. This interview, by the way, was conducted in German with a guard
in attendance. It turned out that I was overly optimistic
and had underrated the capabilities of my informant. She
had placed a price on her information. She would cooperate and tell me everything she knew about Hitler only if I
would promise to help her to get out of the detention
camp. Her plan, in brief, was as follows. She had powerful
connections in Europe through which she could get into
direct contact with Hitler. If General Donovan would arrange her release and place her on the staff of the OSS,
she would act as a go-between in secret negotiations designed to end the war. She would also tell him all she knew
about the Nazi hierarchy, their mode of operation, etc.,
and would cooperate in obtaining any secret information
that he might want. She would cooperate with me now
only on the condition that I would do my utmost to persuade the General to accept her offer. I assured her that I
had no personal influence with General Donovan and that
he was a man who was accustomed to making up his own
mind on such matters. For a time it seemed that I was sty-
mied, but we finally reached a compromise. She agreed to
cooperate on the condition that I personally submit the details of her plan to the General for his consideration. I
agreed, and the interview continued. Upon my return to

Washington I kept my promise. General Donovan was greatly amused but made no comment.

The episode, however, was not yet at an end. When a month or so had passed and no action had been taken to obtain her release, she evidently decided that I had tricked her. As a form of revenge, I suppose, she then reported to the FBI that I had agreed that her arrest had been unjust, that the charges brought against her were all false, and that she was being treated badly. The FBI promptly called me up on the carpet and indignantly demanded to know on what basis I had made these judgments and what was I up to anyway! All I could do was state the nature of my mission and point out that there was a guard in attendance throughout the interview who could attest to the fact that I only listened while she ranted on about her alleged injustices. It turned out that the guard had no knowledge of German!

On another occasion I brought the State Department down on my head. I had learned that Otto Strasser was living in Montreal and, since he had had close contact with Hitler early in his career, I was anxious to interview him. He and his brother Gregor, together with Hitler, were among the founders of the Nazi Party. In the subsequent power struggle, Hitler emerged victorious. Gregor Strasser was murdered, while Otto narrowly escaped and found refuge in Canada. I felt there was much that he could tell me and, being ignorant of international courtesies, I wrote to him directly and arranged an interview. No objections were raised at this time, although it later turned out that all of his mail was being censored by the Canadian authorities. In my innocence I went to Montreal, met Strasser without incident, and enjoyed an interesting interview. Some time later I was severely censured by the State Department. In arranging the interview directly, instead of through official channels, it seems that I had violated a solemn agreement between our State Department and the Canadian authorities. Why somebody had not called my attention to this agreement while I was in the process of arranging the interview was not explained. In any event, my transgression did not result in an international crisis.

Projects of this type always turn out to be much larger and more complicated than one originally anticipates. This one was no exception. A glance at the bibliography will indicate the scope of our research efforts. When a halt was called on further research we had accumulated over eleven hundred single-spaced typewritten pages of excerpted quotations and condensations that appeared to be relevant. This mass of raw material was to serve as the base for our analysis of Hitler and his relationship to the German people. It became known as "The Hitler Source-Book," and the numbers within brackets in the notes section indicate the page on which the original material can be found.

Now came the job of evaluating, digesting, and interpreting this mass of raw material. For this purpose the collaboration of three experienced psychoanalysts was enlisted. The plan was to supply each of the collaborators with a typewritten copy of the material as it was gathered. Each one would work through it independently and form tentative conclusions concerning its reliability, validity, and significance. We would then meet from time to time to compare notes and try to reconcile our differences. These collaborative efforts were to be confined largely to Part V, "Hitler—Psychological Analysis and Reconstruction" and Part VI, "Hitler—His Probable Behavior in the Future." Psychoanalysts were chosen for the difficult task because psychoanalysis, alone, had devised a technique for exploring the deeper regions of the mind and exposing the importance of early experiences and unconscious components as determinants of personality development. It seemed logical to suppose, therefore, that they would be in a position to make the greatest contribution to our attempt to unravel the mysteries of Hitler's psychological make-up.

Many obstacles were to be encountered. The origin of these obstacles can best be demonstrated if we pause for a moment and examine the nature of the psychoanalytic process in its simplest form. Psychoanalysis is, first and foremost, a therapeutic technique. It was originally designed for the purpose of helping individuals who suffered from neurotic or other forms of emotional maladjustment to overcome their difficulties. It is a painstaking and time-consuming process during which the patient, with the help of the analyst, is gradually able to explore the deeper strata of his emotional life. The patient is the sole source of information. He is asked to communicate to the analyst everything that comes to his mind when he suspends all conscious guidance or censorship of his thought processes.

From these "free associations" the analyst is able to make some deductions concerning the unconscious factors which are influencing the patient's current attitudes and behavior. These deductions are then communicated to the patient in the form of interpretations. The objective is to weaken various mechanisms of defense which the patient has unconsciously adopted for the purpose of protecting himself from those feelings, desires, impulses, memories, etc. which he believed, at one time, might endanger his well-being. These interpretations are always tentative, pending additional information which is not yet consciously available to the patient. With the penetration of each successive defense mechanism, however, he is able to recall events further back in his childhood which will eventually throw light on the unsound premises or misconceptions that are the basis of his subsequent adjustments. Gradually the pieces fall into place and the gaps are filled in until, if the analysis is successful, the evolution of his personality becomes clear. This technique of investigating personality structure is, of course, applicable only to living persons who are willing to cooperate in such an undertaking. It has, therefore, no place in the present study.

It is obvious, from this very brief resumé, that the psychoanalyst is accustomed to dealing solely with first-hand information. This information may be fragmentary and incomprehensible at any given time, but at least he can be sure that it is reliable and pertinent to the problem since it originated in the mind of his patient. Furthermore, he has the opportunity of studying the data in detail before arriving at a tentative conclusion concerning its significance. If his conclusion is erroneous or premature, it soon becomes noticeable in the train of thought it arouses in his patient, and he can reevaluate his findings and correct his error in subsequent interpretations. In other words, the psychoanalyst, in the practice of his profession, is working on fairly firm ground which will ultimately lead to a resolution of the problem.

This was not so in this instance. All we could offer the psychoanalyst for his consideration was a mass of raw material that had been gathered from innumerable sources. None of it was first hand, and none was obtained under controlled conditions. Not only was it superficial and fragmentary, but it was static and bore no relationship to the psychic processes of an individual engaged in meeting the exigencies of life at any given moment.

Furthermore, it was almost a foregone conclusion that much of the information would prove to be untrustworthy and irrelevant. This was certainly a far cry from the first-hand data with which a psychoanalyst usually works. There was no firm ground on which to stand and no opportunity to gather additional information which would serve to fill in the gaps that might confirm the validity of our conclusions. This was not a happy situation for the psychoanalyst. The obstacles, at the outset, appeared to be of such magnitude that our ability to make a worthwhile contribution to an understanding of Hitler's psychology was questioned. Since there was no other alternative, we decided to accept the challenge and do the best we could.

The first obstacle to be overcome was that of screening the raw material. How does one screen the wheat from the chaff, fact from fiction, the relevant from the irrelevant, the significant from the insignificant, etc., without a point of reference or orientation? During the forty-five years since Freud had first discovered the psychoanalytic technique of exploration, a considerable number of persons suffering from wide and varied disorders had been psychoanalyzed, and a wealth of clinical findings had been accumulated. From these findings, a theory of personality structure had been developed which sought to explain different character types in terms of early emotional experiences and subsequent cultural influences. This fund of knowledge, together with our own clinical findings, would have to set the guidelines for our screening process. However, in order to do this most effectively, we would have to agree on the fundamental nature of the character structure we proposed to investigate. A survey of the raw material, in conjunction with our knowledge of Hitler's actions as reported in the news, was sufficient to convince us that he was, in all probability, a neurotic psychopath. With this diagnosis as a point of orientation, we were able to evaluate the data in terms of probability. Those fragments that could most easily be fitted into this general clinical category were tentatively regarded as possessing a higher degree of probability—as far as reliability and relevance were concerned—than those which seemed alien to the clinical picture. Each of the collaborators screened the raw material from this point of view, and there was considerable agreement on what was probably pertinent to our study and what was not.

After reading the raw material, one of the collaborators discovered that he was too pressed for time to make the trips to New York to participate in our evaluative meetings. He promised, however, to write down his views and conclusions and submit them for our consideration. Unfortunately, not a word was ever received from him. His only contribution to the study was his agreement with our diagnosis and a verbal affirmation that Hitler's perversion, as reported, was highly probable in the light of his own clinical experience.

We were then confronted with our greatest obstacle. It is one thing to evaluate material in terms of its probable relevance, quite another to evaluate the significance of any particular fragment in terms of the total personality. It is at this point that we become acutely aware of the inadequacy of the information at our disposal. We have many pieces of information which we believe are relevant, but there are so many gaps that it is difficult to tie them together into a meaningful picture. The task was particularly perplexing in the case of Hitler since so little was known about the formative years of his life, and he had gone to great lengths to conceal or distort the little that was known. Under such circumstances, the evaluation of any fragment or group of fragments and their probable influence on his later development becomes a matter of conjecture. This was soon obvious in our group meetings. There was considerable agreement on the interpretation of some of our data, but quite a disparity of opinion concerning the importance or relevance of other information. This disagreement led to lengthy discussions in which the pros and cons of each opinion were examined in detail— particularly in the light of previous clinical findings. These discussions proved invaluable when an attempt was made to put what pieces we had together to form a meaningful picture of the man and his potentialities.

When put into print, this method of screening and evaluating the raw material sounds cumbersome and uncertain, and in the hands of a novice it would probably be so. This is not true with the experienced psychoanalyst. In the course of his daily work he is required to store vast quantities of information pertaining to his respective patients. By some miracle of the mind, information concerning one patient does not get mixed up with that of another. This information, however, does not lie dormant as it would in a filing cabinet. Below the level of consciousness, this material is constantly being worked over in various ways until there is sufficient understanding to warrant an interpretation designed to throw light on some aspect of the patient's problem. At such a time the analyst is able, without effort, to recall all the previously supplied information which lends credence to the validity of his interpretation. In other words, through his training and experience, the analyst has learned to make full use of the psychic processes that take place outside the field of consciousness, and so, while reading the raw material his mind not only screens the information in terms of relevance to his point of orientation, but immediately begins to unconsciously evaluate its significance and relate it to what is already known.

An extraordinary example of the efficacy of this capacity may be of value. Some time after I had completed the Hitler study I was visiting my very good friend, Dr. Jenny Waelder Hall, the noted psychoanalyst, at her home in Bethesda, Maryland. In the course of the conversation, she asked me what I had been able to find out about Hitler's childhood. Without attempting to be orderly I related the material as it came to my mind but omitted any appraisal of its possible significance. She listened intently for awhile and then interrupted me, saying, "Now I know what his perversion is." At first I thought she was joking. She was, however, very serious and insisted that she knew the perversion. To my utter amazement she was right! I asked on what basis she had reached this astonishing conclusion, to which she replied, "It just came to me out of my clinical experience."

Unfortunately Dr. Hall was not among my collaborators, and we were not able to produce such far-reaching insights on so little evidence. This is not to say there was a dearth of potentially significant insights. There were many. The trouble was that we could not check their validity in terms of other known facts, as was possible in her case. It is in this area that the psychoanalyst feels he is standing on very shaky ground. He may have valid insights and formulate hypotheses about various aspects of the personality, but he lacks the corroborative evidence necessary to establish their validity as he does in his daily work. A definitive analysis of an absent person is, consequently, impossible.

The powers-that-be, having little comprehension of the magnitude of the project, were constantly urging that I finish it and turn it in. Assurances that I was doing my best fell on deaf ears. In the late summer of 1943, as nearly as I can now pinpoint it in time, a firm deadline for its termination, whether finished or not, was fixed. The deadline, as I recall it, was little more than a month away, and we were still in the speculative stages. I do not know why it was so important to have the analysis completed on this particular date and, under the circumstances, I did not ask. Perhaps they just wanted to put an end to my suspected procrastination. Since the time was short and our progress as a group was extremely slow, our collaborative efforts had to be abandoned.

Everything was now shifted into high gear. The time for speculation and vacillation was over. With the conjectures and probabilities previously discussed uppermost in my mind, I partitioned the material into sections to meet the requirements set forth in my directives. And the writing began. It ended just one hour before the Federal Express left Boston for Washington on the night before the deadline. Unfortunately, this precluded any possibility of submitting the manuscript to the collaborators for their approval or disapproval. The first draft automatically became the one and only draft. In this way, the study was concluded at the appointed hour.

Looking back on that memorable occasion, I have no recollection of feeling elated at the completion of a major assignment. I do recall that there was a definite feeling of relief at being freed from the constant pressure under which I had been working for eight months. There was also a sense of dissatisfaction with the end result which has stayed with me over the years. There seemed to be so much more that could have been written to tie the strands together and form a more rounded image had I not been restricted by time and the directive to keep it brief and nontechnical. I was also convinced that a revision of the first draft, together with the opportunity to discuss it with my collaborators, would have resulted in a much better product. These, however, are luxuries that had to be sacrificed to meet the exigencies of war. Another luxury that had to be sacrificed in the great rush to meet Donovan's deadline was editorial care. Although I managed to correct some of the errors in the typescript before the printed report was circulated by the OSS to its very select clientele, some errors inevitably got through. In preparing the document for book publication, I have availed myself of the opportunity of rectifying them. These corrections have not altered the substance of the report in any way.

I suppose that every author is curious about the reception his production will receive—How will it sell? Who will the primary readers be? What will the critics say about it? etc. Here, too, I was left with a feeling of frustration. In a hush-hush organization, such as the OSS, in which the left hand rarely knows what the right hand is doing, one is seldom told to whom one's work will be delivered or what use will be made of it. In the present case, General Donovan never said what he planned to do with the analysis. All I know is that he seemed pleased with the final product. From the fact that a very limited number of copies were printed in the OSS and that they were classified "SECRET," I assumed that it was destined for the eyes of the upper echelon of policy makers and others to whom the information might be of value.

How many of those who received a copy actually read it remains a mystery. Recent attempts to obtain information about these matters have been unrewarding since most of the men who held high office during the war are now dead. Inasmuch as there was a wide divergence of opinion concerning Hitler, I like to believe that at least some of our top policy makers gave it more than a passing glance. This belief is reinforced by the fact that one senior diplomat not only read it but remembered it and its author at a later date. This information came to me through an extraordinary coincidence. My older brother William, the historian, was in Washington to attend a reception for Lord Halifax, the British Ambassador to the United States during the war. Upon being introduced to his Lordship, the Ambassador hesitated for a moment, then said: "Langer? Langer? You must be the author of the interesting study of Hitler that I read some time back." This was high praise, and I was flattered.

This event opens new channels for speculation. It seems unlikely that Lord Halifax was on the list of those who received one of the original copies. How then, did it get into his hands? I suppose that under ordinary circumstances the British Ambassador deals primarily with the President and the Secretary of State. Did one or the other of these read the analysis and think it sufficiently important to pass on to the British representative? We have no answer to this question. That somebody found the document of value is evidenced by the fact that shortly after it was submitted I was given the assignment to have it translated into German. This was done, but for whom and for what purpose is still a complete mystery.

I have been asked on a number of occasions what effect this analysis of Hitler had on our subsequent foreign policy or the conduct of the war. It would be very gratifying to me if I could believe that it had any discernible effect on either one. I cannot honestly believe that it did. I am afraid that it came too late. The die had been cast, and the tides of war were gradually turning in our favor. The final outcome would be determined, not at the negotiating table but on the battlefield. I might also point out that this was not its primary objective. The goal we hoped to achieve was the presentation of an unbiased and professional psychological appraisal of Hitler—the man and his relationship to the German people—which might serve as a common basis for decisions in the future. Any impact that it might have, consequently, would be of a subtle nature resulting from a common and more comprehensive understanding of the factors involved.

I have also been asked, "Do you honestly believe that analyses of this kind are worth making?" My answer is a definite yes. The world has become more and more complex with our ever-advancing technology, and revolutions and dictators are becoming more numerous and more dangerous. Too much is at stake to place all of our faith in the personal judgments of individual diplomats or correspondents concerning the nature of the men and their revolutionary movements. This is particularly true in the United States where administrations come and go and many of our top diplomatic posts are entrusted to men without previous experience or training. An objective evaluation of the psychological forces motivating the leaders and their revolutionary movements requires extensive research and expert knowledge.

Our present analysis of Hitler undoubtedly suffers from many shortcomings. Future research may prove it to be erroneous or distorted in many respects. That is to be expected. Nevertheless, had the study been made earlier, under more favorable circumstances, it might have served to provide our policy makers with a single professional evaluation of what was going on in Germany on which they could have based their course of action. With all of its failings, real and imagined, this would have been far better than the broad spectrum of personal judgments—most of which were far wide of the mark—to which they turned for guidance.

I may be naive in diplomatic matters, but I like to believe that if such a study of Hitler had been made years earlier, under less tension, and with more opportunity to gather first-hand information, there might not have been a Munich; a similar study of Stalin might have produced a different Yalta; one of Castro might have prevented the Cuban situation; and one of President Diem might have avoided our deep involvement in Vietnam. Studies of this type cannot solve our international problems. That would be too much to expect. They might, however, help to avoid some of the serious blunders we seemed to have made because we were ignorant of the psychological factors involved and the nature of the leaders with whom we were negotiating. I am not naive enough, however, to believe that even a well-documented study would completely offset the tendency of many policy makers to set their course on the basis of what they want to believe, rather than on what is known.

The existence of this analysis of Hitler has, until very recently, been unknown to scholars and public alike. This was due primarily to the fact that it still carried the "SECRET" classification and, consequently, was not generally available. I assume that the few copies that were distributed during the war were destroyed when hostilities ceased or else are gathering dust in the private libraries of the recipients—just as my own was doing. It is true that over the years a number of my friends and colleagues read it and urged me to publish it in the public interest. I never took this suggestion too seriously since many people feel that they must say something flattering to an author who has loaned them a copy of his book. Moreover, as long as it remained classified there was little that I could do. And so the years have passed. In order that the study might not perish completely I intended to bequeath my personal copy to the Harvard University Library as a curio which some future scholar might find of interest.

Recent events, however, have caused me to view the analysis in a different light. Most important among these was a letter dated March 12, 1969, from a Professor Henderson B. Braddick, of the Department of International Relations at Lehigh University. The letter read, in part:

> Dear Dr. Langer:
>
> As part of my research on international politics prior to the Second World War, I have been trying for years to find if a psychological analysis of Hitler had ever been made for the United States government. Given his extraordinary personality and the general interest in the subject, it seemed logical that a study should have existed. Then, about a month ago, I learned that such a document had been turned over to the National Archives. This is the study you wrote, with the collaboration of three others, for the OSS apparently some time in the first part of 1944. The companion volume of sources was also included.
>
> Seldom have I been so fascinated and impressed. I wonder if there ever has been a psychoanalytic study of the dictator of this depth and based on the sources available to you. It may be unique. The conclusions are absolutely appalling. Certainly this work needs to become known to scholars. Since my own work has been in the areas of politics, law and history, I know that scholars in these fields particularly should become aware of its contents.

I had never thought of the analysis in such a broad context. Since it had been declassified, I investigated its potentialities more fully. An author, in my opinion, is a poor judge of the value of his own work, so I solicited the appraisals of scholars in other fields as well as those of general readers. They were all of the opinion that the study was not without merit, and that it should be published. On the basis of these judgments, I have decided to publish it as an historical document. I trust that other scholars, as well as the reading public, will find it fascinating and impressive.

PART I
卐
HITLER

As He Believes
Himself to Be

AT the time of the reoccupation of the Rhineland in 1936, Hitler made use of an extraordinary figure of speech in describing his own conduct. He said: "I follow my course with the precision and security of a sleepwalker." Even at that time it struck the world as an unusual statement for the undisputed leader of sixty-seven million people to make it the midst of an international crisis. Hitler meant it to be a kind of reassurance for his more wary followers, who questioned the wisdom of his course. It seems, however, that it was a true confession, and had his wary followers only realized its significance and implications they would have had grounds for far greater concern than that aroused by his proposal to reoccupy the Rhineland. For the course of this sleepwalker has carried him over many untraveled roads that finally led him unerringly to a pinnacle of success and power never reached before. And still it lured him on until today he stands on the brink of disaster. He will go down in history as the most worshiped and the most despised man the world has ever known.

Many people have stopped and asked themselves: "Is this man sincere in his undertakings or is he a fraud?" Certainly even a fragmentary knowledge of his past life warrants such a question, particularly since our correspondents have presented us with many conflicting views. At times it seemed almost inconceivable that a man could be sincere and do what Hitler has done in the course of his career. And yet all of his former associates whom we have been able to contact, as well as many of our most capable foreign correspondents, are firmly convinced that Hitler actually does believe in his own greatness. Fuchs reports that Hitler said to Schuschnigg during the Berchtesgaden interviews: "Do you realize that you are in the presence of the greatest German of all time?"

It makes little difference for our own purpose whether

37

he actually spoke these words or not at this particular time, as alleged. In this sentence he has summed up in a very few words an attitude that he has expressed to some of our informants in person. To Rauschning, for example, he once said: "But I do not need your endorsement to convince me of my historical greatness."[1] And to Strasser, who once took the liberty of saying that he was afraid that Hitler was mistaken, he said: "I cannot be mistaken. What I do and say is historical."[2] Many other such personal statements could be given. Oechsner has summed up his attitude in this respect very well in the following words:

> He feels that no one in German history was equipped as he is to bring the Germans to the position of supremacy which all German statesmen have felt they deserved but were unable to achieve.[3]

This attitude is not confined to himself as a statesman. He also believes himself to be the greatest war lord as, for example, when he says to Rauschning:

> I do not play at war. I do not allow the "generals" to give me orders. The war is conducted by *me*. The precise moment to attack will be determined by *me*. There will be only one time that will be truly auspicious, and I will wait for it with inflexible determination. And I will not pass it by. . . .[4]

It seems to be true that he has made a number of contributions to German offensive and defensive tactics and strategy. He believes himself to be an outstanding judge in legal matters and does not blush when he stands before the Reichstag, while speaking to the whole world, and says: "For the last twenty-four hours *I* was the supreme court of the German people."[5]

Then, too, he believes himself to be the greatest of all German architects and spends a great deal of his time in sketching new buildings and planning the remodeling of entire cities. In spite of the fact that he failed to pass the examinations for admission to the Art School, he believes himself to be the only competent judge in this field. A few years ago he appointed a committee of three to act as final judges on all matters of art, but when their verdicts

did not please him he dismissed them and assumed their
duties himself. It makes little difference whether the field
be economics, education, foreign affairs, propaganda,
movies, music, or women's dress. In each and every field
he believes himself to be an unquestioned authority.

He also prides himself on his hardness and brutality.

> I am one of the hardest men Germany has had for
> decades, perhaps for centuries, equipped with the
> greatest authority of any German leader ... but
> above all, I believe in my success. I believe in it
> unconditionally.[6]

This belief in his own power actually borders on a feeling
of omnipotence that he is not reluctant to display.

> Since the events of last year, his faith in his own
> genius, in his instinct, or as one might say, in his star,
> is boundless. Those who surround him are the first to
> admit that he now thinks himself infallible and invin-
> cible. That explains why he can no longer bear either
> criticism or contradiction. To contradict him is in his
> eyes a crime of "lese majeste"; opposition to his
> plans, from whatever side it may come, is a definite
> sacrilege, to which the only reply is an immediate and
> striking display of his omnipotence.[7]

Another diplomat reports a similar impression:

> When I first met him, his logic and sense of reali-
> ties had impressed me, but as time went on he
> appeared to me to become more and more un-
> reasonable and more and more convinced of his
> own infallibility and greatness ...[8]

There seems, therefore, to be little room for doubt concerning Hitler's firm belief in his own greatness. We must
now inquire into the sources of this belief. Almost all writers have attributed Hitler's confidence to the fact that he
is a great believer in astrology and that he is constantly in
touch with astrologers who advise him concerning his
coarse of action. This is almost certainly untrue. All of
our informants who have known Hitler rather intimately
discard the idea as absurd. They all agree that nothing is

more foreign to Hitler's personality than to seek help from outside sources of this type. The informant of the Dutch Legation holds a similar view. He says: "Not only has the Fuehrer never had his horoscope cast, but he is in principle against horoscopes because he feels he might be unconsciously influenced by them."[9] It is also indicative that Hitler, some time before the war, forbade the practice of fortunetelling and star-reading in Germany.

It is true that it looks as though Hitler might be acting under some guidance of this sort that gives him the feeling and conviction of his own infallibility. These stories probably originated in the very early days of the Party. According to Strasser, during the early 1920's Hitler took regular lessons in speaking and in mass psychology from a man named Hanussen, who was also a practicing astrologer and fortuneteller. He was an extremely clever individual who taught Hitler a great deal concerning the importance of staging meetings to obtain the greatest dramatic effect. As far as can be learned, he never had any particular interest in the movement or any say on what course it should follow. It is possible that Hanussen had some contact with a group of astrologers, referred to by von Wiegand, who were very active in Munich at this time. Through Hanussen Hitler, too, may have come in contact with this group, for von Wiegand writes:

> When I first knew Adolf Hitler in Munich, in 1921 and 1922, he was in touch with a circle that believed firmly in the portents of the stars. There was much whispering of the coming of "another Charlemagne and a new Reich." How far Hitler believed in these astrological forecasts and prophecies in those days I never could get out of Der Fuehrer. He neither denied nor affirmed belief. He was not averse, however, to making use of the forecasts to advance popular faith in himself and his then young and struggling movement.

It is quite possible that from these beginnings the myth of his associations with astrologers has grown.

Although Hitler has done considerable reading in a variety of fields of study, he does not in any way attribute his infallibility or omniscience to any intellectual endeavor on his part. On the contrary, he frowns on such sources when it comes to guiding the destiny of nations. His opinion of the intellect is, in fact, extremely low, for in various places he makes such statements as the following:

> Of secondary importance is the training of mental abilities.

> Overeducated people, stuffed with knowledge and intellect, but bare of any sound instincts.

> These impudent rascals (intellectuals) who always know everything better than anybody else. . . .

> The intellect has grown autocratic, and has become a disease of life.

Hitler's guide is something different entirely. It seems certain that Hitler believes that he has been sent to Germany by Providence and that he has a particular mission to perform. He is probably not clear on the scope of this mission beyond the fact that he has been chosen to redeem the German people and reshape Europe. Just how this is to be accomplished is also rather vague in his mind, but this does not concern him greatly because an "inner voice" communicates to him the steps he is to take. This is the guide that leads him on his course with the precision and security of a sleepwalker.

> I carry out the commands that Providence has laid upon me.[10]

> No power on earth can shake the German Reich now, Divine Providence has willed it that I carry through the fulfillment of the Germanic task.[11]

> But if the voice speaks, then I know the time has come to act.[12]

It is this firm conviction that he has a mission and is under the guidance and protection of Providence that is responsible in large part for the contagious effect he has had on the German people.

Many people believe that this feeling of destiny and mission have come to Hitler through his successes. This is probably false. Later in our study (Part V) we will try to show that Hitler has had this feeling for a great many years although it may not have become a conscious conviction until much later. In any case it was forcing its way into consciousness during the last war and has played a dominant role in his actions ever since. Mend (one of his comrades), for example, reports: "In this connection a strange prophecy comes to mind: Just before Christmas (1915) he commented that we would at sometime hear a lot from him. We had only to wait until his time had come."[13] Then, too, Hitler has reported several incidents during the war that proved to him that he was under Divine protection. The most startling of these is the following:

> I was eating my dinner in a trench with several comrades. Suddenly a voice seemed to be saying to me, "Get up and go over there." It was so clear and insistent that I obeyed automatically, as if it had been a military order. I rose at once to my feet and walked twenty yards along the trench carrying my dinner in its tin can with me. Then I sat down to go on eating, my mind being once more at rest. Hardly had I done so when a flash and deafening report came from the part of the trench I had just left. A stray shell had burst over the group in which I had been sitting, and every member of it was killed.[14]

Then, also, there was the vision he had while in hospital at Pasewalk suffering from blindness allegedly caused by gas. "When I was confined to bed, the idea came to me that I would liberate Germany, that I would make it great. I knew immediately that it would be realized."[15]

These experiences must later have fit in beautifully with the views of the Munich astrologers, and it is possible that, underneath, Hitler felt that if there was any truth in their predictions they probably referred to him. But in those days he did not mention any connection between them or dwell on the Divine guidance he believed he possessed. Perhaps he felt that such claims at the beginning of the movement might hinder rather than help it. However, as von Wiegand has pointed out, he was not averse to making use of the forecasts to advance his own ends. At that time he was content with the role of a "drummer" who was heralding the coming of the real savior. Even then, however, the role of drummer was not as innocent or as insignificant in Hitler's mind as might be supposed. This was brought out in his testimony during the trial following the unsuccessful Beer Hall Putsch of 1923. At that time he said:

> You may as well accept the conviction that I do not regard a ministerial position as worth striving for. I do not consider it worthwhile for a great man to want his name in history only by becoming a minister. From the very first day I had a thousand times more in mind: I wanted to be the annihilator of Marxism. I shall solve the task, and when I solve it, then to me the ministerial title would be a trivial matter. The first time when I stood in front of Richard Wagner's tomb my heart was filled with pride. Here rests a man who ruled out an inscription such as: Here rests Privy Councillor Chief Conductor, His Excellency Baron Richard von Wagner. I was proud that this man, and so many men in German history, were satisfied to leave their name to posterity, not their title. It was not modesty that made me want to be the "drummer." *That* is of utmost importance, the rest is a bagatelle.[16]

After his stay in Landsberg Hitler no longer referred to himself as the "drummer." Occasionally he would describe himself in the words of St. Matthew, "as a voice crying in the wilderness," or as St. John the Baptist, whose duty was to hew a path for him who was to come and lead the nation to power and glory. More frequently, however, he referred to himself as "the Fuehrer," a name chosen by Hess during their imprisonment.[17]

As time went on, it became clearer that he was thinking of himself as the Messiah and that it was he who was destined to lead Germany to glory. His references to the Bible became more frequent, and the movement began to take on a religious atmosphere. Comparisons between Christ and himself became more numerous and found their way into his conversation and speeches. For example, he would say:

When I came to Berlin a few weeks ago and looked at the traffic in the Kurfuerstendamm, the luxury, the perversion, the iniquity, the wanton display, and the Jewish materialism disgusted me so thoroughly, that I was almost beside myself. I nearly imagined myself to be Jesus Christ when He came to His Father's temple and found it taken by the money-changers. I can well imagine how He felt when He seized a whip and scourged them out.[18]

During this speech, according to Hanfstaengl, he swung his whip around violently as though to drive out the Jews and the forces of darkness, the enemies of Germany and German honor. Dietrich Eckart, who discovered Hitler as a possible leader and had witnessed this performance, said later, "When a man gets to the point of identifying himself with Jesus Christ, then he is ripe for an insane asylum." The identification in all this was not with Jesus Christ, the Crucified, but with Jesus Christ, the furious, lashing the crowds.

As a matter of fact, Hitler has very little admiration for Christ, the Crucified. Although he was brought up a Catholic and received Communion during the war, he severed his connection with the Church directly afterward. This kind of Christ he considers soft and weak and unsuitable as a German Messiah. The latter must be hard and brutal if he is to save Germany and lead it to its destiny.

My feeling as a Christian points me to my Lord and Saviour as a fighter. It points me to the man who once in loneliness, surrounded by only a few followers, recognized these Jews for what they were and summoned men to fight against them and who, God's truth! was greatest not as a sufferer but as a fighter. In boundless love, as a Christian and as a man, I read through the passage which tells us how the Lord rose at last in His might and seized the scourge to drive out of the Temple the brood of vipers and adders. How terrific was the fight for the world against the Jewish poison.[19]

And to Rauschning he once referred to "the Jewish Christ-creed with its effeminate, pity-ethics."

It is not clear from the evidence whether the new State

Religion was part of Hitler's plan or whether developments were such that it became feasible. It is true that Rosenberg had long advocated such a move, but there is no evidence that Hitler was inclined to take such a drastic step until after he had come to power. It is possible that he felt he needed the power before he could initiate such a change, or it may be that his series of successes were so startling that the people spontaneously adopted a religious attitude toward him, which made the move more or less obvious. In any case he has accepted this Godlike role without any hesitation or embarrassment. White tells us that now when he is addressed with the salutation, "Heil Hitler, our Savior," he bows slightly at the compliment in the phrase—and believes it.[20] As time goes on, it becomes more and more certain that Hitler believes that he is really the "Chosen One" and that in his thinking he conceives of himself as a second Christ, who has been sent to institute in the world a new system of values based on brutality and violence. He has fallen in love with the image of himself in this role and has surrounded himself with his own portraits.

His mission seems to lure him to still greater heights. Not content with the role of transitory savior, it pushes him on to higher goals—he must set the pattern for generations to come. Von Wiegand says: "In vital matters Hitler is far from unmindful of the name and record of success and failure he will leave to posterity."[21] Nor is he content to allow these patterns to evolve in a natural way. In order to guarantee the future he feels that he alone can bind it to these principles. He believes, therefore, that he must become an immortal to the German people. Everything must be huge and befitting as a monument to the honor of Hitler. His idea of a permanent building is one that will endure at least a thousand years. His highways must be known as "Hitler Highways," and they must endure for longer periods of time than the Napoleonic roads. He must always be doing the impossible and leaving his mark on the country. This is one of the ways in which he hopes to stay alive in the minds of the German people for generations to come.

It is alleged by many writers, among them Haffner, Huss, and Wagner,[22] that he has already drawn extensive plans for his own mausoleum. Our informants, who left Germany some time ago, are not in a position to verify these reports. They consider them well within the realm of possibility, however. This mausoleum is to be the mecca of Germany after his death. It is to be a tremendous monument about 700 feet high, with all the details worked out so that the greatest psychological effect might be attained. It is also alleged that his first errand in Paris after the conquest in 1940 was a visit to the Dome des Invalides to study the monument to Napoleon. He found this lacking in many respects. For example, they had put him down in a hole, which forced people to look down rather than high up.

"I shall never make such a mistake," Hitler said suddenly. "I know how to keep my hold on people after I have passed on. I shall be the Fuehrer they look up at and go home to talk of and remember. My life shall not end in the mere form of death. It will, on the contrary, begin then."[23]

It was believed for a time that the Kehlstein had been originally built as an eternal mausoleum by Hitler. It seems, however, that if that was his original intention he has abandoned it in favor of something even more grandiose. Perhaps the Kehlstein was too inaccessible to enable large numbers of people to come and touch his tomb in order to become inspired. In any case it seems that far more extravagant plans have been developed. His plan, if it is to be successful, needs constant emotional play on hysteric mass minds, and the more he can arrange the ways and means of achieving this after he dies, the more assured he is of attaining his final goal.

He is firmly convinced that the furious pace and the epochal age in which he lived and moved (he really is convinced that he is the motivating force and the moulder of that age) will terminate soon after his death, swinging the world by nature and inclination into a long span of digestive process marked by a sort of quiet inactivity. People in his "1000 year Reich" will build monuments to him and go around to touch and look at the things he has built, he thought. He said as much on that glorified visit of his to Rome in 1938, adding that a thousand years hence the greatness and not the ruins of his own time must intrigue

the people of those far-away days. For, believe it or
not, that is how the mind of this man Hitler projects
itself without a blush over the centuries.[24]

There was also a time a few years ago when he spoke a
good deal about retiring when his work was done. It was
assumed that he would then take up his residence in Berchtesgaden and sit as God who guides the destinies of the
Reich until he dies. In July 1933, while visiting the Wagner family, he talked at length about getting old and complained bitterly that ten years of valuable time had been
lost between the Beer Hall Putsch in 1923 and his accession to power. This was all very regrettable since he predicted that it would take twenty-two years to get things in
adequate shape so that he could turn them over to his suc-
cessor.[25] It is supposed by some writers that during this
period of retirement he would also write a book that
would stand for eternity as a great bible of National Socialism.[26] This is all rather interesting in view of Roehm's
statement made many years ago: "Even today, the thing
he would like best, is to sit in the mountains and play
God."[27]

A survey of all the evidence forces us to conclude that
Hitler believes himself destined to become an Immortal
Hitler, chosen by God to be the New Deliverer of Germany and the Founder of a new social order for the
world. He firmly believes this and is certain that in spite
of all the trials and tribulations through which he must
pass he will finally attain that goal. The one condition is
that he follow the dictates of the inner voice that have
guided and protected him in the past. This conviction is
not rooted in the truth of the ideas he imparts but is based
on the conviction of his own personal greatness.[28] Howard
K. Smith makes an interesting observation: "I was convinced that of all the millions on whom the Hitler Myth
had fastened itself, the most carried away was Adolf Hitler, himself."[29]

We will have occasion in Part V to examine the origins
of this conviction and the role it plays in Hitler's psychological economy.

PART II

HITLER

As the German People Know Him

卐

WHEN we try to formulate a conception of Adolf Hitler as
the German people know him we must not forget that
their knowledge of him is limited by a controlled press.
Many thousands of Germans have seen him in person,
particularly in the past, and can use this experience as a
basis for their individual conception of him.

Hitler, from a physical point of view, is not, however, a
very imposing figure—certainly not the Platonic idea of a
great, fighting Leader or the Deliverer of Germany and
the creator of a New Reich. In height he is a little below
average. His hips are wide and his shoulders relatively narrow. His muscles are flabby; his legs short, thin, and spin-
dly, the latter being hidden in the past by heavy boots and
more recently by long trousers. He has a large torso and
is hollow-chested to the point where it is said that he has
his uniforms padded. From a physical point of view he
could not pass the requirements of his own elite guard.

His dress, in the early days, was no more attractive. He
frequently wore the Bavarian mountain costume of leather
shorts with white shirt and suspenders. These were not always too clean, and with his mouth full of brown, rotten
teeth and his long dirty fingernails he presented rather a
grotesque picture. At that time he also had a pointed
beard, and his dark brown hair was parted in the middle
and pasted down flat against his head with oil. Nor was
his gait that of a soldier. "It was a very lady-like walk.
Dainty little steps. Every few steps he cocked his right
shoulder nervously, his left leg snapping up as he did so."[1]
He also had a tic in his face that caused the corner of his
lips to curl upward.[2] When speaking he always dressed in
a common-looking blue suit that robbed him of all distinc-
tiveness. At the trial following the unsuccessful Beer Hall
Putsch Edgar Mowrer, who saw him for the first time,
asked himself:

Was this provincial dandy, with his slick dark hair, his cutaway coat, his awkward gestures and glib tongue, the terrible rebel? He seemed for all the world like a traveling salesman for a clothing firm.[3]

Nor did he make a much better impression later on. Dorothy Thompson, upon her first meeting, described him in the following terms:

He is formless, almost faceless, a man whose countenance is a caricature, a man whose framework seems cartilaginous, without bones. He is inconsequent and voluble, ill poised and insecure. He is the very prototype of the little man.[4]

Smith also found him "the apotheosis of the little man,"[5] funny looking, self-conscious, and unsure of himself.

It may be supposed that this is only the judgment of American journalists who have a different standard of masculine beauty. However, while testifying as a witness in the law court in 1923, Professor Max von Gruber of the University of Munich, the most eminent eugenist in Germany, stated:

It was the first time I had seen Hitler close at hand. Face and head of inferior type, cross-breed; low receding forehead, ugly nose, broad cheekbones, little eyes, dark hair. Expression not of a man exercising authority in perfect self-command, but of raving excitement. At the end an expression of satisfied egotism.[6]

A great deal has been written about his eyes, which have been described in terms of almost every color of the rainbow. As a matter of fact, they seem to be rather a bright blue—bordering on the violet. But it is not the color that has attracted people, but rather their depth and a glint that makes them appear to have a hypnotic quality. One finds stories like the following recurring over and over again in the literature. A policeman who is noted for his antipathy to the Nazi movement is sent to a Hitler meeting to maintain order. While standing at his post Hitler enters:

He gazed into the police officer's eye with that fatal hypnotizing and irresistible glare, which swept the poor officer right off his feet. Clicking to attention he confessed to me this morning: "Since last night I am a National Socialist. Heil Hitler."[7]

These stories are not all from the Nazi propaganda agencies. Very reliable people, now in this country, have reported similar incidents among their own personal acquaintances. Even outstanding diplomats have commented on the nature of his eyes and the way in which he uses them when meeting people, often with disastrous effects.

Then there are others, like Rauschning, who find his look staring and dead—lacking in brilliance and the sparkle of genuine animation.[8] We need not dwell on his eyes and their peculiar quality, however, since relatively few Germans have come in such close contact with him that they could be seriously affected by them.

Whatever effect Hitler's personal appearance may have had on the German people in the past, it is safe to assume that this has been greatly tempered by millions of posters, pasted in every conceivable place, which show the Fuehrer as a fairly good-looking individual with a very determined attitude. In addition, the press, newsreels, and so forth, are continually flooded with carefully prepared photographs showing Hitler at his very best. These have undoubtedly, in the course of time, blotted out any unfavorable impressions he may have created as a real person in the past. The physical Hitler most Germans know now is a fairly presentable individual.

The only other real contact the overwhelming majority of people have had with Hitler is through his voice. He was a tireless speaker, and before he came to power would sometimes give as many as three or four speeches on the same day, often in different cities. Even his greatest opponents concede that he is the greatest orator that Germany has ever known. This is a great concession in view of the fact that the qualities of his voice are far from pleasant—many, in fact, find it distinctly unpleasant. It has a rasping quality that often breaks into a shrill falsetto when he becomes aroused. Nor is it his diction that makes him a great orator. In the early days this was particularly bad. It was a conglomeration of high German with an Austrian dialect, which Tschuppik describes as a "knoed-

lige Sprache."[9] Nor was it the structure of his speeches
that made him a great orator. On the whole, his speeches
were sinfully long, badly structured, and very repetitious.
Some of them are positively painful to read, but, nevertheless, when he delivered them they had an extraordinary effect upon his audiences.

His power and fascination in speaking lay almost wholly
in his ability to sense what a given audience wanted to
hear and then to manipulate his theme in such a way that
he would arouse the emotions of the crowd. Strasser says
of his talent:

> Hitler responds to the vibration of the human heart
> with the delicacy of a seismograph . . . enabling him,
> with a certainty with which no conscious gift could
> endow him, to act as a loudspeaker proclaiming the
> most secret desires, the least permissible instincts, the
> sufferings and personal revolts of a whole nation.[10]

Before coming to power almost all of his speeches centered around the following three themes: (1) the treason
of the November criminals; (2) the rule of the Marxists
must be broken; and (3) the world domination of the
Jews. No matter what topic was advertised for a given
speech he almost invariably would wind up on one or
more of these three themes. And yet people liked it and
would attend one meeting after another to hear him
speak. It was not, therefore, so much what he said that
appealed to his audiences as how he said it.

Even in the early days Hitler was a showman with a
great sense for the dramatic. Not only did he schedule his
speeches late in the evening when his audience would be
tired and their resistance lowered through natural causes,
but he would always send an assistant ahead of time to
make a short speech and warm up the audience. Storm
troopers always played an important role at these meetings and would line the aisle through which he would pass.
At the psychological moment, Hitler would appear in the
door at the back of the hall. Then with a small group behind him, he would march through the rows of S.A. men
to reach the speaker's table. He never glanced to the right
or to the left as he came down the aisle and became
greatly annoyed if anyone tried to accost him or ham-
pered his progress. Whenever possible he would have a

band present, and they would strike up a lively military march as he came down the aisle.

When he began to speak he usually manifested signs of nervousness. Usually he was unable to say anything of consequence until he had gotten the feel of his audience. On one occasion, Heiden reports, he was so nervous that he could think of nothing to say.[11] In order to do something he picked up the table and moved it around on the platform. Then suddenly he got the "feel" and was able to go on. Price describes his speaking in the following way:

> The beginning is slow and halting. Gradually he warms up when the spiritual atmosphere of the great crowd is engendered. For he responds to this metaphysical contact in such a way that each member of the multitude feels bound to him by an individual link of sympathy.[12]

All of our informants report the slow start, waiting for the feel of the audience. As soon as he has found it, the tempo increases in smooth rhythm and volume until he is shouting at the climax. Through all this, the listener seems to identify himself with Hitler's voice, which becomes the voice of Germany.

This is all in keeping with Hitler's own conception of mass psychology as given in *Mein Kampf* where he says:

> The psyche of the broad masses does not respond to anything weak or half-way. Like a woman, whose spiritual sensitiveness is determined less by abstract reason than by an indefinable emotional longing for fulfilling power and who, for that reason, prefers to submit to the strong rather than the weakling—the mass, too, prefers the ruler to a pleader.

And Hitler let them have it. *Newsweek* reported: "Women faint, when, with face purpled and contorted with effort, he blows forth his magic oratory."[13] Flanner says: "His oratory used to wilt his collar, unglue his forelock, glaze his eyes; he was like a man hypnotized, repeating himself into a frenzy."[14] According to Yeates-Brown: "He was a man transformed and possessed. We were in the presence of a miracle."[15]

This fiery oratory was something new to the Germans

and particularly to the slow-tongued, lower-class Bavarians. In Munich his shouting and gesturing were a spectacle men paid to see.[16] It was not only his fiery oratory, however, that won the crowds to his cause. This was certainly something new, but far more important was the seriousness with which his words were spoken.

> Every one of his words comes out charged with a powerful current of energy; at times it seems as if they are torn from the very heart of the man, causing him indescribable anguish.[17]

> Leaning from the tribune, as if he were trying to impel his inner self into the consciousness of all these thousands, he was holding the masses and me with them under a hypnotic spell. . . . It was clear that Hitler was feeling the exaltation of the emotional response now surging up toward him . . . his voice rising to passionate climaxes . . . his words were like a scourge. When he stopped speaking his chest was still heaving with emotion.[18]

Many writers have commented upon his ability to hypnotize his audiences. Stanley High reports:

> When, at the climax, he sways from one side to the other his listeners sway with him; when he leans forward they also lean forward and when he concludes they either are awed and silent or on their feet in a frenzy.[19]

Unquestionably, as a speaker, he has had a powerful influence on the common run of German people. His meetings were always crowded, and by the time he got through speaking he had completely numbed the critical faculties of his listeners to the point where they were willing to believe almost anything he said. He flattered them and cajoled them. He hurled accusations at them one moment and amused them the next by building up straw men that he promptly knocked down. His tongue was like a lash that whipped up the emotions of his audience. And somehow he always managed to say what the majority of the audience were already secretly thinking but could not verbalize. When the audience began to respond, it affected him in return. Before long due to this reciprocal relationship, he and his audience became intoxicated with the emotional appeal of his oratory.[20]

It was this Hitler that the German people knew at first-hand. Hitler, the fiery orator, who tirelessly rushed from one meeting to another, working himself to the point of exhaustion in their behalf. Hitler, whose heart and soul were in the Cause and who struggled endlessly against overwhelming odds and obstacles to open their eyes to the true state of affairs. Hitler, who could arouse their emotions and channelize them toward goals of national aggrandizement. Hitler the courageous, who dared to speak the truth and defy the national authorities as well as the international oppressors. It was a sincere Hitler that they knew, whose words burned into the most secret recesses of their minds and rebuked them for their own shortcomings. It was the Hitler who would lead them back to self-respect because he had faith in them.

This fundamental conception of Hitler made a beautiful foundation for a propaganda build-up. He was so convincing on the speaker's platform and appeared to be so sincere in what he said that the majority of his listeners were ready to believe almost anything good about him because they wanted to believe it. The Nazi propaganda agencies were not slow in making the most of their opportunities.

Hitler himself had provided an excellent background for propaganda build-up. From the earliest days of his political career he had steadfastly refused to divulge anything about his personal life, past or present. To his most immediate associates he was, in reality, a man of mystery. There was no clearing away of unpleasant incidents to be done before the building-up process could begin. In fact, the more secrecy he maintained about his personal life the more curious his followers became. This was, indeed, fertile ground on which to build a myth or legend.

The Nazi propaganda machine devoted all its efforts to the task of portraying Hitler as something extrahuman. Everything he did was written up in such a way that it portrayed his superlative character. If he does not eat meat, drink alcoholic beverages, or smoke, it is not due to the fact that he has some kind of inhibition or does it because he believes it will improve his health. Such things are not worthy of the Fuehrer. He abstains from these because he is following the example of the great German, Richard

Wagner, or because he has discovered that it increases his energy and endurance to such a degree that he can give much more of himself to the creation of the new German Reich.

Such abstinence also indicates, according to the propaganda, that the Fuehrer is a person with tremendous will power and self-discipline. Hitler himself fosters this conception, according to Hanfstaengl, for, when someone asked him how he managed to give up these things, he replied: "It is a matter of will. Once I make up my mind not to do a thing, I just don't do it. And once that decision is made, it is taken for always. Is that so wonderful?"

The same is true with regard to sex. As far as the German people know he has no sex life and this, too, is clothed, not as an abnormality, but as a great virtue. The Fuehrer is above human weaknesses of this sort, and von Wiegand tells us that he "has profound contempt for the weakness in men for sex and the fools that it makes of them."[21] Hanfstaengl reports that Hitler frequently makes the statement that he will never marry a woman since Germany is his only bride. However, Hitler, with his deep insight into human nature, appreciates these weaknesses in others and is tolerant of them. He does not even condemn them or forbid them among his closest associates.

He is also portrayed in the propaganda as the soul of kindliness and generosity. Endless stories that illustrate these virtues are found over and over again in the literature. Price[22] cites a typical example: an attractive young peasant girl tries to approach him but is prevented from doing so by the guards. She bursts into tears and Hitler, seeing her distress, inquires into the cause. She tells him that her fiancé had been expelled from Austria for his Nazi principles and that he cannot find work and consequently they cannot get married. Hitler is deeply touched. He promises to find the young man a job and, in addition, completely furnishes a flat for them to live in, even down to a baby's cot. Every attempt is made to present him as extremely human, with a deep feeling for the problems of ordinary people.

A great many writers, both Nazi and anti-Nazi, have written extensively about his great love for children and the Nazi press is certainly full of pictures showing Hitler in the company of little tots. It is alleged that when he is at Berchtesgaden he always has the children from the

neighborhood visit him in the afternoon and that he serves
them candy, ice cream, and cake. Phayre says, "Never
was there a middle-aged bachelor who so delighted in the
company of children."[23] Princess Olga reported that when
she visited Hitler in Berlin and the topic of children came
up during the conversation, Hitler's eyes filled with tears.
The Nazi press had made extremely good use of this and
endless stories accompany the pictures. Likewise, a great
deal is written about his fondness for animals, particularly
dogs. Here again, there are numberless pictures to prove it
is so. The propaganda build-up is Hitler's modesty and
simplicity. One writer even went so far as to attribute his
vegetarianism to his inability to tolerate the thought of animals being slaughtered for human consumption.[24] Hitler is
pictured as an "affable lord of the manor," full of
gentleness, kindliness and helpfulness, or, as Oechsner puts
it, he is the Great Comforter—father, husband, brother,
or son to every German who lacks or has lost such a relative.[25]

Another trait that has received a great deal of comment
in the propaganda is that power has never gone to his
head. At bottom he is still the simple soul he was when he
founded the Party and his greatest joy is to be considered
as "one of the boys." As proof of this they point to the
fact that he has never sought a crown, that he never appears in gaudy uniforms or does a great deal of entertaining. Even after he came to power he continued to wear
his old trench coat and slouch hat and when he donned a
uniform it was always that of a simple storm trooper.
Much was written about his fondness for visits from early
acquaintances and about how he loved to sit down in the
midst of his busy day in order to talk over old times.
There was really nothing he liked better than to frequent
his old haunts and meet old friends while he was in Munich, or to take part in their festivities. At heart he was
still a worker, and his interests were always with the
working classes with whom he felt thoroughly at home.

Hitler is also a man of incredible energy and endurance.
His day consists of sixteen and eighteen hours of uninter-
rupted work. He is absolutely tireless when it comes to
working for Germany and its future welfare, and no personal pleasures are permitted to interfere with the
carrying out of his mission. The ordinary man in the street
cannot imagine a human being in Hitler's position not tak-

ing advantage of his opportunity. He can only imagine himself in the same position reveling in luxuries, and yet here is Hitler who scorns them all. His only conclusion is that Hitler is not an ordinary mortal. Phillips reports the case of a young Nazi who once confided to him: "I would die for Hitler, but I would not change places with Hitler. At least when I wake up every morning I can say, 'Heil Hitler! but this man, he has no fun in life. No smoking, no drinking, no women!—only work, until he falls asleep at night!"[26]

A great deal is made of Hitler's determination. It is pointed out, over and over again, that he never gives up once he has made up his mind to attain a particular goal. No matter how rough the road, he plods along in unswerving determination. Even though he receives serious setbacks and the situation appears to be hopeless, he never loses faith and always gets what he goes after. He refuses to be coerced into compromises of any sort and is always ready to assume the full responsibility for his actions. The great trials and tribulations through which the Party had to pass on its way to power are cited over and over again, and all the credit is given to Hitler and his fanatical faith in the future. Even his refusal to permit ordinary scruples to get in his way is cited as a sign of his greatness. The fact that he did not communicate with his family for over ten years becomes a great virtue since it meant a severe deprivation to the young man who was determined to make something of himself before he returned home!

A great deal of publicity has also been given to his breadth of vision, ability to penetrate the future, and his ability to organize both the Party and the country in preparation for obstacles they will have to overcome. According to the propagandists, Hitler is the soul of efficiency and has an extraordinary power of resolving conflicts and simplifying problems that have stumped all experts in the past. In fact, his infallibility and incorruptibility are not only implied but openly stated in no uncertain terms.

He is also a person of great patience who would never spill a drop of human blood if it could possibly be avoided. Over and over again one hears of his great patience with the democracies, with Czechoslovakia and with Poland. But here, as in his private life, he never loses control of his emotions. Fundamentally, he is a man of peace who desires nothing quite so much as to be left alone to work out the destiny of Germany in a quiet and constructive manner. For he is a builder at heart and an artist, and these prove that the creative and constructive elements in his nature are predominant.

This does not mean, however, that he is a coward. On the contrary, he is a person of outstanding courage. His way of life is proof of this, as well as his enviable record during the last war. A great many stories about his decorations for bravery have been circulated, stressing his outstanding heroism for which he was awarded the Iron Cross First Class. The fact that the stories of his performance vary from one time to another does not seem to disturb the people in the least.

Fundamentally, according to the Nazi press, Hitler is a man of steel. He is well aware of his mission, and no amount of persuasion, coercion, sacrifices, or unpleasant duties can persuade him to alter his course. In the face of all sorts of disasters and disagreeable happenings, he never loses his nerve for a moment. But he is not hard in human qualities. He places loyalty and justice as the two greatest virtues and observes them with scrupulous care. Loyalty means so much to him that the inscription over his door at Berchtesgaden reads, "My honor is called loyalty." He is the acme of German honor and purity; the Resurrector of the German family and home. He is the greatest architect of all time; the greatest military genius in all history. He has an inexhaustible fount of knowledge. He is a man of action and the creator of new social values. He is, indeed, according to the Nazi propaganda bureau, the paragon of all virtues. A few typical examples may illustrate the extent to which they are carried in their praise of him.

Next comes Hitler himself: Hitler is a man without compromise. Above all he knows no compromise with himself. He has one single thought that guides him: to resurrect Germany. This idea suppresses everything else. He knows no private life. He knows family life no more than he knows vice. He is the embodiment of the National will.

The knighthood of a holy goal which can be climaxed by no man: Germany! ... Hitler ... surprises (with) his geniality. The tranquility and strength radiate, almost physically, from this man. In his presence others grow. How he reacts to everything! ... His features harden and the words drop as stones. ... The classical solemnity with which Hitler and his surrounding group of co-workers consider their mission has very few parallels in world history.[27]

... Also in private matters of exemplary behavior and human greatness ... whether Hitler ... is met with cheers by streetworkers, or moved and shocked stands at the bed of his murdered companions, he is always surrounded by this grandeur and deepest humaneness ... this unique personality ... a great and good human being. Hitler's spirit is universal. Not even in 100 pictures is it possible to give justice to the manifoldness of his being. In these fields too (architecture and history) Hitler is an unassailable expert. Perhaps in our time this outstanding man will be honored and loved, but nobody will be able to measure his great depth.[28]

Hitler is a modest man—and the world needs modest men. Therefore the people love him. Like every good leader, he must be an efficient follower. He makes himself the humblest disciple of himself, the severest of all disciplinarians with himself. In fact, Hitler is a modern monk, with the three knots of Poverty, Chastity, and Obedience tied in his invisible girdle. A zealot among zealots. He eats no meat, drinks no wine, does not smoke. I am told he takes for himself no salary but lives privately from the income of his book, *Mein Kampf*. ... Surplus funds he turns back to the S.A. His work day consists of eighteen hours, usually, and he often falls asleep in the last hour of his work. There have been four women in his life—but only to help him along with service and money. ... He once gave a lecture at Bayreuth on Wagner and "Deutsche Lieder" that astounded the musical critics and revealed him as a musical scholar of parts. ... Sheer opportunism never lured him as much as the opportunity to preach his doctrines. His quality is Messianic; his spiritual trend is ascetic; his reaction is medieval. ...[29]

Hitler not only knows about all these writings, but since he has always been the guiding spirit in all German propaganda and usually plans the broad lines that are to be followed, it is safe to assume that he himself is responsible for the instigation and development of this mythical personality. When we look back over the development of this build-up we can see clearly that Hitler, from the very beginning, planned on making himself a mythological figure. He opens *Mein Kampf* with the following passage:

> In this little town on the river Inn, Bavarian by blood and Austrian by nationality, gilded by the light of German martyrdom, there lived, at the end of the 80's of the last century, my parents: the father a faithful civil servant, the mother devoting herself to the cares of the household and looking after her children with eternally the same loving kindness.

This is the classic way of beginning a fairy tale rather than a serious autobiography or a political treatise. In the very first sentence of the book he implies that Fate was already smiling on him at the time of his birth, for it reads: "Today I consider it my good fortune that Fate designated Braunau on the Inn as the place of my birth."

As soon as Hitler came to power new weapons for self-aggrandizement were put into the hands of the propagandists and they made good use of them. Unemployment dropped off rapidly, roads that the Germans never dreamed of sprung up overnight, new and imposing buildings were erected with astounding rapidity. The face of Germany was being lifted at an incredible speed. Hitler was keeping his promises; he was accomplishing the impossible. Every success in diplomacy, every social reform was heralded as world-shaking in its importance. And for each success, Hitler modestly accepted all the credit. It was always Hitler that did this, and Hitler who did that, provided these acts were spectacular and met with the approval of the public. If they happened to meet with disapproval, it was always one of his assistants who was to blame. Every effort was made to cultivate the attitude that Hitler was infallible and was carrying through his mission of saving Germany.

It was not long before the German people were prepared to take the short step of seeing Hitler, not as a man, but as a Messiah of Germany. Public meetings and particularly the Nuremberg rally took on a religious atmosphere. All the stagings were designed to create a supernatural and religious atmosphere, and Hitler's entry was more befitting a god than a man. In Berlin one of the large art shops on Unter den Linden exhibited a large portrait of Hitler in the center of its display window. Hitler's portrait was entirely surrounded, as though by a halo, with various copies of a painting of Christ.[30] Notes appeared in the press to the effect that, "As he spoke, one heard God's mantle rustle through the room!" Ziemer reports that on the side of a hill in Odenwald, conspicuous as a waterfall, painted on white canvas were the black words:

> We believe in Holy Germany
> Holy Germany is Hitler!
> We believe in Holy Hitler! ![31]

Roberts reports:

> In Munich in the early autumn of 1936 I saw colored pictures of Hitler in the actual silver garments of the Knights of the Grail; but these were soon withdrawn. They gave the show away; they were too near the truth of Hitler's mentality.[32]

Teeling writes that at the Nuremberg Nazi Party Rally in September 1937, there was a huge photograph of Hitler underneath which was the inscription, "In the beginning was the Word. ..." He also says that the Mayor of Hamburg assured him, "We need no priests or parsons. We communicate direct with God through Adolf Hitler. He has many Christ-like qualities."[33] Soon these sentiments were introduced by official circles. Rauschning reports that the Party has adopted this creed: "We all believe, on this earth, in Adolf Hitler, our Fuehrer, and we acknowledge that National Socialism is the only faith that can bring salvation to our country."[34] A Rhenish group of German "Christians" in April 1937 passed this resolution: "Hitler's word is God's law, the decrees and laws which represent it possess divine authority."[35] And Reichminister for Church Affairs, Hans Kerrl, says: "There has arisen a new authority as to what Christ and Christianity really are—that is Adolf Hitler. Adolf Hitler ... is the true Holy Ghost."[36]

This is the way Hitler hopes to pave his path to immortality. It has been carefully planned and consistently executed in a step-by-step fashion. The Hitler the German people know is fundamentally the fiery orator who fascinated them, and this has gradually been embroidered by the propaganda until he is now presented to them as a full-fledged deity. Everything else is carefully concealed from them as a whole. How many Germans believe it we do not know. Some, certainly, believe it wholeheartedly. Dorothy Thompson writes of such a case:

> At Garmisch I met an American from Chicago. He had been at Oberammergau, at the Passion Play. "These people are all crazy," he said. "This is not a revolution, it's a revival. They think Hitler is God. Believe it or not, a German woman sat next to me at the Passion Play and when they hoisted Jesus on the Cross, she said, 'There he is. That is our Fuehrer, our Hitler.' And when they paid out the thirty pieces of silver to Judas, she said: 'That is Roehm, who betrayed the Leader.' "[37]

Extreme cases of this kind are probably not very numerous, but it would be amazing if a small degree of the same type of thinking had not seeped into the picture of Hitler that many Germans hold.

PART III

卐

HITLER

As His Associates
Know Him

THE picture the Nazi propaganda machine has painted of Hitler certainly seems like an extravagant one. Even if we ignore the deifying elements, it seems like the fantasy of a superman—the paragon of all virtues. Extraordinary as it may seem, however, there are times at which he approximates such a personality and wins the respect and admiration of all his associates.

At such times he is a veritable demon for work and often works for several days on end with little or no sleep. His powers of concentration are extraordinary, and he is able to penetrate very complex problems and reduce them to a few simple, fundamental factors. He prides himself on this talent and has said to various people: "I have the gift of reducing all problems to their simplest foundations. . . . A gift for tracing back all theories to their roots in reality." And he really has it. Unencumbered with abstract theories or traditional points of view and prejudices he is able to look at complex problems in a rather naive way and pick out the most salient and significant elements and apply them to the present situation in a fairly simple and workable manner. To be sure, he never solves the entire problem in this way but only the human elements involved. Since this is the part that interests him most, and produces immediate results, it has been rated very highly and has won the admiration of his close associates from the earliest days of his political career.

During these periods of activity Hitler is completely absorbed in the task confronting him. Conference follows conference with great rapidity. His judgments are quick and decisive. He is impatient to get things done and expects everyone to apply himself with an ardor equal to his own. He, therefore, demands great sacrifices from his associates.

At such times, however, he is also very human. He

shows an unusual degree of considerateness toward others
and a certain tolerance of their weaknesses. When he calls
a halt for meals he will not eat until his entire staff has
been served. When an overzealous servant insists on serv-
ing him before others he will often get up and take the
plate over to one of his lowly assistants. During all of this
he is in the best of spirits and jokes with everyone around
him.

He has an extraordinary memory and continually recalls
amusing incidents from the past lives of those around him.
These he tells to his staff at large. He is an excellent
mimic and often plays out the role of the individual involved to the great amusement of the staff while the individual must sit by and witness the performance much to
his own embarrassment. Nevertheless, he is thoroughly
flattered that the Fuehrer should single him out and
remember him and his actions in such detail. During these
periods Hitler is also the soul of kindliness and generosity.
He acts more like a big brother to his staff than as a
Fuehrer and manages to endear himself to each and every
one of them.

But, underneath, he is every inch the Fuehrer. He displays extraordinary courage and determination. He shows
a great deal of initiative and is willing to assume full responsibility for the wisdom of the course he has mapped
out. He is very persuasive and is able to muster and organize his people into an efficient smooth-running unit. Personal frictions disappear, for the time being, and everybody has but a single thought in mind: to do what the
Fuehrer wishes.

He works with great certainty and security and appears
to have the situation entirely in hand. All kinds of facts
and figures relevant to the problem flow from him without
the slightest hesitation or effort, much to the amazement
of those about him. He can cite the tonnages of ships in
various navies:

He knows exactly what kind of armament, the kind
of armor plates, the weight, the speed, and the number of the crew of every ship in the British Navy. He
knows the number of rotations of airplane motors in
every model and type existent. He knows the number
of shots a machine gun fires a minute, whether it is a

light, medium, or heavy one, whether it was made in the United States, Czechoslovakia, or France.[1]

Then, too, his staff has learned from past experience that when Hitler is in one of these moods he approximates infallibility particularly when the support of the people is needed to carry through the project on which he is engaged. This may seem like an unwarranted statement, but, if our study is to be complete, we must appraise his strengths as well as his weaknesses. It can scarcely be denied that he has some extraordinary abilities where the psychology of the average man is concerned. He has been able, in some manner or other, to unearth and apply successfully many factors pertaining to group psychology, the importance of which has not been generally recognized and some of which we might adopt to good advantage. These might be briefly summarized as follows:

1. Full appreciation of the importance of the masses in the success of any movement. Hitler has phrased this very well in *Mein Kampf*:

> The lack of knowledge of the internal driving forces of great changes led to an insufficient evaluation of the importance of the great masses of the people; from this resulted the scanty interest in the social question, the deficient courting of the soul of the nation's lower classes.[2]

2. Recognition of the inestimable value of winning the support of youth; realization of the immense momentum given a social movement by the wild fervor and enthusiasm of young people as well as the importance of early training and indoctrination.

3. Recognition of the role of women in advancing a new movement and of the fact that the reactions of the masses as a whole have many feminine characteristics. As early as 1923, he said to Hanfstaengl:

> Do you know the audience at a circus is just like a woman (Die Masse, das Volk is wie ein Weib). Someone who does not understand the intrinsically feminine character of the masses will never be an effective speaker. Ask yourself: 'What does a woman

expect from a man?' Clearness, decision, power, and
action. What we want is to get the masses to act.
Like a woman, the masses fluctuate between ex-
tremes. ... The crowd is not only like a woman, but
women constitute the most important element in an
audience. The women usually lead, then follow the
children, and at last, when I have already won over
the whole family—follow the fathers.[3]

And in *Mein Kampf*, he writes:

The people, in an overwhelming majority, are so
feminine in their nature and attitude that their activities and thoughts are motivated less by sober consideration than by feeling and sentiment.[4]

4. The ability to feel, identify with, and express in pas-
sionate language the deepest needs and sentiments of the
average German and to present opportunities or possibilities for their gratification.

5. Capacity to appeal to the most primitive, as well as
the most ideal inclinations in man, to arouse the basest instincts and yet cloak them with nobility, justifying all actions as means to the attainment of an ideal goal. Hitler
realized that men will not combine and dedicate themselves to a common purpose unless this purpose be an
ideal one capable of survival beyond their generation. He
has also perceived that although men will die only for an
ideal their continued zest and enterprise can be maintained
only by a succession of more immediate and earthly satis-
factions.

6. Appreciation of the fact that the masses are as hungry for a sustaining ideology in political action as they are
for daily bread. Any movement that does not satisfy this
spiritual hunger in the masses will not mobilize their
wholehearted support and is destined to fail.

All force which does not spring from a firm spiritual foundation will be hesitating and uncertain. It
lacks the stability which can only rest on a fanatical
view of life.[5]

Every attempt at fighting a view of life by means of
force will finally fail, unless the fight against it rep-

resents the form of an attack for the sake of a new spiritual direction. Only in the struggle of two views of life with each other can the weapon of brute force, used continuously and ruthlessly, bring about the decision in favor of the side it supports.[6]

7. The ability to portray conflicting human forces in vivid, concrete imagery that is understandable and moving to the ordinary man. This comes down to the use of metaphors in the form of imagery, which, as Aristotle has said, is the most powerful force on earth.

8. The faculty of drawing on the traditions of the people and by reference to the great classical mythological themes evoking the deepest unconscious emotions of the audience. The fact that the unconscious mind is more intensely affected by the great eternal symbols and themes is not generally understood by most modern speakers and writers.

9. Realization that enthusiastic political action does not take place if the emotions are not deeply involved.

10. Appreciation of the willingness, almost desire, of the masses to sacrifice themselves on the altar of social improvement or spiritual values.

11. Realization of the importance of artistry and dramatic intensity in conducting large meetings, rallies, and festivals. This involves not only an appreciation of what the artist—the writer, musician, and painter—can accomplish in the way of evoking emotional responses but also the leader's recognition of the necessity of his participation in the total dramatic effect as chief character and hero. Hitler has become master of all the arts of highlighting his own role in the movement for a Greater Germany. Lochner describes this very well:

> A searchlight plays upon his lone figure as he slowly walks through the hall, never looking to right or left, his right hand raised in salute, his left hand at the buckle of his belt. He never smiles—it is a religious rite, this procession of the modern Messiah incarnate. Behind him are his adjutants and secret service men. But his figure alone is flooded with light.

By the time Hitler has reached the rostrum, the masses have been so worked upon that they are ready to do his will. . . .[7]

12. A keen appreciation of the value of slogans, catch-words, dramatic phrases, and happy epigrams in penetrating the deeper levels of the psyche. In speaking to Hanfstaengl on this point he once used the following figure of speech:

> "There is only so much room in a brain, so much wall space, as it were, and if you furnish it with your slogans, the opposition has no place to put up any pictures later on, because the apartment of the brain is already crowded with your furniture." Hanfstaengl adds that Hitler has always admired the use the Catholic Church made of slogans and has tried to imitate it.[8]

13. Realization of a fundamental loneliness and feeling of isolation in people living under modern conditions and a craving to "belong" to an active group that carries a certain status, provides cohesiveness, and gives the individual a feeling of personal worth and belongingness.

14. Appreciation of the value underlying a hierarchical political organization that affords direct contact with each individual.

15. Ability to surround himself with and maintain the allegiance of a group of devoted aides whose talents complement his own.

16. Appreciation of winning confidence from the people by a show of efficiency within the organization and government. It is said that foods and supplies are already in the local warehouses when the announcement concerning the date of distribution is made. Although they could be distributed immediately the date is set for several weeks ahead in order to create an impression of superefficiency and win the confidence of the people. Every effort is made to avoid making a promise that cannot be fulfilled at precisely the appointed time.

17. Appreciation of the important role played by little things that affect the everyday life of the ordinary man in building up and maintaining the morale of the people.

18. Full recognition of the fact that the overwhelming majority of the people want to be led and are ready and willing to submit if the leader can win their respect and confidence. Hitler has been very successful in this respect because he has been able to convince his followers of his

own self-confidence and because he has guessed right on
so many occasions that he has created the impression of
infallibility.

19. This was largely possible because he is naturally a
tactical genius. His timing of decisions and actions has almost been uncanny. As Thyssen puts it:

> Sometimes his intelligence is astonishing ... mirac-
> ulous political intuition, devoid of all moral sense, but
> extraordinarily precise. Even in a very complex situa-
> tion he discerns what is possible and what is not.

20. Hitler's strongest point is, perhaps, his firm belief in
his mission and, in public, the complete dedication of his
life to its fulfillment. It is the spectacle of a man whose
convictions are so strong that he sacrifices himself for the
cause that appeals to others and induces them to follow
his example. This demands a fanatical stubbornness that
Hitler possesses to a high degree. "Only a storm of glow-
ing passion can turn the destinies of nations, but this
passion can only be roused by a man who carries it within
himself."

21. He also has the ability to appeal to and arouse the
sympathetic concern and protectiveness of his people, to
represent himself as the bearer of their burdens and their
future, with the result that he becomes a personal concern
to individuals, and many, particularly the women, feel tenderly and compassionately about him. They must always
be careful not to inflict undue annoyance or suffering on
the Fuehrer.

22. Hitler's ability to repudiate his own conscience in
arriving at political decisions has eliminated the force that
usually checks and complicates the forward-going thoughts
and resolutions of most socially responsible statesmen. He
has, therefore, been able to take that course of action that
appeals to him as most effective without pulling his
punches. The result has been that he has frequently out-
witted his adversaries and attained ends that would not
have been as easily attained by a normal course. Nevertheless, it has helped to build up the myth of his infallibility and invincibility.

23. Equally important has been his ability to persuade
others to repudiate their individual consciences and allow
him to assume that role. He can then decree for the indi-

vidual what is right and wrong, permissible or unpermissible, and can use them freely in the attainment of his own ends. As Goering has said: "I have no conscience. My conscience is Adolf Hitler."

24. This has enabled Hitler to make full use of terror and mobilize the fears of the people, which he evaluated with an almost uncanny precision.

25. He has a capacity for learning from others even though he may be violently opposed to everything they believe and stand for. The use of terror, for example, he says he learned from the Communists, the use of slogans from the Catholic Church, the use of propaganda from the democracies, and so forth.

26. He is a master of the art of propaganda. Ludecke writes:

> He has a matchless instinct for taking advantage of every breeze to raise a political whirlwind. No official scandal was so petty that he could not magnify it into high treason; he could ferret out the most deviously ramified corruption in high places and plaster the town with the bad news.[9]

His primary rules were: never allow the public to cool off; never admit a fault or wrong; never concede that there may be some good in your enemy; never leave room for alternatives; never accept blame; concentrate on one enemy at a time and blame him for everything that goes wrong; people will believe a big lie sooner than a little one; and if you repeat it frequently enough people will sooner or later believe it.

27. He has the "never-say-die" spirit. After some of his severest set-backs he has been able to get his immediate associates together and begin making plans for a "comeback." Events that would crush most individuals, at least temporarily, seem to act as stimulants to greater efforts in Hitler.

These are some of Hitler's outstanding talents and capacities. They have enabled him to attain a position of unprecedented power in an incredibly short period of time, over a rarely used route. No other Nazi in a high position possesses these abilities in any comparable degree, and consequently they could not displace him in the minds of the masses.

His associates recognize these capacities in Hitler, and they admire and respect his extraordinary leadership qualities, particularly the influence he has over people. In addition they love him for his very human qualities when he is at his best and is engaged in some important undertaking. These are aspects of Hitler's personality we should never lose sight of when evaluating his hold on his associates or on the German people. He has a magnetic quality about him that, together with his past accomplishments, wins the allegiance of people and seems to rob them of their critical functions. It is a bond that does not easily dissolve even in the face of evidence that he is not always what he pretends to be—in fact is more often than not the exact opposite.

We have reviewed Hitler's strength and briefly portrayed his character when he is at his best. It is now time to look at the other side of his personality—the side that is known only to those who are on fairly intimate terms with him.

Perhaps the truest words that Goebbels ever wrote are: "The Fuehrer does not change. He is the same now as he was when he was a boy."[10] If we glance at his boyhood we find that Hitler was far from a model student. He studied what he wanted to study and did fairly well in these subjects. Things that did not interest him he simply ignored even though his marks were "unsatisfactory" or "failing." For over a year before his mother died, he did nothing, as far as can be determined, except lie around the house or occasionally paint a few watercolors. Although they were in difficult financial circumstances he did not seek work or try to improve himself in school. He was self-willed, shy, and inactive. In Vienna, after his mother died, he continued this pattern even though he was frequently on the verge of starvation and reduced to begging on the streets. Hanisch, who was his flophouse buddy, reports that "he was never an ardent worker, was unable to get up in the morning, had difficulty in getting started, and seemed to be suffering from a paralysis of the will." As soon as he had sold a picture and had a little money in his pocket he stopped work and spent his time listening to parliament, reading newspapers in the cafés, or delivering lengthy political dissertations to his fellows in the hostel. This behavior he justified on the grounds that "he must have leisure, he was not a coolie." When Hanisch asked him one day what he was waiting for, Hitler replied: "I don't know myself."

As an adult he is still this little boy except when he is in one of his active moods. In 1931 Billing wrote: "The inner difficulties of a Hitler government will be found in the person of Hitler himself. Hitler will be unable to adjust to any regulated intellectual activity."[11] Ludecke also wrote: "He had a typical Austrian 'Schlamperei.' He suffered from an all-embracing disorderliness. Naturally this grew less in time but in the beginning it was apparent in everything."[12] It was indeed so apparent that early in the history of the movement the Party engaged a secretary whose duty it was to keep track of Hitler and see to it that he fulfilled his duties and obligations. The move was only partially successful, however: "Hitler was always on the go but rarely on time."[13] He is still rarely on time and frequently keeps important foreign diplomats, as well as his own staff, waiting for considerable periods of time.

He is unable to maintain any kind of a working schedule. His hours are most irregular, and he may go to bed any time between midnight and seven o'clock in the morning and get up anywhere from nine o'clock in the morning to two in the afternoon. In later years the hours tended to get later, and it was unusual for him, just before the war, to go to bed before daybreak. The night, however, was not spent in working, as his propaganda agents allege, but in viewing one or two feature movies, endless newsreels, listening to music, entertaining film stars, or just sitting around chatting with his staff. He seemed to have a violent dislike for going to bed or being alone. Frequently, he would ring for his adjutants in the middle of the night, after his guests had gone home, and demand that they sit up and talk to him. It was not that he had anything to say and often the adjutants would fall asleep listening to him talk about nothing of importance. As long as one of them remained awake, however, he would not be offended. There was an unwritten law among his immediate staff never to ask a question at these early morning sessions because to do so might get Hitler off on another subject and force them to remain for another hour.

Hitler sleeps very badly and has been in the habit for some years of taking a sleeping powder every night before retiring. It is possible that he demands someone to be with him in the hope that the powder will take effect and he will be overcome with sleep. His behavior, however, is not in keeping with this hypothesis for he carries on a monologue and frequently gets very much stirred up about the topic. This is hardly conducive to sleep, and we must suppose that there is some other reason for his late hours. Even after he has dismissed his adjutants and goes to bed he usually takes an armful of illustrated periodicals with him. These are usually magazines with pictures concerning naval and military matters, and American magazines are usually included. Shirer reports that he has been informed that since the war broke out Hitler has been keeping better hours and regularly has his first breakfast at seven A.M. and his second breakfast at nine A.M.[14] This may have been so during the early days of the war, but it is very doubtful that Hitler could keep up this schedule for any length of time. Rauschning claims that Hitler has a bed compulsion, which demands that the bed be made in a particular way with the quilt folded according to a prescribed pattern and that a man must make the bed before he can go to sleep.[15] We have no other information on this subject, but from his general psychological structure such a compulsion would be possible.

His working day before the war was equally disorderly. Rauschning reports, "He does not know how to work steadily. Indeed, he is incapable of working." He dislikes desk work and seldom glances at the piles of reports that are placed on his desk daily. No matter how important these may be or how much his adjutants may urge him to attend to a particular matter, he refuses to take them seriously unless it happens to be a project that interests him. On the whole, few reports interest him unless they deal with military or naval affairs or political matters. He seldom sits in a cabinet meeting because they bore him. On several occasions when sufficient pressure was brought to bear he did attend but got up abruptly during the session and left without apology. Later it was discovered that he had gone to his private theater and had the operator show some film that he liked particularly. On the whole, he prefers to discuss cabinet matters with each member in person and then communicate his decision to the group as a whole.

He has a passion for the latest news and for photographs of himself. If Hoffmann, the official Party photographer, happens to appear or someone happens to enter his office with a newspaper he will interrupt the most important meeting in order to scan through it. Very frequently he becomes so absorbed in the news or in his own photographs that he completely forgets the topic under discussion. Ludecke writes:

> Even on ordinary days in those times, it was almost impossible to keep Hitler concentrated on one point. His quick mind would run away with the talk, or his attention would be distracted by the sudden discovery of the newspaper and he would stop to read it avidly, or he would interrupt your carefully prepared report with a long speech as though you were an audience.[16]

And Hanfstaengl reports that "his staff is usually in despair on account of his procrastination. . . . He never takes their protests in this respect very seriously and usually brushes them aside by saying, 'Problems are not solved by getting fidgety. If the time is ripe, the matter will be settled one way or another.' "[17]

Although Hitler tries to present himself as a very decisive individual who never hesitates when he is confronted by a difficult situation, he is usually far from it. It is at just these times that his procrastination becomes most marked. At such times it is almost impossible to get him to take action on anything. He stays very much by himself and is frequently almost inaccessible to his immediate staff. He often becomes depressed, is in bad humor, talks little, and prefers to read a book, look at movies, or play with architectural models. According to the Dutch report his hesitation to act is not due to divergent views among his advisers.[18] At such times he seldom pays very much attention to them and prefers not to discuss the matter.

> What is known as the mastery of material was quite unimportant to him. He quickly became impatient if the details of a problem were brought to him. He was greatly adverse to experts and had little regard for their opinion. He looked upon them as mere hacks, as brush-cleaners and color grinders.[19]

On some occasions he has been known to leave Berlin
without a word and go to Berchtesgaden where he spends
his time walking in the country entirely by himself. Rauschning, who has met him on such occasions, says: "He recog-
nizes nobody then. He wants to be alone. There are times
when he flees from human society."[20] Roehm frequently
said, "Usually he solves suddenly, at the very last minute, a
situation that has become intolerable and dangerous only
because he vacillates and procrastinates."[21]

It is during these periods of inactivity that Hitler is
waiting for his "inner voice" to guide him. He does not
think the problem through in a normal way but waits until
the solution is presented to him. To Rauschning he said:

> Unless I have the incorruptible conviction: *This is
> the solution,* I do nothing. Not even if the whole
> party tried to drive me to action. I will not act; I will
> wait, no matter what happens. But if the voice
> speaks, then I know the time has come to act.[22]

These periods of indecision may last from a few days to
several weeks. If he is induced to talk about the problem
during this time he becomes ill-natured and bad-tempered.
However, when the solution has been given to him he has
a great desire to express himself. He then calls in his
adjutants, and they must sit and listen to him until he is
finished no matter what time it happens to be. On these occasions he does not want them to question him or even to
understand him. It seems that he just wants to talk.

After this recital to his adjutants Hitler calls in his advisers and informs them of his decision. When he has finished they are free to express their opinions. If Hitler
thinks that one of these opinions is worthwhile he will listen for a long time, but usually these opinions have little
influence on his decision when this stage has been reached.
Only if someone succeeds in introducing new factors is
there any possibility of getting him to change his mind. If
someone voices the opinion that the proposed plan is too
difficult or onerous he becomes extremely angry and frequently says: "I do not look for people having clever ideas
of their own but rather people who are clever in finding
ways and means of carrying out my ideas."[23]

As soon as he has the solution to a problem his mood
changes very radically. He is again the Fuehrer we have

described at the beginning of this section. "He is very cheerful, jokes all the time and does not give anybody an opportunity to speak, while he himself makes fun of everybody." This mood lasts throughout the period when necessary work has to be done. As soon as the requisite orders have been given to put the plan into execution, however, Hitler seems to lose interest in it. He becomes perfectly calm, occupies himself with other matters, and sleeps unusually long hours.[24]

This is a very fundamental trait in Hitler's character structure. He does not think things out in a logical and consistent fashion, gathering all available information pertinent to the problem, mapping out alternative courses of action, and then weighing the evidence pro and con for each of them before reaching a decision. His mental processes operate in reverse. Instead of studying the problem, as an intellectual would do, he avoids it and occupies himself with other things until unconscious processes furnish him a solution. Having the solution he then begins to look for facts that will prove that it is correct. In this procedure he is very clever, and by the time he presents it to his associates, it has the appearance of a rational judgment. Nevertheless, his thought processes proceed from the emotional to the factual instead of starting with the facts as an intellectual normally does. It is this characteristic of his thinking process that makes it difficult for ordinary people to understand Hitler or to predict his future actions. His orientation in this respect is that of an artist and not that of a statesman.

Although Hitler has been extremely successful in using this inspirational technique to determine his course of action (and we are reminded of his following his course with the precision of a sleepwalker) it is not without its shortcomings. He becomes dependent on his inner guide, which makes for unpredictability on the one hand and rigidity on the other. The result is that he cannot modify his course in the face of unexpected developments or firm opposition. Strasser tell us that: "When he was then confronted by contradictory facts he was left floundering."[25] And Roehm says that there is: "No system in the execution of his thoughts. He wants things his own way and gets mad when he strikes firm opposition on solid ground."[26] This rigidity of mental functioning is obvious even in ordinary everyday interviews. When an unexpected question is asked, he is completely at a loss. Lochner supplies us with an excellent description of this reaction:

> I saw this seemingly super-self-confident man actually blush when I broached the theme of German-American relations. . . . This evidently caught him off-guard. He was not used to having his infallibility challenged. For a moment he blushed like a school-boy, hemmed and hawed, then stammered an embarrassed something about having so many problems to ponder that he had not yet had time to take up America.[27]

Almost everyone who has written about Hitler has commented upon his rages. These are well-known to all of his associates, and they have learned to fear them. The descriptions of his behavior during these rages vary considerably. The more extreme descriptions claim that at the climax he rolls on the floor and chews on the carpets. Shirer reports that in 1938 he did this so often that his associates frequently refer to him as "Teppichfresser."[28] Not one of our informants who has been close to Hitler, people like Hanfstaengl, Strasser, Rauschning, Hohenlohe, Friedelinde Wagner, and Ludecke, have ever seen him behave in this manner. Morever, they are all firmly convinced that this is a gross exaggeration, and the informant of the Dutch Legation says that this aspect must be relegated to the domain of "Greuelmaerchen" ("atrocity tales").[29]

Even without this added touch of chewing the carpet, his behavior is still extremely violent and shows an utter lack of emotional control. In the worst rages he undoubtedly acts like a spoiled child who cannot have his own way and bangs his fists on the tables and walls. He scolds and shouts and stammers, and on some occasions foaming saliva gathers in the corners of his mouth. Rauschning, in describing one of these uncontrolled exhibitions, says: "He was an alarming sight, his hair disheveled, his eyes fixed, and his face distorted and purple. I feared that he would collapse or have a stroke."[30]

It must not be supposed, however, that these rages occur only when he is crossed on major issues. On the contrary, very insignificant matters might call out this reaction. In general they are brought on whenever anyone contradicts him, when there is unpleasant news for which he might feel responsible, when there is any skepticism concerning his judgment, or when a situation arises in which his infallibility might be challenged or belittled. Von Wiegand reports that among his staff there is a tacit understanding: "For God's sake don't excite the Fuehrer—which means do not tell him bad news—do not mention things which are not as he conceives them to be."[31] Voigt says that: "Close collaborators for many years said that Hitler was always like this—that the slightest difficulty or obstacle could make him scream with rage."[32]

Many writers believe that these rages are just play acting. There is much to be said for this point of view since Hitler's first reaction to the unpleasant situation is not indignation, as one would ordinarily expect. He goes off into a rage or tirade without warning. Similarly, when he has finished there is no aftermath. He immediately cools down and begins to talk about other matters in a perfectly calm tone of voice as though nothing had happened. Occasionally he will look around sheepishly, as if to see if anyone is laughing, and then proceeds with other matters, without the slightest trace of resentment.

Some of his closest associates have felt that he induces these rages consciously to frighten those about him. Rauschning, for example, says it is a "... technique by which he would throw his entire entourage into confusion by well-timed fits of rage and thus make them more submissive."[33] Strasser also believes this to be the case for he says: "Rage and abuse became the favorite weapons in his armory."[34] This is not the time to enter into a detailed discussion concerning the nature and purpose of the rages. It is sufficient, for the present time, to realize that his associates are well aware that Hitler can and does behave in this way. It is a part of the Hitler they know and are forced to deal with. We may point out, however, that these rages are not conscious acting alone since it is almost impossible for an actor to actually become purple in the face unless he really is in an emotional state.

There are many other aspects of Hitler's personality, as it is known to his associates, that do not fit into the picture of the Fuehrer as it is presented to the German people. A few of the more important of these merit mention. Hitler is represented as a man of great courage, with nerves of steel who is always in complete control of every situation. Nevertheless, he often runs away from an unpleasant, unexpected, or difficult situation.

Bayles reports two incidents that illustrate this reaction:

> Particularly noticeable is his inability to cope with unexpected situations, this having been amusingly revealed when he laid the cornerstone of the House of German Art in Munich. On this occasion he was handed a dainty, rococo hammer for delivering the three traditional strokes to the cornerstone, but not realizing the fragility of the rococo, he brought the hammer down with such force that at the very first stroke it broke into bits. Then, instead of waiting for another hammer, Hitler completely lost his composure, blushed, looked wildly about him in the manner of a small boy caught stealing jam, and almost ran from the scene leaving the cornerstone unlaid. His enjoyment of the Berlin Olympic Games was completely spoilt when a fanatical Dutch woman who had achieved a personal presentation suddenly clasped him in two hefty arms and tried to kiss him in plain view of 100,000 spectators. Hitler could not regain his composure or stand the irreverent guffaws of foreign visitors, and left the Stadium.[35]

This type of behavior is illustrated even more clearly in relation to Gregor Strasser because the occasion was one of extreme importance to Hitler. Strasser threatened to split the Party if a definite program could not be agreed upon. Hitler avoided the situation as long as he possibly could in the hope that something might happen, that the situation would somehow solve itself. When it did not he agreed to Strasser's demand for a meeting in Leipzig at which their differences could be thrashed out. Strasser was in the restaurant at the appointed hour. Hitler came late. Hardly had he sat down to the table when he excused himself in order to go to the toilet. Strasser waited for some time and when Hitler did not return he began making inquiries. To his amazement he discovered that instead of going to the toilet Hitler had slipped out of the back door and driven back to Munich without discussing a single point.[36]

Heiden also tells us that in 1923 he was in conference with Ludendorff when he suddenly rushed off without as much as an apology.[37] In the spring of 1932 he ran out on a meeting of the Verband Bayrischer Industrieller before which he was to speak. This group was not kindly disposed to him, but it was important for Hitler to win them over. He got up to speak: ". . . He stops, looks at the table in perplexing silence. An embarrassing moment. Suddenly Hitler turns on his heel and without a word goes to the door."[38] The same thing happened a year later when, as Chancellor, he was to speak to the Reichsverband der Deutschen Presse. Again he sensed opposition in the group and again he fled from the scene. Olden says: "This is a trick which the Fuehrer will use often: when the situation becomes embarrassing he hides."[39]

At other times, when he finds himself in difficult situations, the great dictator who prides himself on his decisiveness, hardness, and other leadership qualities, breaks down and weeps like a child appealing for sympathy. Rauschning writes:

> In 1934 as in 1932 he complained of the ingratitude of the German people in the sobbing tones of a down-at-the-heel music-hall performer! A weakling who accused and sulked, appealed and implored, and retired in wounded vanity ("If the German people don't want me!") instead of acting.[40]

Otto Strasser reports that on one occasion:

> He seized my hands, as he had done two years before. His voice was choked with sobs, and tears flowed down his cheeks.[41]

Heiden reporting a scene at which the Party leaders were waiting for the arrival of Gregor Strasser:

> "Never would I have believed it of Strasser," he (Hitler) cried, and he laid his head on the table and sobbed. Tears came to the eyes of many of those present, as they saw their Fuehrer weeping. Julius Streicher, who had been snubbed by Strasser for years, called out from his humble place in the background: "Shameful that Strasser should treat our Fuehrer like that!"[42]

In extremely difficult situations he has openly threatened to commit suicide. Sometimes it seems that he used
this as a form of blackmail while at other times the situation seems to be more than he can bear. During the Beer
Hall Putsch he said to the officials he was holding as
prisoners: "There are still five bullets in my pistol—four
for the traitors, and one, if things go wrong, for myself."[43] He also threatened to commit suicide before
Mrs. Hanfstaengl directly after the failure of the Putsch,
while he was hiding from the police in the Hanfstaengl
home. Again in Landsberg he went on a hunger strike and
threatened to martyr himself—in imitation of the Mayor
of Cork. In 1930 he threatened to commit suicide after the
strange murder of his niece, Geli, of whom we shall speak
later.[44] In 1932 he again threatened to carry out this action
if Strasser split the Party.[45] In 1933 he threatened to do so
if he was not appointed Chancellor,[46] and in 1936, he promised to do so if the occupation of the Rhineland failed.[47]

These, however, are relatively infrequent exhibitions although his associates have learned that they are always a
possibility and that it is wise not to push the Fuehrer too
far. More frequent are his depressions about which a great
deal has been written. It is certain that he does have very
deep depressions from time to time. During his years in
Vienna (1907-1912), he undoubtedly suffered from them
a great deal. Hanisch reports: "I have never seen such
helpless letting down in distress."[48] It is probably also true
that he suffered from depressions during the war as Mend
reports.[49]

After the death of his niece, Geli (1930), he also went
into a severe depression, which lasted for some time. Gregor Strasser actually feared that he might commit suicide
during this period and stayed with him for several days.
There is some evidence that he actually tried to do so and
was prevented from carrying it out.[50] It is also interesting
to note that for several years after her death he went into
a depression during the Christmas holidays and wandered
around Germany alone for days on end.[51]

Rauschning gives us a vivid description of his condition
after the Blood Purge of 1934. He writes:

But for the present he did not give the impression
of a conqueror. With his face puffed up and his features distorted, he sat opposite me as I reported to

him. His eyes were dim. He did not look at me. He played with his fingers. I did not get the impression that he listened to me. ... All the time it seemed to me that he wrangled with disgust, weariness, and contempt, and that in his thoughts he was far away. ... I had heard that he was able to sleep by the hour only. . . . At night he wandered around, restlessly. Sleeping pills did not help. . . . Supposedly he awoke from the short sleep in crying fits. Repeatedly he had vomited. Shivering he sat in an armchair, covered with blankets. ... Sometimes he wanted everything lit up and to be surrounded by people, many people; in the next moment, however, he did not want to see anybody.[52]

These were major crises in his life, and we can assume that they probably represent his worst depressions. Undoubtedly he very frequently has minor ones when he withdraws from his associates and broods by himself, or periods when he refuses to see anyone and is irritable and impatient with those around him. On the whole, however, it appears that the reports of Hitler's depressions have been grossly exaggerated. Not one of our informants who has had close contact with him has any knowledge of his ever retiring to a sanatorium during such times and there is only one source that indicates that he ever sought psychiatric help and that was not accepted. We must assume that the many reports that have flourished in the newspapers have been plants by the Nazi Propaganda agencies to lure us into false expectations.

There are a number of other respects in which Hitler does not appear before his associates as the self-confident Fuehrer he likes to believe himself to be. One of the most marked of these is his behavior in the presence of accepted authority. Under these circumstances he is obviously nervous and very ill at ease. Many times he is downright submissive. As far back as 1923, Ludecke reports that: "In conference with Poehner, Hitler sat with his felt hat crushed shapeless in his hands. His mien was almost humble."[53] Fromm writes that at a dinner:

Hitler's eagerness to obtain the good graces of the princes present was subject to much comment. He bowed and clicked and all but knelt in his zeal to please oversized, ugly Princess Luise von Sachsen-Meiningen, her brother, hereditary Prince George, and their sister, Grand Duchess of Sachsen-Weimar. Beaming in his servile attitude he dashed personally to bring refreshments from the buffet.[54]

On his visit to Rome, Huss writes: "When leading Queen Helene in Rome he was like a fish out of water. He didn't know what to do with his hands."[55] To Hindenburg he was extremely submissive. Pictures taken of their meetings illustrate his attitude very clearly. In some of them it looks almost as though he were about to kiss the President's hand. Flannery also reports that when Hitler first met Petain he took him by the arm and escorted him to his car.[56] Hanfstaengl reports that he found Hitler outside the door of the banquet hall in which a dinner and reception were being given to the former Kaiser's wife. He was unable to bring himself to go in and meet her Highness alone. When Hanfstaengl finally persuaded Hitler to go in he was so ill at ease that he could only stammer a few words to Hermine and then excused himself.[57] Many other examples could be cited. From the weight of evidence it seems certain that Hitler does lose his self-confidence badly when he is brought face to face with an accepted authority of high standing, particularly royalty.

This subservient attitude is also obvious in his use of titles. This is well described by Lania reporting on Hitler's trial:

> In the course of his peroration he came to speak of Generals Ludendorff and von Seeckt; at such moments, he stood at attention and trumpeted forth the words "General" and "Excellency." It made no difference that one of the generals was on his side, while the other, von Seeckt, Commander-in-Chief of the Reichswehr, was his enemy; he abandoned himself entirely to the pleasure of pronouncing the high-sounding titles. He never said "General Seeckt," he said "His Excellency Herr Colonel General von Seeckt," letting the words melt on his tongue and savoring their aftertaste.[58]

Many others have also commented on this tendency to use the full title. It also fits in with his very submissive behavior to his officers during the last war, which has been commented upon by several of his comrades. It seems safe to assume that this is a fundamental trait in his character that becomes less obvious as he climbs the ladder but is present nevertheless.

The Fuehrer is also ill at ease in the company of diplomats and avoids contact with them as much as possible. Fromm describes his behavior at a diplomatic dinner in the following words:

> The corporal seemed to be ill at ease, awkward and moody. His coat-tails embarrassed him. Again and again his hand fumbled for the encouraging support of his sword belt. Each time he missed the familiar cold and bracing support, his uneasiness grew. He crumpled his handkerchief, tugged it, rolled it, just plain stage-fright.[59]

Henderson writes:

> It will always be a matter of regret to me that I was never able to study Hitler in private life, as this might have given me the chance to see him under normal conditions and to talk with him as man to man. Except for a few brief words at chance meetings, I never met him except upon official and invariably disagreeable, business. He never attended informal parties at which diplomats might be present, and when friends of mine did try to arrange it, he always got out of meeting me in such a manner on the ground of precedent. . . . But he always looked self-conscious when he had to entertain the diplomatic corps, which happened normally three times a year.[60]

Hitler also becomes nervous and tends to lose his composure when he has to meet newspapermen. Being a genius of propaganda he realizes the power of the press in influencing public opinion and he always provides the press with choice seats at all ceremonies. When it comes to interviews, however, he feels himself on the defensive and insists that the questions be submitted in advance. When the interview takes place he is able to maintain considerable poise because he has his answers prepared. Even then he gives no opportunity to ask for further clarification because he immediately launches into a lengthy dissertation, which sometimes develops into a tirade. When this is finished, the interview is over.[61]

He is also terrified when he is called upon to speak to intellectuals or any group in which he feels opposition or the possibility of criticism.[62]

Hitler's adjustment to people in general is very poor. He is not really on intimate terms with any of his associates. Hess is the only associate, with the possible exception of Streicher, who has ever had the privilege of addressing him with the familiar "Du." Even Goering, Goebbels, and Himmler must address him with the more formal "Sie" although each of them would undoubtedly be willing to sacrifice his right hand for the privilege of addressing him in the informal manner. It is true that outside of his official family there are a few people in Germany, notably Mrs. Bechstein and the Winifred Wagner family who address him as "Du" and call him by his nickname, "Wolf," but even these are few and far between. On the whole, he always maintains a considerable distance from other people. Ludecke, who was very close to him for a while, writes:

> Even in his intimate and cozy moments, I sensed no attitude of familiarity towards him on the part of his staff; there was always a certain distance about him, that subtle quality of aloofness. . . .[63]

And Fry says: "He lives in the midst of many men and yet he lives alone."[64]

It is well-known that he cannot carry on a normal conversation or discussion with people. Even if only one person is present he must do all the talking. His manner of speech soon loses any conversational qualities it might have had and takes on all the characteristics of a lecture and may easily develop into a tirade. He simply forgets his companions and behaves as though he were addressing a multitude. Strasser has given a good, brief description of his manner:

> Now Hitler drew himself erect and by the far-away look in his eyes showed plainly that he was not speaking merely to me; he was addressing an imaginary

audience that stretched far beyond the walls of the living room.[65]

This is not only true in connection with political matters. Even when he is alone with his adjutants or immediate staff and tries to be friendly he is unable to enter into a give-and-take conversation. At times he seems to want to get closer to people and relates personal experiences, such as "When I was in Vienna," or "When I was in the Army." But under these circumstances, too, he insists on doing all the talking and always repeats the same stories over and over again in exactly the same form, almost as though he had memorized them. The gist of most of these stories is contained in *Mein Kampf*. His friends have all heard them dozens of times, but this does not deter him from repeating them again with great enthusiasm. Nothing but the most superficial aspects of these experiences are ever touched upon. It seems as though he is unable to give more of himself than that.[66]

Price says: "When more than two people are present, even though they are his intimate circle, there is no general discourse. Either Hitler talks and they listen, or else they talk among themselves and Hitler sits silent."[67] And this is the way it seems to be. He is not at all annoyed when members of the group talk to each other unless, of course, he feels like doing the talking himself. But ordinarily he seems to enjoy listening to others while he makes believe that he is attending to something else. Nevertheless, he overhears everything that is being said and often uses it later on.[68] However, he does not give credit to the individual from whom he has learned it but simply gives it out as his own. Rauschning says: "He has always been a *poseur*. He remembers things that he has heard and has a faculty for repeating them in such a way that the listener is led to believe that they are his own."[69]   Roehm also complained of this:

If you try to tell him anything, he knows everything already. Though he often does what we advise, he laughs in our faces at the moment, and later does the very thing as if it were all his own idea and creation. He doesn't even seem to be aware of how dishonest he is.[70]

Another one of his tricks that drives people and particularly his associates to distraction is his capacity for forgetting. This trait has been commented upon so much that it scarcely needs mentioning here. We all know how he can say something one day and a few days later say the opposite, completely oblivious of his earlier statement. He does not only do this in connection with international affairs but also with his closest associates. When they show their dismay and call his attention to the inconsistency he flies off into a rage and demands to know if the other person thinks he is a liar. Evidently the other leading Nazis have also learned the trick, for Rauschning says: "Most of the Nazis with Hitler at their head, literally forget, like hysterical women, anything they have no desire to remember."[71]

Although Hitler almost invariably introduces a few humorous elements into his speeches and gives the impression of considerable wit, he seems to lack any real sense of humor. He can never take a joke on himself. Heyst says, "He is unable to purify his gloomy self with self-irony and humor."[72] Von Wiegand says he is extremely sensitive to ridicule,[73] and Huss says, "He takes himself seriously and will flare up in a temperamental rage at the least impingement by act or attitude on the dignity and holiness of state and Fuehrer."[74] When everything is going well he sometimes gets into a gay and whimsical mood in a circle of close friends. His humor then is confined almost wholly to a kind of teasing or ribbing. The ribbing is usually in connection with alleged love affairs of his associates but are never vulgar and only hint at sexual factors.[75] Friedelinde Wagner provides us with an example of his teasing. Goering and Goebbels were both present at the time that he said to the Wagner family:

> You all know what a volt is and an ampere, don't you? Right. But do you know what a goebbels, a goering are? A goebbels is the amount of nonsense a man can speak in an hour and a goering is the amount of metal that can be pinned on a man's breast.[76]

His other form of humor is mimicking. Almost everyone concedes that he has great talent along these lines, and he frequently mimics his associates in their presence much to the amusement of everyone except the victim. He also loved to mimic Sir Eric Phipps and later Chamberlain.

Hitler's poor adaptation to people is perhaps most obvious in his relations to women. Since he has become a political figure, his name has been linked with a great many women, particularly in the foreign press. Although the German public seem to know very little about this phase of his life, his associates have seen a great deal of it and the topic is always one for all kinds of conjectures. Roughly speaking, his relations to women fall into three categories: (1) much older women, (2) actresses and passing fancies, and (3) more or less enduring relationships.

1. As early as 1920 Frau Carola Hofman, a sixty-one-year-old widow, took him under her wing and for years played the part of foster mother. Then came Frau Helena Bechstein, the wife of the famous Berlin piano manufacturer, who took over the role. She spent large quantities of money on Hitler in the early days of the Party, introduced him to her social circle, and lavished maternal affection on him. She often said that she wished that Hitler were her son, and while he was imprisoned in Landsberg she claimed that she was his adopted mother in order that she might visit him. Strasser says that Hitler would often sit at her feet and lay his head against her bosom while she stroked his hair tenderly and murmured, "Mein Woelfchen."[77] Since he came to power things have not gone so smoothly. She seemed to find fault with everything he did and would scold him unmercifully, even in public. According to Friedelinde Wagner,[78] she is the one person in Germany who can carry on a monologue in Hitler's presence and who would actually tell him what she thought. During these violent scoldings Hitler would stand there like an abashed schoolboy who had committed a misdemeanor. According to Hanfstaengl, Mrs. Bechstein had groomed Hitler in the expectation that he would marry her daughter, Lottie, who was far from attractive. Out of sense of obligation, Hitler did ask Lottie, but was refused.[79] Mrs. Bechstein was disconsolate over the failure of her plans and began to criticize Hitler's social reforms as well as his actions. Nevertheless, Hitler made duty calls fairly regularly even though he postponed them as long as possible.[80]

Then there was also Frau Victoria von Dirksen, who is alleged to have spent a fortune on him and his career,[81] and a number of others. In more recent years, Mrs. Goebbels has taken over the role of foster mother and looks after his comforts, supervises his household, and bakes delicacies of which he is particularly fond. She, too, has been acting as a matchmaker in the hope that he might marry one of her friends and thereby draw the bond between them even tighter. To Ludecke, she complained, "I am no good as a matchmaker. I would leave him alone with my most charming friends, but he wouldn't respond."[82] There was also his older half-sister, Angela, who kept house for him at Munich and Berchtesgaden and, for a time, seemed to play a mother's role.

Winifred Wagner, the daughter-in-law of Richard Wagner, has also caused a great deal of comment. She is English by birth, and, from all accounts, is very attractive and about Hitler's own age. She met Hitler in the early 1920's and since that time has been one of his staunch supporters. He became a frequent visitor at the Wagner home in Bayreuth and after his accession to power built a house on the Wagner estate for himself and his staff. After the death of Siegfried Wagner, reports all over the world had it that she would become Hitler's wife. But nothing happened in spite of the fact that it seemed like an ideal union from the point of view of both parties.

Nevertheless, Hitler continued to be a frequent guest at the Wagners'. It probably was the nearest thing to a home he has known since his own home broke up in 1907. Mrs. Wagner undoubtedly did everything in her power to make him comfortable, and Hitler felt very much at home. There were three small children, a boy and two girls (one of them is our informant, Friedelinde), which added considerably to the home atmosphere. The entire family called him by his nickname "Wolf" and addressed him as "Du." He felt so secure in this house that he often came and stayed without his bodyguard. He sometimes spent his Christmas holidays with the family and became very much a part of it. But further than that he was unwilling to go, even though the marriage would have been exceedingly popular with the German people.

2. Then there were a long line of "passing fancies." For the most part these were screen and stage stars. Hitler likes to be surrounded with pretty women and usually requests the moving picture companies to send over a number of actresses whenever there is a party in the Chancel-

lory. He seems to get an extraordinary delight in fascinating these girls with stories about his past life. He also likes to impress them with his power by ordering the studios to provide them with better roles, or promising that he will see to it that they are starred in some forthcoming picture. Most of his associations with women of this type, and their number is legion, do not go beyond this point as far as we have been able to discover. On the whole he seems to feel more comfortable in the company of stage people than with any other group and often went down to the studio restaurants for lunch.

3. There have been several other women who have played a more or less important role in Hitler's life. The first of which we have any knowledge was Henny Hoffmann, the daughter of the official Party photographer. Henny, according to reports, was little more than a prostitute and spent most of her time among the students in Munich, who alleged that she could be had for a few marks. Heinrich Hoffmann, her father, was a member of the Party and a close friend of Hitler. By a queer twist of Fate, Hoffmann had taken a picture of the crowds in Munich at the outbreak of the last war. Later, when Hitler became prominent in Munich politics, Hoffmann discovered Hitler in the picture and called it to his attention. Hitler was delighted, and a close relationship sprung up between them. Hoffmann's wife was also very fond of Hitler and played a mother role toward him for a time.

With the death of Mrs. Hoffmann, the home went to pieces from a moral point of view and became a kind of meeting place for homosexuals of both sexes. There was a good deal of drinking and great freedom in sexual activities of all kinds. Hitler was frequently present at parties given in the Hoffmann home and became very friendly with Henny. The relationship continued for some time until Henny, who was a very garrulous person by nature, got drunk one night and began to talk about her relationship to Hitler. Her father became enraged and for a time had little to do with Hitler.

Up to this time Hitler had steadfastly refused to have his photograph taken for publication on the grounds that it was better publicity to remain a mystery man and, also, because if his picture appeared it would be too easy to identify him when he crossed Communist territories. Shortly after the above described episode, Hitler named

Hoffmann as the official Party photographer and gave him
the exclusive right to his photographs. These privileges, so
it is alleged, have, in the course of years, netted Hoffmann
millions of dollars. Among Hitler's associates, it was supposed that Hitler had committed some kind of sexual indiscretion with Henny and bought Hoffmann's silence by
granting him these exclusive rights. In any event, Henny
was soon married to Baldur von Schirach, the Leader of
the Nazi Youth Movement, who is reputed to be a homosexual. His family was violently opposed to the marriage but Hitler insisted. All differences between Hitler
and Hoffmann seem to have disappeared, and today he is
one of Hitler's closest associates and exerts a great personal influence on the Fuehrer. We shall consider the
nature of Hitler's indiscretion later in our study since it is
not a matter of common knowledge and would lead us too
far afield at the present time.

After the Henny Hoffmann episode, Hitler began to appear in public with his niece, Geli, the daughter of his
half-sister, Angela, who had come to keep house for Hitler
in 1924. At the time this relationship matured her mother
had gone to Berchtesgaden, and Hitler and Geli were living alone in his Munich flat. They became inseparable
companions and the subject of much comment in Party
circles. Many of the members, particularly Gregor Strasser, felt that this was poor publicity and was creating a
good deal of unfavorable talk. Other members had Hitler
brought on the carpet to explain where he was getting the
money to clothe Geli and sport her around if he was not
using Party funds for this purpose.

Hitler became very jealous of Geli's attention and refused to let her go out with any other men. Some claim
that he kept her locked in during the day when he could
not take her with him. For several years the relationship
continued over the opposition of the Party. Then one day
Geli was found dead in Hitler's apartment—she had died
from a bullet fired from Hitler's revolver. There was considerable commotion. The coroner's verdict was suicide
but Geli was buried in hallowed ground by a Catholic
clergy. There was much speculation whether she killed
herself or was killed by Hitler. Whatever the facts may be,
Hitler went into a profound depression that lasted for
months. During the first days after the funeral, Gregor
Strasser remained with him in order to prevent him from

committing suicide. Ludecke says: "The special quality of Hitler's affection (for Geli) is still a mystery to those closest to him."[83]

For a few years after Geli's death, Hitler had little to do with women except in a very superficial way. Along about 1932, however, he became interested in Eva Braun, Hoffmann's photographic assistant. This relationship did not develop very rapidly, but it has continued. In the course of time, Hitler has bought her many things, including high-powered automobiles and a house between Munich and Berchtesgaden where, it is alleged, he frequently spends the night on the way to or from his country estate. Eva Braun is also frequently a guest at Berchtesgaden and in Berlin. Oechsner was told that after one of her visits in Berchtesgaden, some of her underwear was found in Hitler's bedroom. Wiedemann, according to Hohenlohe, says that she has sometimes spent the entire night in Hitler's bedroom in Berlin. It is reported by Norburt that Eva moved into the Chancellory on December 16, 1939, and it is said that Hitler intends to marry her when the war is over.[84] Beyond that, we know nothing about this affair except that Eva Braun has twice tried to commit suicide and that one of Hitler's bodyguards hurled himself from the Kehlstein because he was in love with her but could not trespass on the Fuehrer's domain.

The affair with Eva Braun was not exclusive, however. During this period he has also seen a good deal of at least two moving picture actresses. These have been more enduring than most of his associations with actresses and much more intimate. Both of these girls were frequently invited alone to the Chancellory late at night and departed in the early hours of the morning. During their stay they were alone with Hitler behind closed doors so that not even his immediate staff knew what transpired between them. The first of these relationships was with Renarte Mueller, who committed suicide by throwing herself from the window of a Berlin hotel. The other was with Leni Riefenstahl, who continued to be a guest at the Chancellory up to the outbreak of the war.

Hitler's associates know that in respect to women Hitler is far from the ascetic he and the Propaganda Bureau would like to have the German public believe. None of them, with the possible exception of Hoffmann and Schaub (his personal adjutant), know the nature of his sexual activities. This has led to a great deal of conjecture in Party circles. There are some who believe that his sex life is perfectly normal but restricted. Others, that he is immune from such temptations and that nothing happens when he is alone with girls. Still others believe that he is homosexual.

The latter belief is based largely on the fact that during the early days of the Party many of the inner circle were well-known homosexuals. Roehm made no attempt to hide his homosexual activities, and Hess was generally known as "Fraulein Anna." There were also many others, and it was supposed, for this reason, that Hitler, too, belonged in this category.

In view of Hitler's pretense at purity and the importance of his mission for building a Greater Germany, it is extraordinary that he should be so careless about his associates. He has never restricted them in any way except at the time of the Blood Purge in 1934 when his excuse was that he had to purge the Party of these undesirable elements. At all other times, he has been liberal to a fault. Lochner reports:

> The only criterion for membership in the Party was that the applicant be "Unconditionally obedient and faithfully devoted to me." When someone asked if that applied to thieves and criminals, Hitler said, "Their private lives don't concern me."[85]

Ludecke claims that in speaking of some of the moralists who were complaining about the actions of his S.A. men, Hitler said:

> He would rather his S.A. men took the women than some fat-bellied moneybag. "Why should I concern myself with the private lives of my followers. ... Apart from Roehm's achievements, I know that I can absolutely depend on him. . . ."[86]

Rauschning says that the general attitude in the Party was: "Do anything you like but don't get caught at it."[87]

This attitude toward his associates certainly did not make for high standards in the Party. Captain von Mueke resigned from the Party on the grounds that: "The People's Party no longer is the party of respectable people; it has deteriorated and it is corrupt. In one word: it is a pig-sty."[88] Rauschning expresses a similar sentiment:

> Most loathsome of all is the reeking miasma of furtive, unnatural sexuality that fills and fouls the whole atmosphere around him, like an evil emanation. Nothing in this environment is straightforward. Surreptitious relationships, substitutes and symbols, false sentiments and secret lusts—nothing in this man's surroundings is natural and genuine, nothing has the openness of a natural instinct.[89]

One of Hitler's hobbies that is carefully hidden from the public is his love for pornography. He can scarcely wait for the next edition of *Der Stuermer* to appear, and when it reaches him he goes through it avidly. He seems to get great pleasure out of the dirty stories and the cartoons that feature this sheet.[90] To Rauschning Hitler said that the *Stuermer* "was a form of pornography permitted in the Third Reich." In addition, Hitler has a large collection of nudes and, according to Hanfstaengl and others, he also enjoys viewing lewd movies in his private theater, some of which are prepared by Hoffmann for his benefit.

He also likes to present himself as a great authority and lover of good music. One of his favorite pastimes is to lecture on Wagner and the beauty of his operatic music. There can be no doubt that he enjoys Wagnerian music and gets considerable inspiration from it. Oechsner reports that he has been able to observe Hitler closely while he was listening to music and saw, "grimaces of pain and pleasure contort his face, his brows knit, his eyes close, his mouth contract tightly."[91] Hitler has said, "For me, Wagner is something godly, and his music is my religion. I go to his concerts as others go to church." According to Hanfstaengl, however, he is not a lover of good music in general.[92] He says that about 85 percent of Hitler's preferences in music are the normal program music in Viennese cafés. This is probably why Hitler rarely attends concerts and in later years seldom goes to the opera. His preferences now seem to run to musical comedies and cabarets in addition to the movies he sees at the Chancellory. Pope says that Hitler frequently visited *The Merry Widow* in which an American actress played the lead. He says, "I have seen Hitler nudge his gauleiter, Wagner, and smirk when Dorothy does her famous backbending number in the spotlight." In this number, Dorothy's costume consists of a pair of transparent butterfly wings, or sometimes nothing at all. Hitler watches the performance through opera glasses and sometimes has command performances for his private benefit.[93]

Much has been written by the Nazi propaganda bureau about his modest way of living. This, through the eyes of his associates, has also been vastly overrated. Although he is a vegetarian, most of them feel that his meals are scarcely to be considered as a form of deprivation. He eats large quantities of eggs prepared in 101 different ways by the best chef in Germany, and there are always quantities and a large variety of fresh vegetables prepared in unusual ways. In addition, Hitler consumes incredible quantities of pastries and often as much as two pounds of chocolates in the course of a single day. Nor are his personal tastes particularly inexpensive. Although his clothes are simple, he has an incredible number of each article of clothing. All are made of the finest materials that can be procured and made up by the best workmen. He also has a passion for collecting paintings, and when he has his heart set on one the sky is the limit as far as price is concerned. The only thing that is really modest about his living arrangements is his bedroom, which is extremely simple and contains only a white metal bed (decorated with ribbons at the head), a painted chest of drawers, and a few straight chairs. Friedelinde Wagner and Hanfstaengl, both of whom have seen the room with their own eyes, have described it in identical terms: namely, that it is a room that one would expect a maid to have and not a Chancellor.

Although he is presented to the German public as a man of extraordinary courage, his immediate associates frequently have occasion to question this. Several occasions have been reported on which he has not carried through his own program because he feared opposition. This is particularly true in connection with his gauleiters. He seems to have a particular fear of these people, and rather than meet opposition from them he usually tries to find out on which side of an issue the majority have aligned themselves before he meets with them. When the meeting takes place, he proposes a plan or course of action that will fit in with the sentiments of the majority.[94]

According to Hohenlohe he also backed down before three Army generals when they protested against the rapid developments in the Danzig question, and before Munich he decided to postpone the war because he discovered that the crowds watching the troops marching under the Chancellory windows were unenthusiastic.[95]

Furthermore, they must wonder about the necessity of the extreme precautions that are taken for his safety. Most of these are carefully concealed from the German public. When Hitler appears he looks for all the world like an extremely brave man as he stands up in the front seat of his open car and salutes. The people do not know of the tremendous number of secret service men who constantly mingle with the crowds in addition to the guards who line the streets through which he is to pass. Neither do they know of all the precautions taken at the Chancellory or at Berchtesgaden. Before the war his house at Berchtesgaden was surrounded with eight miles of electrified wire. Pillboxes and antiaircraft batteries were set up in the surrounding hills.[96] When he visited at Bayreuth, troops were sent in weeks in advance to set up machine-gun nests and antiaircraft batteries in the hills immediately adjoining.[97] Lochner reports that when he travels in a special train he is accompanied by 200 SS guards who are more heavily armed than the retinue of any German emperor.[98] After the war started, his train was heavily armored and equipped with antiaircraft fore and aft. And, yet, when the newsreels show him at the front, he is the only one who does not wear a steel helmet.

There is, consequently, a considerable discrepancy between Hitler as he is known to the German people and Hitler as he is known to his associates. Nevertheless, it appears that most of his associates have a deep allegiance to Hitler personally and are quite ready to forgive or ignore his shortcomings. In many cases it seems as though his associates are quite oblivious to the contradictory traits in his character—to them he is still the Fuehrer and they live for the moments when he actually plays this role.

PART IV

卐

HITLER

As He Knows Himself

✤

HITLER has always been extremely secretive in all his dealings. Hanfstaengl tells us that this trait is carried to such a degree that he never tells one of his immediate associates what he has been talking about or arranged with another. His mind is full of compartments, Hanfstaengl says, and his dealings with every individual are carefully pigeonholed. What has been filed in one pigeonhole is never permitted to mix with that in another. Everything is scrupulously kept locked up in his mind and is only opened when he needs the material.

This is also true of himself. We have already seen how he has steadfastly refused to divulge anything about his past to his associates. This, he believed, was something that did not concern them in any way, and consequently he has kept the pigeonhole tightly closed. He talks almost continually about everything under the sun—except himself. What really goes on in his mind is almost as great a mystery as his past life.

Nevertheless, it would be helpful and interesting to open this pigeonhole and examine its contents. Fortunately, a few fragments of information concerning his past life have been unearthed in the course of time, and these are extremely valuable as a background for understanding his present behavior. Then, too, we have records of attitudes and sentiments expressed in speeches and writings. Although these utterances are confined to a rather limited area, they do represent the products of some of his mental processes and consequently give us some clue to what goes on behind those much discussed eyes, of which Rauschning writes:

> Anyone who has seen this man face to face, has met his uncertain glance, without depth or warmth, from eyes that seem hard and remote, and has then

seen that gaze grow rigid, will certainly have experienced the uncanny feeling: "That man is not
normal."[1]

In addition, we have descriptions of his overt behavior in
the face of varied circumstances. We must assume that
these, too, are the products of his psychological processes
and that they reflect what is going on behind the scenes.

All of this, however, would be insufficient data for an
adequate picture of Hitler, as he knows himself, in everyday life. Fortunately, patients with behavior patterns, tendencies, and sentiments very similar to those that Hitler
has expressed are not unknown in psychoanalytical practice. From our knowledge of what goes on in the minds of
these patients, together with a knowledge of their past his-
tories, it may be possible to fill in some of the gaps and
make some deductions concerning his extraordinary mode
of adjustment.

We have learned from the study of many cases that the
present character of an individual is the product of an
evolutionary process, the beginnings of which are to be
found in infancy. The very earliest experiences in the lifetime of the individual form the foundation upon which the
character is gradually structured as the individual passes
through successive stages of development and is exposed
to the demands and influences of the world around him. If
this is true, it would be well for us to review briefly Hitler's past history, as far as it is known, in the hope that it
may cast some light upon his present behavior and the
course he is most likely to pursue in the future. Such a review of his past is also pertinent to our study insofar as it
forms the background through which Hitler sees himself.
It is a part of him he must live with, whether he likes it or
not.

The Hitler Family

FATHER

There is a great deal of confusion in studying Hitler's
family tree. Much of this is due to the fact that the name
has been spelled in various ways: Hitler, Hidler, Hiedler,
and Huettler. It seems reasonable to suppose, however,
that it is fundamentally the same name spelled in various

ways by different members of what was basically an illiterate peasant family. Adolf Hitler himself signed his name Hittler on the first Party membership blanks, and his sister usually spells her name as Hiedler. Another element of confusion is introduced by the fact that Adolf's mother's mother was also named Hitler, which later became the family name of his father. Some of this confusion is dissipated, however, when we realize that Adolf's parents had a common ancestor (father's grandfather and mother's great-grandfather), an inhabitant of the culturally backward Waldviertel district of Austria.

Adolf's father, Alois Hitler, was the illegitimate son of Maria Anna Schicklgruber. It is generally supposed that the father of Alois Hitler was a Johann Georg Hiedler, a miller's assistant. Alois, however, was not legitimized, and he bore his mother's name until he was forty years of age when he changed it to Hitler. Just why this was done is not clear, but it is generally said among the villagers that it was necessary in order to obtain a legacy. Where the legacy came from is unknown. One could suppose that Johann Georg Hiedler relented on his deathbed and left an inheritance to his illegitimate son together with his name. It seems strange, however, that he did not legitimize the son when he married Anna Schicklgruber thirty-five years earlier. Why the son chose to take the name Hitler instead of Hiedler, if this is the case, is also a mystery that has remained unsolved. Unfortunately, the date of the death of Hiedler has not been established, and consequently we are unable to relate these two events in time. A peculiar series of events, prior to Hitler's birth, furnishes plenty of food for speculation.

There are some people who seriously doubt that Johann Georg Hiedler was the father of Alois. Thyssen and Koehler, for example, claim that Chancellor Dollfuss had ordered the Austrian police to conduct a thorough investigation into the Hitler family. As a result of this investigation a secret document was prepared that proved that Maria Anna Schicklgruber was living in Vienna at the time she conceived. At that time she was employed as a servant in the home of Baron Rothschild. As soon as the family discovered her pregnancy she was sent back to her home in Spital where Alois was born. If it is true that one of the Rothschilds is the real father of Alois Hitler, it would make Adolf a quarter Jew. According to these sources, Adolf Hitler knew of the existence of this document and the incriminating evidence it contained. In order to obtain it he precipitated events in Austria and initiated the assassination of Dollfuss. According to this story, he failed to obtain the document at that time since Dollfuss had secreted it and had told Schuschnigg of its whereabouts so that in the event of his death the independence of Austria would remain assured. Several stories of this general character are in circulation.

Those who lend credence to this story point out several factors that seem to favor its plausibility.

1. That it is unlikely that the miller's assistant in a small village in this district would have very much to leave in the form of a legacy.

2. That it is strange that Johann Hiedler should not claim the boy until thirty-five years after he had married the mother and the mother had died.

3. That if the legacy were left by Hiedler on the condition that Alois take his name, it would not have been possible for him to change it to Hitler.

4. That the intelligence and behavior of Alois, as well as that of his two sons, is completely out of keeping with that usually found in Austrian peasant families. They point out that their ambitiousness and extraordinary political intuition are much more in harmony with the Rothschild tradition.

5. That Alois Schicklgruber left his home village at an early age to seek his fortune in Vienna where his mother had worked.

6. That it would be peculiar for Alois Hitler, while working as a customs official in Braunau, to choose a Jew named Prinz, of Vienna, to act as Adolf's godfather unless he felt some kinship with the Jews himself.

This is certainly a very intriguing hypothesis, and much of Adolf's later behavior could be explained in rather easy terms on this basis. However, it is not absolutely necessary to assume that he has Jewish blood in his veins in order to make a comprehensive picture of his character with its manifold traits and sentiments. From a purely scientific point of view, therefore, it is sounder not to base our reconstruction on such slim evidence but to seek firmer

foundations. Nevertheless, we can leave it as a possibility
that requires further verification.

In any event Maria Anna Schicklgruber died when
Alois was five years of age. When he was thirteen he left
the Waldviertel and went to Vienna where he learned to
be a cobbler. The next twenty-three years of his life are
largely unaccounted for. It seems probable that during this
time he joined the army and had perhaps been advanced
to the rank of noncommissioned officer. His service in the
army may have helped him to enter the Civil Service as
Zollamtsoffizial later on.

His married life was stormy. His first wife (born Glasl-
Hoerer) was about thirteen years older than himself. She
is alleged to have been the daughter of one of his superiors and seems to have been in poor health. In any event
the marriage turned out badly, and they finally separated
since, as Catholics, a complete divorce was not possible.
His first wife died on April 6, 1883.

In January 1882 Franziska Matzelsberger gave birth to
an illegitimate son, who was named Alois. After the death
of his first wife, Alois Hitler married Franziska
Matzelsberger on May 22, 1883, and legitimized his son.
On July 28, 1883, his second wife bore him another child,
Angela, and a year later, on August 10, 1884, she died.
During the time of his first marriage the couple had taken
as a foster daughter Klara Poelzl, Alois Hitler's second
cousin once removed. He had reared her up to the time of
the separation from his first wife when she went to Vienna
as a servant. During the last months of the life of his second wife, Klara Poelzl returned to his home to look after
the invalid and the two children. She remained in his
home as housekeeper after the death of his second wife
and on January 7, 1885, he married her. On May 17, 1885,
she gave birth to a son who died in infancy. It is alleged
by William Patrick Hitler, Adolf's nephew, that an illegitimate child was born previously, but we have no other record of this. In any event at least one child was conceived
out of wedlock. Four more children were born of this
union. This is certainly a tempestuous married life for a
customs officer—three wives, seven or possibly eight children, one divorce, at least one birth and possibly two before marriage, two directly after the wedding, one wife
thirteen years older than himself and another twenty-three
years younger, one the daughter of a superior, one a wait-

ress, and the third a servant and his foster daughter. All of this, of course, has never been mentioned by Hitler. In *Mein Kampf* he gives a very simple picture of conditions in his father's home.

Relatively little is known about Alois Hitler. It seems that he was very proud of his achievements in the civil service, and yet he retired from this service at the astonishing age of fifty-six, four years after Adolf was born. In very rapid succession the family moved into several different villages, and the father tried his hand at farming. It is said, however, that he always wore his customs official's uniform and insisted on being addressed as Herr Oberoffizial Hitler. According to reports, he liked to lord it over his neighbors, whom he may have looked down upon as "mere" peasants. In any event it seems quite certain that he enjoyed sitting in the tavern and relating his adventures as a customs official and also discussing political topics. He died on his way to the tavern in Leonding from a stroke of apoplexy in 1903.

He is generally described as a very domineering individual who was a veritable tyrant in his home. William Patrick Hitler says that he has heard from his father, Adolf's elder half-brother, that he used to beat the children unmercifully. On one occasion it is alleged he beat the older son into a state of unconsciousness and on another occasion beat Adolf so severely that he left him for dead. It is also alleged that he was somewhat of a drunkard and that frequently the children would have to bring him home from the taverns. When he reached home a grand scene would take place during which he would beat wife, children, and dog rather indiscriminately. Although this story is rather generally accepted, Heiden, who interviewed a number of the villagers in various places where the family had lived, could not find substantiating evidence. Many found the old man rather amusing and claimed that his home life was fairly happy and quiet except when his wife's sister came to visit with the family. Why this should be a disturbing factor is unknown. Heiden suspects that the legacy was a bone of contention. However, many things may have taken place in the home that the villagers were unaware of or reluctant to talk about.

There is also some doubt about the complexion of Alois Hitler's political sentiments. Hanisch reports: "Hitler heard from his father only praise of Germany and all the

faults of Austria." According to Heiden, more reliable informants claim that the father, though full of complaints
and criticisms of the government he served, was by no
means a German nationalist. They say he favored Austria
against Germany, and this coincides with William Patrick
Hitler's information that his grandfather was definitely
anti-German just as his own father was.

MOTHER

Klara Poelzl, as has been said, was the foster daughter of
her husband and twenty-three years his junior. She came
from old peasant stock, was hard-working, energetic,
pious, and conscientious. Whether it was due to her years
of domestic service or to her upbringing, her home was always spotlessly clean, everything had its place, and not a
speck of dust was to be found on the furniture. She was
very devoted to her children and, according to William
Patrick Hitler, was a typical stepmother to her stepchildren. According to Dr. Bloch, who treated her, she was a
very quiet, sweet, and affectionate woman whose life centered around her children and particularly Adolf, who was
her pet. She spoke highly of her husband and the life they
had had together. She felt it was a real deprivation for the
children to have lost their father while they were still so
young.

One could question her background. Her sister is married and has two sons, one of whom is a hunchback and
has an impediment in his speech. When we consider that
Klara Poelzl may have lost one child before her marriage
to Alois Hitler, another son born in 1885 died in 1887, another son born in 1894 died in 1900, and a girl born in
1886 died in 1888, one has grounds to question the purity
of the blood. There is even cause for greater suspicion
when we learn from Dr. Bloch that he is certain that there
was a daughter slightly older than Adolf who was an imbecile. He is absolutely certain of this because he noticed
at the time that the family always tried to hide the child
and keep her out of the way when he came to attend the
mother. It is possible that this is Ida, who was born in
1886 and who is alleged to have died in 1888, except that
Dr. Bloch believes that this girl's name was Klara. He
may, however, be mistaken in this, particularly since both
names end in "a" and he never had any close contact with

her. There is no other mention of a Klara anywhere in the records. The younger sister, Paula, is also said to be a little on the stupid side, perhaps a high-grade moron. This is certainly a poor record, and one is justified in suspecting some constitutional weakness. A syphilitic taint is not beyond the realm of possibility. The mother died following an operation for cancer of the breast on December 21, 1907. All biographers have given the date of her death as December 21, 1908, but Dr. Bloch's records show clearly that she died in 1907 and John Gunther's record of the inscription on her tombstone corroborates this. The last six months of her life were spent in extreme pain, and during the last weeks it was necessary to give her injections of morphine daily.

It is often alleged that she was of Czech origin and spoke only a broken German and that consequently Adolf may have been ashamed of her among his playmates. This is almost certainly untrue. Dr. Bloch reports that she did not have any trace of an accent of any kind, nor did she show any Czech characteristics. Alois Hitler's first wife was of Czech origin, and later writers may have confused her with Adolf's mother.

ALOIS, JR.

Alois Hitler, Jr., was born January 13, 1882; he was the illegitimate son of the father's second wife, but was born during the lifetime of the first wife. He is the father of William Patrick Hitler, one of our informants. He seems to have taken very much after his father in some respects. He left the parental home before the death of his father because, according to his son, he could tolerate it no longer. His stepmother, according to the story, made life very difficult for him and continually antagonized her husband against him. It seems that Alois, Jr., had considerable talent for mechanical pursuits, and his father had planned on sending him to a technical school for training as an engineer. Until his third marriage the father was very fond of his oldest boy, and all his ambitions were wrapped up in him. But the stepmother systematically undermined this relationship and finally persuaded the father that Alois, Jr., was unworthy and that he should save his money for the education of her son Adolf. She was finally successful and Alois, Jr. was sent away from home as an apprentice waiter.

Evidently the profession of waiter did not interest him, for in 1900 he received a five-months' sentence for thievery and in 1902 he was sentenced to eight months in jail for the same reason. He then went to London, where he obtained a position as a waiter and in 1909 married Bridget Dowling, an Irish girl. In 1911 William Patrick Hitler was born, and in 1913 his father deserted the family and returned to Germany. The family was not a happy one and broke up several times in the course of these four years. It is alleged that the father drank quite frequently and would then come home and create tremendous scenes during which he frequently beat his wife and tried to beat the small infant. During these four years when his mother and father had separated for a time, his father did go to Vienna. This would agree with Hanfstaengl's conviction that Alois, Jr., was in Vienna at the same time that Adolf was there.

In 1924 Alois, Jr., was brought before the court of Hamburg charged with bigamy. He was sentenced to six months in prison, but since his first wife did not prosecute the sentence was suspended. He has an illegitimate child by the second wife who lives in Germany. During all these years he has never sent any money for the support of his first wife or child. Up until the time of the inflation it is alleged that he had a very successful business in Germany. The business failed, and he has had various jobs up until 1934 when he opened a restaurant in Berlin that became a popular meeting place for S.A. men.

According to his son, Alois, Jr., heartily disliked Adolf as a boy. He always felt that Adolf was spoiled by his mother and that he was forced to do many of the chores that Adolf should have done. Furthermore, it seems that Adolf occasionally got into mischief that his mother would blame on Alois, and Alois would have to take the punishment from his father. He used to say that as a boy he would have liked to have wrung Adolf's neck on more than one occasion, and considering the circumstances this is probably not far from the truth. Since Hitler came to power, the two brothers have practically no contact with each other. They have come together a few times, but the meeting is usually unpleasant, with Adolf taking a very high-handed attitude and laying down the law to the rest of the family. Alois, Jr., is not mentioned in *Mein Kampf*, and only a few people in Germany know of his relationship to Hitler. According to a newspaper report he was sent to a concentration camp in 1942 because he talked too much.

WILLIAM PATRICK HITLER

The son of Alois, Jr., is a young man of thirty-two, who has not amounted to much. Before his uncle came to power he worked as a bookkeeper in London. When his uncle became famous he obviously expected that something would be done for his family. He gave up his job in London and went to Germany where he had some contact with Adolf Hitler. The latter, however, was chiefly interested in keeping him under cover and provided him with a minor job in the Opel Automobile Company. It is my impression that William Patrick was quite ready to blackmail both his father and his uncle but that things did not work out as planned. He returned to England and as a British subject came to this country where he is a professional speaker. He is also engaged in writing a book about his associations and experiences in Hitler Germany.

ANGELA

She is an elder half-sister of Adolf. She seems to be the most normal one in the family and from all reports is rather a decent and industrious person. During her childhood she became very fond of Adolf despite the fact that she had the feeling that his mother was spoiling him. She is the only one of the family with whom Adolf has had any contact in later years and the only living relative Hitler ever mentioned. When his mother died in 1907 there was a small inheritance that was to be divided among the children. Since the two girls had no immediate means of earning a livelihood, the brothers turned over their share to help the girls along. Adolf turned his share over to Angela while Alois turned his over to a younger sister, Paula. Angela later married an official named Raubal in Linz who died not long afterward. She then went to Vienna where after the war she was manager of the Mensa Academica Judaica. Some of our informants knew her during this time and report that in the student riots Angela defended the Jewish students from attack and on several occasions beat the Aryan students off the steps of the dining hall with a club. She is a rather large, strong peasant type of person who is well able to take an active part.

After Adolf was discharged from the army at the close of the last war, it is alleged that he went to Vienna and visited Angela with whom he had had no contact for ten years. While he was confined in Landsberg she made the trip from Vienna to visit him. In 1924 she moved to Munich with her daughter, Geli, and kept house for Adolf. Later, she took over the management of Berchtesgaden. In 1936 friction developed between Adolf and Angela, and she left Berchtesgaden and moved to Dresden where she married Professor Hamitsch. It is reported by William Patrick that the cause of the break was the discovery by Hitler that she was in a conspiracy with Goering to purchase the land adjoining Hitler's house at Berchtesgaden. This enraged Hitler to the extent that he ordered her from the house and has had little contact with her since. In any case, Adolf did not attend her second wedding.

GELI RAUBAL

Hitler's relationship with Geli, Angela's daughter, has already been described in the previous section. She died in 1930.

LEO RAUBAL

It has been generally assumed that Geli was the only child of Angela. William Patrick Hitler, however, reports that there was also a son named Leo. Not much is known of him except that he refused to have anything to do with his uncle Adolf after the death of Geli. He had a job in Salzburg and frequently came to Berchtesgaden to visit his mother when Hitler was in Berlin, but would leave again just as soon as word was received that Hitler was on his way there. According to William Patrick, he openly accused Hitler of causing Geli's death and refused to speak to him again as long as he lived. Word has been received that he was killed in 1942 while in the Balkans.

PAULA HITLER

Paula Hitler, or Hiedler, is Adolf's real sister and is seven years younger. What happened to her after her mother's death is a mystery until she was discovered living very poorly in an attic in Vienna where she has a position addressing envelopes for an insurance company. She now lives under the name of Frau Wolf (Hitler's nickname is Wolf). Dr. Bloch went to visit her in the hope that she might intercede with her brother and obtain permission for him to take some money out of the country when he was exiled. He rapped on her door a number of times but received no answer. Finally, the neighbor on the same landing came to the door and asked who he was and what he wanted. The neighbor explained that Frau Wolf never received anyone and intimated that she was very queer (other writers have also reported this). She promised, however, to deliver any message he might give her. Dr. Bloch explained his predicament in detail. The next day when he returned, hoping that he would have an opportunity of speaking to Paula Hitler personally, the neighbor reported that Paula was very glad to hear from him and that she would do everything she could to help him. Nothing more.

During her childhood, according to William Patrick Hitler, she and Adolf did not get on very well together. There seems to have been considerable friction and jealousy between them, particularly since Alois, Jr., was always taking her side. As far as is known, Hitler had no contact with her whatever from the time his mother died until 1933, when he became Chancellor. He has never mentioned her anywhere, as far as can be determined. It is alleged that he now sends her a small allowance each month to alleviate her poverty and keep her out of the limelight. According to William Patrick Hitler, his uncle became more interested in her as the friction with Angela increased. It is said that he has had her visit him at Berchtesgaden, and William Patrick met her at the Bayreuth Festival in 1939 where she went by the name of Frau Wolf, but Hitler did not mention to anyone that it was his sister. He said she is a little on the stupid side and not very interesting to talk to since she rarely opens her mouth.

This is Adolf Hitler's family, past and present. It is possible that there is another sister, Ida, an imbecile, who is still living, but if so we have no knowledge of her whereabouts. On the whole it is nothing to be proud of, and Hitler may be wise in keeping it well under cover.

If we let our imaginations carry us back into the early 1890's it is not difficult to picture what life was like for Adolf in his earliest years. His father was probably not much company for his mother. Not only was he twenty-three years older but, it seems, he spent most of his spare time in the taverns or gossiping with the neighbors. Furthermore, his mother knew only too well the past history of her husband, who was also her foster father, and one can imagine that for a twenty-five-year-old woman this was not what might be called a romantic marriage. Moreover, Klara Hitler had lost her first two children, and possibly a third, in the course of three or four years. Then Adolf arrived. Under these circumstances it is almost inevitable that he became the focal point in her life and that she left no stone unturned to keep him alive. All of the affection that normally would have gone to her husband and to her other children now became lavished on this newly born son.

It is safe to assume that for five years little Adolf was the center of attraction in this home. But then a terrible event happened in Adolf's life—another son was born. No longer was he the center of attraction, no longer was he the king of the roost. The newcomer usurped all this, and little Adolf, who was on his way to growing up, was left to shift more or less for himself—at least so it probably seemed to him. Sharing was something he had not learned up to this time, and it was probably a bitter experience for him as it is for most childen who have a sibling born when they are in this age period. In fact, in view of the earlier experiences of his parents it is reasonable to suppose that it was probably more acute in his case than it is with the average boy.

For two years he had to put up with this state of affairs. Then matters went from bad to worse—a baby sister was born. More competition and still less attention, for the baby sister and the ailing brother were consuming all of his mother's time while he was being sent off to school and made to take care of himself. Four years later tragedy again visited the Hitler household. When Adolf was eleven years old (in 1900) his baby brother, Edmund, died. Again we can imagine that Adolf reaped an additional harvest of affection and again became the apple of his mother's eye.

This extraordinary series of events certainly must have

left their mark on Adolf's immature personality. What probably went on in his mind during these years we shall consider later on. It is sufficient at the moment to point out the extraordinary sequences of events and the probable effects they had on the members of the family and their relations with each other.

When Adolf was six years old he was sent off to school. The first school was a very small Volkschule where three grades met in the same room and were taught by the same teacher. In spite of the fact that he had to change schools several times in the course of the next few years, due to the fact that his father kept buying and selling his property and moving from one place to another, he seems to have done quite well in his studies. When he was eight years old he attended a Benedictine Monastery in Lamback. He was very much intrigued with all this—it gave him his first powerful impression of human achievement. At that time his ambition was to become an abbot. But things did not work out very well. He was dismissed from the monastery because he was caught smoking in the gardens. His last year in Volkschule was in Leonding where he received high marks in all his subjects with the occasional exception of singing, drawing, and physical exercises.

In 1900, the year his brother Edmund died, he entered the Realschule in Linz. To the utter amazement of all who knew him his school work was so poor that he failed and had to repeat the class another time. Then there was a gradual improvement in his work, particularly in history, freehand drawing, and gymnastics. In these subjects he was marked "excellent" several times. Mathematics, French, German, and so forth, remained mediocre, sometimes satisfactory, sometimes unsatisfactory. On "Effort" he was frequently marked "irregular." When he was fourteen years of age his father died suddenly. The following year he left the Realschule in Linz and attended the one in Steyr. We do not know why this change was made. Dr. Bloch is under the impression that he was doing badly toward the end of the year in the Linz school and was sent to Styria because it had the reputation of being easier. But his performance there was very mediocre. The only two subjects in which he excelled were freehand drawing, in which he was marked "praiseworthy," and gymnastics, in which he received the mark of "excellent."

In the first semester German Language was "unsatisfactory" and "History" was "adequate."

All this is beautifully glossed over in Hitler's description of these years. According to his story he was at odds with his father concerning his future career as artist, and in order to have his own way he sabotaged his studies—except those he felt would contribute to an artist's career, and History, which he says always fascinated him. In these studies, according to his own story, he was always outstanding. An examination of his report cards reveals no such thing. History, even in his last year in Realschule, is adequate or barely passing, and other subjects that might be useful to an artist are in the same category. A better diagnosis would be that he was outstanding in those subjects that did not require any preparation or thought while in those that required application he was sadly lacking. We frequently find report cards of this type among our patients who are very intelligent but refuse to work. They are bright enough to catch on to a few of the fundamental principles without exerting themselves and clever enough to amplify these sufficiently to obtain a passing grade without ever doing any studying. They give the impression of knowing something about the subject, but their knowledge is very superficial and is glossed over with glib words and terminology.

This evaluation of Hitler's school career fits in with the testimony of former fellow students and teachers. According to their testimony he never applied himself and was bored with what was going on. While the teacher was explaining new material, he read the books of Karl May (Indian and Wild West stories), which he kept concealed under his desk. He would come to school with bowie knives, hatchets, and the like, and was always trying to initiate Indian games in which he was to be the leader. The other boys, however, were not greatly impressed by him and his big talk or by his attempts to play the leader. On the whole, they preferred to follow the leadership of boys who were more socially minded, who were more realistic in their attitudes, and who held greater promise of future achievements than Hitler, who gave every indication of being lazy and uncooperative, who lived in a world of fantasy, who talked big but did nothing of merit. He probably did not improve his standing with the other boys, when in his twelfth year he was found guilty of a "Sittlichkeitsvergehen" in the school. Just what the sexual indiscretion consisted of we do not know, but Dr. Bloch, who remembers that one of the teachers in the school told him about it, feels certain that he had done something with a little girl. He was severely censured for this and barely missed being expelled from school. It is possible that he was ostracized by his fellow students and that this is the reason he changed schools the following year.

In September 1905 he stopped going to school altogether and returned to Leonding where he lived with his mother and sister. According to his biographers, he was suffering from lung trouble during this period and had to remain in bed the greater part of the time. Dr. Bloch, who was the family doctor at this time, is at a loss to understand how this story ever got started because there was no sign of lung trouble of any sort. Adolf came to his office now and then with a slight cold or a sore throat, but there was nothing else wrong with him. According to Dr. Bloch, he was a very quiet boy at this time, rather slight in build but fairly wiry. He was always very courteous and patiently waited for his turn. He made no fuss when the doctor looked into his throat or when he swabbed it with an antiseptic. He was very shy and had little to say except when spoken to. But there was no sign of lung trouble.

During this time, however, he frequently went with his mother to visit his aunt in Spital, Lower Austria, where he also spent vacations. The doctor who treated him there is alleged to have said to the aunt: "From this illness Adolf will not recover." It has been assumed that he referred to a lung condition, but he may have been referring to something else entirely. In any event Dr. Bloch is convinced that there were no indications of lung trouble a few months later when Adolf returned to Leonding.

Although the mother's income was extremely modest, Adolf made no attempt to find work. There is some evidence that he went to a Munich art school for a short time during this period. Most of his time, however, was evidently spent in loafing around and daubing paints and water colors. He took long walks into the hills, supposedly to paint, but it is reported that he was seen there delivering speeches to the rocks of the countryside in a most energetic tone of voice.

In October 1907, when he was eighteen years old, he went to Vienna to prepare himself for the state examinations for admission as a student to the Academy of Art. He qualified for admission to the examination but failed to be accepted as a student. He returned home to Linz but there is no indication that he communicated to anybody the results of the examination. It was undoubtedly a severe blow to him, for he tells us himself that he couldn't understand it, "he was so sure he would succeed." At this time his mother had already undergone an operation for cancer of the breast. She was failing rather rapidly, and little hope was held for her recovery. She died on December 21, 1907 and was buried on Christmas Eve. To preserve a last impression, he sketched her on her deathbed. Adolf, according to Dr. Bloch, was completely broken: "In all my career I have never seen anyone so prostrate with grief as Adolf Hitler." Although his sisters came to Dr. Bloch a few days after the funeral and expressed themselves fully, Adolf remained silent. As the little group left, he said: "I shall be grateful to you forever."[2] After the funeral he stood at her grave for a long time after the sisters had left. The bottom had obviously fallen out of his world. Tears came into Dr. Bloch's eyes as he described the tragic scene. "His mother would turn over in her grave if she knew what he turned out to be."[3] This was the end of Adolf Hitler's family life.

Later Experiences

VIENNA

Shortly after his mother's death the family broke up, and Adolf went to Vienna to make his way in the world as his father had done before him. This was early in 1908. How much money he took with him, if any, is not known. The records here are very vague particularly since all biographers have gone on the supposition that his mother died a year later than she actually did. This leaves an entire year unaccounted for since the next thing we hear of Adolf, he has again applied for admission to the examinations for the Academy of Art. One of the conditions for reexamination was that he submit to the Board some of the paintings he had done previously. This he did but the Board was not impressed with them and refused to allow him to enter the examination. This, it seems, was even a greater shock than his failure to pass the examinations a year earlier.

After he had received notification to the effect that his work was of such a nature that it did not warrant his admission to the second examination, he interviewed the Director. He claims that the Director told him that his drawings showed clearly that his talents lay in the direction of architecture rather than pure art and advised him to seek admission to the Architectural School. This he applied for but was not admitted, according to his story, because he had not satisfactorily finished his course in the Realschule. To be sure, this was one of the general requirements but exceptions could be made in the case of boys who showed unusual talent. Hitler's rejection, therefore, was on the grounds of insufficient talent rather than for failure to complete his school course.

He was now without hope. All his dreams of being a great artist seemed to be nipped in the bud. He was without money and without friends. He was forced to go to work and found employment as a laborer on construction jobs. This, however, did not suit him. Friction developed between himself and his fellow workmen. It seems logical to suppose that he was working beneath his class and refused to mingle with them, for he tells us that he sat apart from the others and ate his lunch. Further difficulties developed inasmuch as the workmen tried to convert him to a Marxian point of view. Their attitudes and arguments jarred him since they were far from the ideal Germany that had been portrayed by his favorite Linz teacher, Ludwig Poetsch, an ardent German nationalist. But Hitler found himself unable to answer their arguments. He made the unpleasant discovery that the workmen knew more than he did. He was fundamentally against everything they said, but he was unable to justify his point of view on an intellectual level—he was at a terrible disadvantage. In order to remedy the situation he began reading all kinds of political pamphlets and attending political meetings but not with the idea of understanding the problem as a whole, which might have enabled him to form an intelligent opinion, but to find arguments that would support his earlier conviction. This is a trait that runs throughout his life. He never studies to learn but only to justify what he feels. In other words, his judgments are based wholly on emotional factors and are then clothed with an intellectual argument. Soon, he tells us, he knew more than they did about their own political ideology and was able to tell them things about it that they did not know themselves.

It was this, according to Hitler, that antagonized the workmen against him. In any case he was run off the job with the threat that if he appeared again they would push him off the scaffold. This must have been during the first half of 1909 when he was twenty years old. Without a job he sunk lower and lower in the social scale and at times must have been on the verge of starvation. At times he found an odd job such as carrying luggage, shoveling snow, or running errands, but a large part of his time was spent in breadlines or begging on the streets. In November 1909 he was ousted from his room because he did not pay his rent and was forced to seek refuge in a flophouse. Here he met Reinhold Hanisch, who was in much the same predicament. Years later, Hanisch wrote a long book about his associations with Hitler during this period. It is a gruesome story of unbelievable poverty. Hitler must have been a sorry sight during these days with a full black beard, badly clothed and haggard. Hanisch writes: "It was a miserable life and I once asked him what he was really waiting for. The answer: 'I don't know myself.' I have never seen such hopeless letting down in distress."[4] Hanisch took him in hand and encouraged him to do some painting. The difficulty was that neither one had the money with which to buy materials. When Hanisch discovered that Hitler had signed over his inheritance to his sister, he persuaded Hitler to write her and obtain a small loan. This was presumably his half-sister, Angela. When the money was received Hitler's first thought was to take a week's vacation in order to recuperate. At this time he moved into the Maennerheim Brigittenau, which was slightly better than the flophouses in which he had been staying.

He and Hanisch went into business together. It was Hitler's job to paint post cards, posters, and water colors, which Hanisch then took around Vienna and peddled to art dealers, furniture stores, and so forth. In this he was quite successful, but his difficulties were not at an end. The moment Hitler got a little money, he refused to work. Hanisch describes this vividly:

> But unfortunately Hitler was never an ardent worker. I often was driven to despair by bringing in

orders that he simply wouldn't carry out. At Easter, 1910, we earned forty kronen on a big order and we divided it equally. The next morning, when I came downstairs and asked for Hitler, I was told he had already left with Neumann, a Jew. . . . After that I couldn't find him for a week. He was sightseeing Vienna with Neumann and spent much of the time in the museum. When I asked him what the matter was and whether we were going to keep on working, he answered that he must recuperate now, that he must have some leisure, that he was not a coolie. When the week was over, he no longer had any money.[5]

At this time Hitler was not a Jew-hater. There were a number of Jews living in the Men's Home with whom he was on excellent terms. Most of his paintings were sold to Jewish dealers, who paid just as much for them as the Aryans. He also admired Rothschild for sticking to his religion even if it prevented him from entering court. During this time he also sent two post cards to Dr. Bloch, in Linz, who was a Jew. One of these was just a picture post card of Vienna; the other, a copy that he had painted. On both of them he wrote of his deep gratitude to the doctor. This is mentioned because it is one of the very few cases of which we have any record where Hitler showed any lasting gratitude. During this time Hitler himself looked very Jewish. Hanisch writes:

> Hitler at that time looked very Jewish, so that I often joked with him that he must be of Jewish blood, since such a large beard rarely grows on a Christian's chin. Also he had big feet, as a desert wanderer must have.[6]

In spite of his close association with Hanisch the relationship ended in a quarrel. Hitler accused Hanisch of withholding some of the money he had received for a picture. He had Hanisch arrested and appeared as a witness against him. We have little knowledge of what happened to Hitler after this time. According to Hanfstaengl the home in which Hitler lived had the reputation of being a place where homosexual men frequently went to find companions. Jahn said that he had information from a Viennese official that on the police record Hitler was listed as a

sexual pervert, but it gave no details of offenses. It is possible that the entry may have been made solely on suspicion. Simone claims that the Viennese police file in 1912
recorded a charge of theft against Hitler and that he
moved from Vienna to Munich in order to avoid arrest.[7]
This would fit in with Hanfstaengl's suspicion that Hitler's
elder half-brother (who was twice convicted for theft)
was in Vienna at that time and that they may have become involved in some minor crime. This would not be
impossible, for Hanisch tells us that Hitler frequently spent
his time figuring out shady ways of making money. One
example may be of interest:

> He proposed to fill old tin cans with paste and sell
> them to shopkeepers, the paste to be smeared on win-
> dowpanes to keep them from freezing in winter. It
> should be sold . . . in the summer, when it couldn't be
> tried out. I told him it wouldn't work because the
> merchants would just say, come back in the winter.
> . . . Hitler answered that one must possess a talent for
> oratory.[8]

Since Hitler could only be brought to work when he
was actually hungry he spent a good deal of time reading
political pamphlets, sitting in café houses, reading newspapers, and delivering speeches to the other inmates of the
home. He became a great admirer of Georg von Schoenerer and the Viennese mayor, Karl Lueger. It was presumably from them that he learned his anti-Semitism and
many of the tricks of a successful politician. According to
Hanisch his companions were greatly amused by him and
often ridiculed him and his opinions. In any event it seems
that he got a good deal of practice in speechmaking during these years that stood him in good stead later on.
Even in these days he talked about starting a new party.

It is not clear why he remained in Vienna and lived in
such poverty for five years when he had such a deep love
for Germany and could have gone there with relatively little difficulty. It is also not clear why he went when he did
unless there is some truth in the supposition that he fled
Vienna to avoid arrest. His own explanation is that he
could not tolerate the mixture of people, particularly the
Jews and always more Jews, and says that for him Vienna
is the symbol of incest.

But according to Hitler's account this time was not lost. As he looks back over that period he can say:

> So in a few years I built a foundation of knowledge from which I still draw nourishment today.[9]

> At that time I formed an image of the world and a view of life which became the granite foundation for my actions.[10]

PREWAR MUNICH

In Munich before the war things were no better for him. As far as poverty is concerned he might as well have stayed in Vienna. He earned a little money painting post cards and posters and at times painting houses. Early in 1913 he went to Salzburg to report for duty in the army but was rejected on the grounds of poor physical condition. He returned to Munich and continued to work at odd jobs and sit in café houses where he spent his time reading newspapers. Nothing that is pertinent to our present study of which we have any knowledge happened during this time. The prospects of ever making anything out of himself in the future must have been very bleak at that time.

WORLD WAR

Then came the World War. He writes of this occasion:

> The struggle of the year 1914 was forsooth, not forced on the masses, but desired by the whole people.

> To myself those hours came like a redemption from the vexatious experiences of my youth. Even to this day I am not ashamed to say that, in a transport of enthusiasm, I sank down on my knees and thanked Heaven from an overflowing heart.

On August 3, 1914, at age twenty-five, Hitler joined a Bavarian regiment as a volunteer. During the first days of the war his regiment suffered very heavy losses and was not particularly popular among the Bavarian people. Hitler became an orderly in Regimental Headquarters as well as a runner. The one thing that all his comrades comment-

ed on was his subservience to superior officers. It seems
that he went out of his way to court their good graces, offering to do their washing and other menial tasks much to
the disgust of his comrades. He was not popular with the
other men and always remained aloof from them. When
he did join them he usually harangued about political matters. During the four years of war he received no packages or mail from anyone. In this he was unique. At
Christmas time when everyone else was receiving gifts and
messages he withdrew from the group and sulked moodily
by himself. When his comrades encouraged him to join the
group and share their packages, he refused. On October 7,
1916, he was wounded by a piece of shrapnel and sent to a
hospital. It was a light wound, and he was soon discharged
and sent to Munich as a replacement. After two days
there he wrote his commanding officer, Captain Wiedemann, asking that he be reinstated in his regiment because
he could not tolerate Munich when he knew his comrades were at the Front. Wiedemann had him returned to
the regiment where he remained until October 14, 1918,
when he was exposed to mustard gas and sent to a hospital in Pasewalk. He was blind and, according to Friedelinde Wagner, also lost his voice.

It seems that mystery always follows Hitler. His career
in the army is no exception. There are several things that
have never been satisfactorily explained. The first is that
he spent four years in the same regiment but was never
advanced beyond the rank of First Class Private or Lance
Corporal. The second is the Iron Cross First Class that he
constantly wears. This has been the topic of much discussion, but the mystery has never been solved. There is no
mention of the award in the history of his regiment. This
is rather amazing inasmuch as other awards of this kind
are listed. Hitler is mentioned in a number of other connections but not in this one, although it is alleged that it
was awarded to him for capturing twelve Frenchmen, including an officer, singlehanded. This is certainly no ordinary feat in any regiment, and one would expect that it
would at least merit some mention, particularly in view of
the fact that Hitler had considerable fame as a politician
when the book went to press.

The Nazi propaganda agencies have not helped to
clarify the situation. Not only have a number of different
versions of the story appeared in the press, but each gives

a different number of Frenchmen he is alleged to have captured. They have also published alleged facsimiles of his war record that do not agree. The Berlin *Illustrierte Zeitung* of August 10, 1939, printed a facsimile in which the date of award for this decoration was clearly August 4, 1918. Yet the *Voelkische Beobachter* of August 14, 1934, had published a facsimile in which the date of award was October 4, 1918. Although these alleged facsimiles mentioned other citations, they did not include the date of award of the Iron Cross Second Class. From all that can be learned the First Class Cross was never awarded unless the recipient had already been awarded the Second Class decoration.

Just what the facts are it is impossible to determine. It is alleged that his war record has been badly tampered with and that von Schleicher was eliminated during the Blood Purge because he knew the true facts. Strasser, who served in the same division, has probably as good an explanation as any. He says that during the last months of the war there were so many First Class Crosses being given out that General Headquarters was no longer able to pass on the merits of each individual case. To facilitate matters a number of these decorations were allotted to each regiment every month to be issued by the Commanding Officers. They, in turn, notified the High Command of the award and the deed that merited it. According to Strasser, when the army began to collapse, the Regimental Headquarters had in their possession a number of decorations that had not been awarded. Since few members of the Headquarters Staff ever received an award of this type, they took advantage of the general melee and gave them to each other and forged the signature of the Commanding Officer in sending it to the High Command. The thing that speaks in favor of this explanation is the curious bond that exists between Hitler and his regimental sergeant-major, Max Amann, who was later to become the head of the Nazi Eher Verlag. This is one of the most lucrative positions in the entire Nazi hierarchy, and Amann was called to the position by Hitler.

The only explanation for the lack of promotion that has been published is the comment of one of his officers to the effect that he would never make a noncommissioned officer "out of that neurotic fellow, Hittler." Rauschning gives a different explanation.[11] He claims that a high Nazi had

Mother, Klara Hitler (née Poelzl), twenty-three years younger than her husband. Father, Alois Hitler, the illegitimate son of Maria Anna Schicklgruber.

Hitler as an infant.

With wartime comrades (extreme left, front row). *International News Photo*

Hitler, Ludendorff, and other conspirators in the unsuccessful Beer Hall Putsch of 1923. *Keystone Photo*

In Landsberg prison after the failure of the Putsch. *AP Photo*

Hitler in Bavarian peasant garb. *Keystone Photo*

With his half-sister, Angela. "The only living relative Hitler ever mentioned." *AP Photo*

With favorite film stars—from left to right: Else Elster, Leni Marenbach, Hitler, Lilian Harvey, Karin Hardt, Dinah Grace, Willi Fritsch, Leni Riefenstahl, and Dinah Grace's sister. *AP Photo*

Reviewing an SA parade. *AP Photo*

With President Hindenburg at ceremonies marking the opening of the Reichstag at Potsdam. *Wide World Photo*

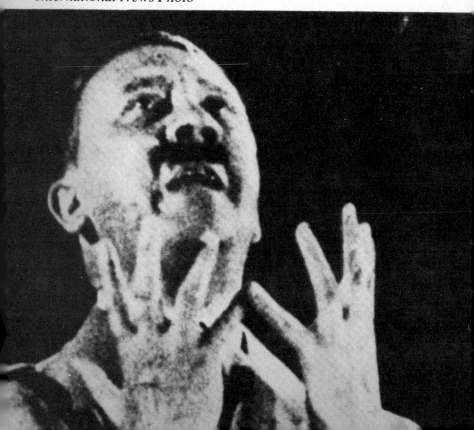

once confided in him that he had seen Hitler's military record and that it contained an item of a court martial that found him guilty of pederastic practices with an officer, and that it was for this reason that he was never promoted. Rauschning also claims that in Munich Hitler was found guilty of a violation of paragraph 175, which deals with pederasty. No other evidence of either of these two charges has been found.

The mystery becomes even deeper when we learn from a great many informants that Hitler was quite courageous and never tried to evade dangerous assignments. It is said that he was unusually adept at running and then falling or seeking shelter when the fire became intense. It also seems that he was always ready to volunteer for special assignments and was considered exceedingly reliable in the performance of all his duties by his own officers.

It may be well to mention at this point that when Hitler entered the army he again became a member of a recognized and respected social institution. No longer did he have to stand in breadlines or seek shelter in flophouses. For the first time since his mother died did he really belong to a group of people. Not only did this provide him with a sense of pride and security, but at last he had achieved his great ambition, namely, to be united with the German nation. It is also interesting to note a considerable change in his appearance. From the dirty, greasy, castoff clothes of Jews and other charitable people he was now privileged to wear a uniform. Mend, one of his comrades, tells us that when Hitler came out of the trenches or back from an assignment he spent hours cleaning his uniform and boots until he became the joke of the regiment.[12] Quite a remarkable change for one who for almost seven years refused to exert himself just a little in order to pull himself out of the pitiful conditions in which he lived among the dregs of society.

POSTWAR

Then came the armistice and all this was over. Adolf Hitler, from a psychological point of view, was in exactly the same position as the one in which he found himself eleven years before when his mother died. He faced the future alone. The army, his home for four years, was breaking up. Again he stood alone before a dismal future—a world in which he could not find a niche, a world that did not care for him, a world of aimless existence fraught with hardships. It was almost more than he could bear, and he went into a deep depression that continued for a considerable period of time.

Where to go and what to do. Having no home or family to greet him he returned to Munich, not because it had been kind to him in the past, but because he had no other place to go. He could take up his life again where he had left off four years earlier. He wandered around Munich for a short time, "a stray dog looking for a master." Then it is reported that he went to Vienna to visit his half-sister, Angela, with whom he had had no contact for many years. If he actually made this trip he did not stay long, for soon he was back in the reserve army, stationed at Traunstein. Here he could wear the uniform and eat the food of the army, and he stayed there until April 1920, when the camp was broken up. He then returned to Munich still attached to the army and living in the barracks. During this time he seems to have continued his political discussions with his comrades, siding with the Social Democrats against the Communists. According to the *Muenchener Post* he actually affiliated himself with the Social Democratic Party.[18] After the counterrevolution every tenth man in the barracks was shot, but Hitler was singled out beforehand and asked to stand to one side. At the inquiry he appeared before the board with "charge-lists" against some of his comrades that can only signify denunciations for Communistic activities. He had been spying on his comrades and now assigned them to the executioner. In *Mein Kampf* he refers to this occupation as his "first more or less political activity."

The army now undertook to educate its soldiers in the proper political philosophy, and Hitler was assigned to such a course. He spoke so ably in this group that his talent for speaking impressed an officer who was present, and Hitler was appointed "education officer." His hour had struck—he was discovered and appreciated, singled out for his talent. He threw himself into this work with great enthusiasm, always speaking to larger groups. His confidence grew with his success in swaying people. He was on his way to becoming a politician. From here on his career is a matter of history and need not be reviewed here.

This is the foundation of Hitler's character. Whatever

he tried to be afterward is only superstructure, and the superstructure can be no firmer than the foundations on which it rests. The higher it goes the more unstable it becomes—the more it needs to be propped up and patched up in order to make it hold together. This is not an easy job. It requires constant vigilance, strong defenses, and heavy losses in time and energy.

There was general agreement among the collaborators that Hitler is probably a neurotic psychopath bordering on schizophrenia. This means that he is not insane in the commonly accepted sense of the term, but a neurotic who lacks adequate inhibitions. He has not lost complete contact with the world about him and is still striving to make some kind of psychological adjustment that will give him a feeling of security in his social group. It also means that there is a definite moral component in his character no matter how deeply it may be buried or how seriously it has been distorted.

With this diagnosis established, we are in a position to make a number of surmises concerning the conscious mental processes that ordinarily take place in Hitler's mind. These form the nucleus of the "Hitler" he consciously knows and must live with. It is in all probability not a happy "Hitler," but one harassed by fears, anxieties, doubts, misgivings, uncertainties, condemnations, feelings of loneliness and of guilt. From our experience with other neurotic psychopaths we are probably on firm ground when we suppose that Hitler's mind is like a battle royal most of the time with many conflicting and contradictory forces and impulses pulling him this way and that.

Such a state of confusion is not easy to bear. A large part of his energies are usually wasted in wrestling with himself instead of being directed toward the external world. He can see possibilities for gratifications about him, but only rarely can he muster enough energy to make a consistent effort. Fears, doubts, and implications obstruct his thinking and acting, he becomes indecisive, and he frequently ends up doing nothing. Vicarious gratifications through fantasies become substitutes for the satisfaction obtained from real achievements. We must suppose that Hitler was in this state during the seven years that elapsed between the death of his mother and the outbreak of the war when he was wasting his time lying around in flophouses and sitting in cafés in Vienna. Only when his hunger became acute could he muster the energy necessary to apply himself to a few hours of work. As soon as this hunger was appeased he lapsed back into his former state of procrastination and indecision.

We can assume that the periods of procrastination at the present time have a similar origin. He withdraws from society, is depressed, and dawdles away his time until "the situation becomes dangerous," then he forces himself to action. He works for a time, and as soon as the job is under way "he loses interest in it" and slips back into his leisurely life in which he does nothing except what he is forced to do or likes to do. Now, of course, it is no longer hunger that drives him to work but another motive, even more powerful, of which he is not fully conscious. The nature of this motive will be discussed in the next section.

As one surveys Hitler's behavior patterns, as his close associates observe them, one gets the impression that this is not a single personality, but two that inhabit the same body and alternate back and forth. The one is a very soft, sentimental, and indecisive individual who has very little drive and wants nothing quite so much as to be amused, liked, and looked after. The other is just the opposite—a hard, cruel, and decisive person with considerable energy—who seems to know what he wants and is ready to go after it and get it regardless of cost. It is the first Hitler who weeps profusely at the death of his canary and the second Hitler who cries in open court: "Heads will roll." It is the first Hitler who cannot bring himself to discharge an assistant, and it is the second Hitler who can order the murder of hundreds, including his best friends, and can say with great conviction: "There will be no peace in the land until a body hangs from every lamppost." It is the first Hitler who spends his evenings watching movies or going to cabarets, and it is the second Hitler who works for days on end with little or no sleep, making plans that will affect the destiny of nations.

Until we understand the magnitude and implications of this duality in his nature we can never understand his actions. It is a kind of "Dr. Jekyll and Mr. Hyde" personality structure in which two wholly different personalities oscillate back and forth and make the individual almost unrecognizable. This characteristic is common to many psychopaths. Under these circumstances it is extremely difficult to predict from one moment to the next what his reactions to a given situation are going to be. An illustration may be helpful. According to Russell extravagant preparations were made for the commemorative services for the Germans who died when the battleship *Deutschland* was bombed. Hitler spoke long and passionately to those attending, as well as over the radio. It was then arranged that he should walk down the line of survivors and review the infantry and naval units drawn up at attention. Newsreel cameramen were stationed at all crucial points:

> The first widow to whom Hitler spoke a few words cried violently. Her child, who was 10 years old and who stood next to his bereaved mother, began to cry heartrendingly. Hitler patted him on the head and turned uncertainly to the next in line. Before he could speak a word, he was suddenly overcome. He spun completely around, left the carefully prepared program flat. Followed by his utterly surprised companions he walked as fast as he could to his car and had himself driven away from the parade grounds.[14]

This sudden alternation from one to the other is not uncommon. Close associates have commented on it time and time again. Ludecke writes:

> There were times when he gave an impression of unhappiness, of loneliness, of inward searching. . . . But in a moment, he would turn again to whatever frenzied task . . . with the swift command of a man born for action.[15]

Rauschning says: "Almost anything might suddenly inflame his wrath and hatred. . . . But equally, the transition from anger to sentimentality or enthusiasm might be quite sudden."[16] Huddleston writes: "His eyes, soft and dreamy as he spoke to me, suddenly flashed and hardened. . . ."[17] Voigt says: "Close collaborators for many years said that Hitler was always like this—the slightest difficulty or obstacle could make him scream with rage or burst into tears."[18] Heiden has commented upon the duality of Hitler's character and has suggested that the procrastinating side is "Hitler" while the fiery personality that erupts from time to time is "the Fuehrer." Although this may not be strictly true from a psychological point of view, it may be helpful to think of him in these terms.

There is not, however, a complete dissociation of the personality. In such a case we would expect to find the personalities alternating with each other quite beyond the voluntary control of the individual. This is clearly not the case with Hitler, who can adopt either role more or less at will. At least he is able on occasion to induce the Fuehrer personality to come into existence when the occasion demands. That is what he does at almost every speech. At the beginning as previously mentioned he is nervous and insecure on the platform. At times he has considerable difficulty in finding anything to say. This is "Hitler." But under these circumstances the "Hitler" personality does not usually predominate for any length of time. As soon as he gets the feel of the audience the tempo of the speech increases, and the "Fuehrer" personality begins to assert itself. Heiden says: "The stream of speech stiffens him like a stream of water stiffens a hose." As he speaks he hypnotizes himself into believing that he is actually and fundamentally the "Fuehrer," or as Rauschning says: "He doses himself with the morphine of his own verbiage."[19] It is this transformation of the little Hitler into the great Fuehrer, taking place under the eyes of his audience, that probably fascinates them. By complicated psychological processes they are able to identify themselves with him, and as the speech progresses they themselves are temporarily transformed and inspired.

He must also undergo a transformation of this kind when he is expected to make a decision or take definite action. As we have seen, Hitler procrastinates until the situation becomes dangerous and intolerable. When he can procrastinate no longer, he is able to induce the Fuehrer personality to assert itself. Rauschning has put this well:

> He is languid and apathetic by nature and needs the stimulus of nervous excitement to rouse him out of chronic lethargy to a spasmodic activity.[20]

> Before Hitler can act he must lash himself out of lethargy and doubts into a frenzy.[21]

Having lashed himself into this state of mind he can play the "Fuehrer" to perfection. When the transformation takes place in his personality all his views, sentiments, and values are also transformed. The result is that as "Fuehrer" he can make statements with great conviction that flatly contradict what "Hitler" said a few minutes earlier. He can grapple with the most important problems and in a few minutes reduce them to extremely simple terms; he can map out campaigns, be the supreme judge, deal with diplomats, ignore all ethical and moral principles, order executions or the destruction of cities without the slightest hesitation. And he can be in the best of humor while he is doing it. All of this would have been completely impossible for "Hitler."

Hitler likes to believe that this is his true self, and he has made every effort to convince the German people that it is his only self. But it is an artifact. The whole "Fuehrer" personality is a grossly exaggerated and distorted conception of masculinity as Hitler conceives it. The "Fuehrer" personality shows all the earmarks of a reaction formation that has been created unconsciously as a compensation and cover-up for deep-lying tendencies that he despises. This mechanism is very frequently found in psychopaths and always serves the purpose of repudiating the true self by creating an image that is diametrically opposite and then identifying oneself with the image. The great difference between Hitler and thousands of other psychopaths is that he has managed to convince millions of other people that the fictitious image is really himself. The more he was able to convince them, the more he became convinced of it himself on the theory that eighty million Germans cannot be wrong. And so he has fallen in love with the image he himself created and does his utmost to forget that behind it there is quite another Hitler who is a very despicable fellow. It is his ability to convince others that he is what he is not that has saved him from insanity.

This psychological maneuver, however, is never entirely successful. Secret fears and anxieties that belie the reality of the image keep cropping up to shake his confidence and security. He may rationalize these fears or displace them, but they continue to haunt him. Some are at least partially justified, others seem to be groundless. For example, he has had a fear of cancer for many years. Ordinarily he fears that he has a cancer in his stomach, since he is always bothered with indigestion, and all the assurances of his doctors have not been sufficient to dispel this fear. A few years ago a simple polyp grew on his larynx. Immediately his fear shifted to the throat, and he was sure that he had developed a throat cancer. When Dr. von Eicken diagnosed it as a simple polyp, Hitler at first refused to believe him.

Then he has fears of being poisoned, fears of being assassinated, fears of losing his health, fears of gaining weight, fears of treason, fears of losing his mystical guidance, fears of anesthetics, fears of premature death, fears that his mission will not be fulfilled. Every conceivable precaution must be taken to reduce these dangers, real and imagined, to a minimum. In later years the fear of betrayal and possible assassination by one of his associates seems to have grown considerably. Thyssen claims that it has reached the point where he no longer trusts the Gestapo.[22] Frank reports that even the generals must surrender their swords before they are admitted into conferences with him.[23]

Sleep is no longer a refuge from his fears. He wakes up in the night shaking and screaming. Rauschning claims that one of Hitler's close associates told him that:

> Hitler wakes at night with convulsive shrieks; shouts for help. He sits on the edge of his bed, as if unable to stir. He shakes with fear, making the whole bed vibrate. He shouts confused, unintelligible phrases. He gasps, as if imagining himself to be suffocating. On one occasion Hitler stood swaying in his room, looking wildly about him. "He! He! He's been here!" he gasped. His lips were blue. Sweat streamed down his face. Suddenly he began to reel off figures, and odd words and broken phrases, entirely devoid of sense. It sounded horrible. He used strangely composed and entirely un-German word formations. Then he stood still, only his lips moving. . . . Then he suddenly broke out—"There, there! In the corner! Who's that?" He stamped and shrieked in the familiar way.[24]

Zeissler also reports such incidents.[25] It would seem that Hitler's late hours are very likely due to the fact that he is afraid to go to sleep.

The result of these fears, as it is with almost every psychopath, is a narrowing of the world in which he lives. Haunted by secret misgivings, he distrusts everyone, even

those closest to him. He cannot establish any close friend-
ships for fear of being betrayed or being discovered as he
really is. As his world becomes more and more circum-
scribed he becomes lonelier and lonelier. He feels himself
to be a captive and often compares his life to that of the
Pope.[26] Fry says, "spiritual loneliness must be Hitler's
secret regret,"[27] and von Wiegand writes:

> Perhaps the snow-crowned peaks of the Alps glis-
> tening in the moonlight remind Adolf Hitler of the
> glittering but cold, lonely heights of fame and
> achievement to which he has climbed. "I am the lone-
> liest man on earth" he said to an employee of his
> household.[28]

Psychopaths, however, are not discouraged by all this.
On the contrary, they interpret their fears as proof of
their own importance, rather than as signs of their fundamental weakness. As Hitler's personal world becomes
smaller he must extend the boundaries of his physical
domains. Meanwhile, his image of himself must become
evermore inflated in order to compensate for his deprivations and to maintain his repressions. He must build bigger
and better buildings, bridges, stadia, and what not as tangible symbols of his power and greatness and then use
these as evidence that he really is what he wants to believe
he is.

There is, however, little gratification in all this. No matter what he achieves or what he does it is never sufficient
to convince him that things are what they seem to be. He
is always insecure and must bolster up his superstructure
by new acquisitions and more defenses. But the more he
gets and the higher he builds, the more he has to worry
about and defend. He is caught in a vicious circle, which
grows bigger and bigger as time goes on but never brings
him the sense of security he craves above everything else.

People of this type have a tendency to bark up the
wrong tree. The security they seek is not to be found in
the outside world but in themselves. Had they conquered
their own unsocial impulses, their real enemy, when they
were young, they would not need to struggle with such
subterfuges when they are mature. The dangers they fear
in the world around them are only the shadows of the
dangers they fear will creep up on them from within if

they do not maintain a strict vigilance over their actions. Repudiation is not synonymous to annihilation. These unsocial impulses, like termites, gnaw away at the foundations of the personality, and the higher the superstructure is built, the shakier it becomes.

In most psychopaths these unsocial impulses, which they consciously regard as dangers, have been fairly successfully repressed. The individual may feel himself to be despicable without being conscious of the whys and wherefores of this feeling. The origins of the feeling remain almost wholly unconscious or are camouflaged in such a way that they are not obvious to the individual himself. In Hitler's case, however, this is not so—at least not entirely. He has good cause for feeling himself to be despicable and he is partially aware of its origins. The repression has not been completely successful, and consequently some of the social tendencies do from time to time assert themselves and demand satisfaction.

Hitler's sexual life has always been the topic of much speculation. As pointed out in the previous chapter, most of his closest associates are absolutely ignorant on this subject. This has led to conjectures of all sorts. Some believe that he is entirely immune from such impulses. Some believe that he is a chronic masturbator. Some believe that he derives his sexual pleasure through voyeurism. Many believe that he is completely impotent. Others, and these are perhaps in the majority, think that he is homosexual. It is probably true that he is impotent, but he is certainly not homosexual in the ordinary sense of the term. His perversion has quite a different nature, which few have guessed. It is an extreme form of masochism in which the individual derives sexual gratification from the act of having a woman urinate or defecate on him.[29]

Although this perversion is not a common one, it is not unknown in clinical work, particularly in its incipient stages. The four collaborators on this study, in addition to Dr. de Saussure, who learned of the perversion from other sources, have all had experience with cases of this type. All five agree that the information as given is probably true in view of their clinical experience and their knowledge of Hitler's character. In the following chapter further evidence of its validity will be cited together with a consideration of the influence it has had on his personality and actions. At the present time it is sufficient to recognize

that these tendencies represent a constant threat to him
that disturbs the equilibrium of his conscious mental life.
Not only must he be continually on his guard against any
overt manifestation, but he must struggle with the
intolerable feelings of guilt that are generated by his secret
and unwelcome desires. These, together with his fears,
haunt him day and night and incapacitate him as far as consistent and constructive work is concerned.

Surely Hitler has externalized his own problem and its
supposed solution when he writes:

> Only when the time comes when the race is no
> longer overshadowed by the consciousness of its own
> guilt, then it will find internal peace and external en-
> ergy to cut down regardlessly and brutally the wild
> shoots, and to pull up the weeds.

PART V

✠

HITLER

Psychological Analysis
and Reconstruction

Tнᴇ world has come to know Adolf Hitler for his insatiable greed for power, his ruthlessness, his cruelty, his utter lack of feeling, his contempt for established institutions, and his lack of moral restraints. In the course of relatively few years he has contrived to usurp such tremendous power that a few veiled threats, accusations, or insinuations were sufficient to make the world tremble. In open defiance of treaties he occupied huge territories and conquered millions of people without even firing a shot. When the world became tired of being frightened and concluded that it was all a bluff, he initiated the most brutal and devastating war in history—a war that for a time threatened the complete destruction of our civilization. Human life and human suffering seem to leave this individual completely untouched as he plunges along the course he believes he was predestined to take.

Earlier in his career the world had watched him with amusement. Many people refused to take him seriously on the grounds that "he could not possibly last." As one action after another met with amazing success and the measure of the man became more obvious, this amusement was transformed into incredulousness. To most people it seemed inconceivable that such things could actually happen in our modern civilization. Hitler, the leader of these activities, became generally regarded as a madman, if not inhuman. Such a judgment, concerning the nature of our enemy, may be satisfactory to the man in the street. It gives him a feeling of satisfaction to pigeonhole an incomprehensible individual in one category or another, and having classified him in this way, he feels that the problem is solved. All we need to do is to eliminate the madman from the scene of activities, replace him with a sane individual, and the world will again return to a normal and peaceful state of affairs.

This naive view, however, is wholly inadequate for those who are delegated to conduct the war against Germany or for those who will be delegated to deal with the situation when the war is over. They cannot content themselves with simply regarding Hitler as a personal devil and condemning him to an Eternal Hell in order that the remainder of the world may live in peace and quiet. They will realize that the madness of the Fuehrer has become the madness of a nation, if not of a large part of the continent. They will realize that these are not wholly the actions of a single individual but that a reciprocal relationship exists between the Fuehrer and the people and that the madness of the one stimulates and flows into the other and vice versa. It was not only Hitler, the madman, who created German madness, but German madness that created Hitler. Having created him as its spokesman and leader, it has been carried along by his momentum, perhaps far beyond the point where it was originally prepared to go. Nevertheless, it continues to follow his lead in spite of the fact that it must be obvious to all intelligent people now that his path leads to inevitable destruction.

From a scientific point of view, therefore, we are forced to consider Hitler, the Fuehrer, not as a personal devil, wicked as his actions and philosophy may be, but as the expression of a state of mind existing in millions of people, not only in Germany, but to a smaller degree in all civilized countries. To remove Hitler may be a necessary first step, but it would not be the cure. It would be analogous to removing a chancre without treating the underlying disease. If similar eruptions are to be prevented in the future, we cannot content ourselves with simply removing the overt manifestations of the disease. On the contrary, we must ferret out and seek to correct the underlying factors that produced the unwelcome phenomenon. We must discover the psychological streams that nourish this destructive state of mind in order that we may divert them into channels that will permit a further evolution of our form of civilization.

The present study is concerned wholly with Adolf Hitler and the social forces that impinged upon him in the course of his development and produced the man we know. One may question the wisdom of studying the psychology of a single individual if the present war represents a rebellion by a nation against our civilization. To understand the one does not tell us anything about the millions of others. In a sense this is perfectly true. In the process of growing up we are all faced with highly individual experiences and exposed to varying social influences. The result is that when we mature no two of us are identical from a psychological point of view. In the present instance, however, we are concerned not so much with distinct individuals as with a whole cultural group. The members of this group have been exposed to social influences—family patterns, methods of training and education, opportunities for development, and so forth—that are fairly homogeneous within a given culture or strata of a culture. The result is that the members of a given culture tend to act, think, and feel more or less alike, at least in contrast to the members of a different cultural group. This justifies to some extent our speaking of a general cultural character. On the other hand, if a large section of a given culture rebels against the traditional pattern, then we must assume that new social influences have been introduced that tend to produce a type of character that cannot thrive in the old cultural environment.

When this happens it may be extremely helpful to understand the nature of the social forces that influenced the development of individual members of the group. These may serve as clues to an understanding of the group as a whole inasmuch as we can then investigate the frequency and intensity of these same forces in the group and draw deductions concerning their effect upon its individual members. If the individual being studied happens to be the leader of the group, we can expect to find the pertinent factors in an exaggerated form that would tend to make them stand out in sharper relief than would be the case if we studied an average member of the group. Under these circumstances the action of the forces may be more easily isolated and subjected to detailed study in relation to the personality as a whole as well as to the culture in general. The problem of our study should be, then, not only whether Hitler is mad or not, but what influences in his development have made him what he is.

If we scan the tremendous quantities of material and information that have been accumulated on Hitler, we find little that is helpful in explaining why he is what he is. One can, of course, make general statements as many authors have done and say, for example, that his five years in Vi-

enna were so frustrating that he hated the whole social order and is now taking his revenge for the injustices he suffered. Such explanations sound very plausible at first
glance, but we would also want to know why, as a young
man, he was unwilling to work when he had the opportunity and what happened to transform the lazy Vienna beg-
gar into the energetic politician who never seemed to tire
from rushing from one meeting to another and who was
able to work thousands of listeners into a state of frenzy.
We would also like to know something about the origins
of his peculiar working habits at the present time, his firm
belief in his mission, and so on. No matter how long we
study the available material we can find no rational explanation of his present conduct. The material is descriptive
and tells us a great deal about how he behaves under
varying circumstances, what he thinks and feels about various subjects, but it does not tell us why. To be sure, he
himself sometimes offers explanations for his conduct, but
it is obvious that these are either built on flimsy rational
foundations or else they serve to push the problem further
back into his past. On this level we are in exactly the same
position in which we find ourselves when a neurotic patient first comes for help.

In the case of an individual neurotic patient, however,
we can ask for a great deal more first-hand information,
which gradually enables us to trace the development of his
irrational attitudes or behavioral patterns to earlier experiences or influences in his life history and to study the effects of these on his later behavior. In most cases the
patient will have forgotten these earlier experiences, but
nevertheless he still uses them as premises in his present
conduct. As soon as we are able to understand the premises underlying his conduct, then his irrational behavior
becomes comprehensible to us.

The same finding would probably hold in Hitler's case
except that here we do not have the opportunity of obtaining the additional first-hand information that would enable us to trace the history of his views and behavioral
patterns to their early origins in order to discover the
premises on which he is operating. Hitler's early life, when
his fundamental attitudes were undoubtedly formed, is a
closely guarded secret, particularly as far as he himself is
concerned. He has been extremely careful and has told us
exceedingly little about this period of his life, and even

that is open to serious questioning. A few fragments have, however, been unearthed that are helpful in reconstructing his past life and the experiences and influences that have determined his adult character. Nevertheless, in themselves they would be wholly inadequate for our purposes.

Fortunately, there are other sources of information. One of them is Hitler himself. In every utterance a speaker or writer unknowingly tells us a great deal about himself of which he is entirely unaware. The subjects he chooses for elaboration frequently reveal unconscious factors that make these seem more important to him than many other aspects that would be just as appropriate to the occasion. Furthermore, the method of treatment, together with the attitudes expressed toward certain topics, usually reflect unconscious processes that are symbolically related to his own problems. The examples he chooses for purposes of illustration almost always contain elements from his own earlier experiences that were instrumental in cultivating the view he is expounding. The figures of speech he employs reflect unconscious conflicts and linkages, and the incidence of particular types or topics can almost be used as a measure of his preoccupation with problems related to them. A number of experimental techniques have been worked out that bear witness to the validity of these methods of gathering information about the mental life, conscious and unconscious, of an individual in addition to the findings of psychoanalysts and psychiatrists.

Then, too, we have our practical experience in studying patients whose difficulties were not unlike those we find in Hitler. Our knowledge of the origins of these difficulties may often be used to evaluate conflicting information, check deductions concerning what probably happened, or to fill in gaps where no information is available. It may be possible with the help of all these sources of information to reconstruct the outstanding events in his early life that have determined his present behavior and character structure. However, our study must of necessity be speculative and inconclusive. It may tell us a great deal about the mental processes of our subject, but it cannot be as comprehensive or conclusive as the findings of a direct study conducted with the cooperation of the individual. Nevertheless, the situation is such that even an indirect study of this kind is warranted.

Freud's earliest and greatest contribution to psychiatry in particular and to an understanding of human conduct in general was his discovery of the importance of the first years of a child's life in shaping his future character. It is during these early years, when the child's acquaintanceship with the world is still meager and his capacities are still undeveloped, that the chances of misinterpreting the nature of the world about him are the greatest. The mind of the child is inadequate for understanding the demands that a complex culture makes upon him or the host of confusing experiences to which he is exposed. In consequence, as has been shown over and over again, a child during his early years frequently misinterprets what is going on about him and builds his personality structure on false premises. Even Hitler concedes that this finding is true, for he says in *Mein Kampf:*

> There is a boy, let us say, of three. This is the age at which a child becomes conscious of his first impressions. In many intelligent people, traces of these early memories are found even in old age.[1]

Under these circumstances it will be well for us to inquire into the nature of Hitler's earliest environment and the impressions that he probably formed during this period. Our factual information on this phase of his life is practically nil. In *Mein Kampf* Hitler tries to create the impression that his home was rather peaceful and quiet, his "father a faithful civil servant, the mother devoting herself to the cares of the household and looking after her children with eternally the same loving care." It would seem that if this is a true representation of the home environment there would be no reason for his concealing it so scrupulously. This is the only passage in a book of a thousand pages in which he even intimates that there were other children for his mother to take care of. No brother and no sister are mentioned in any other connection, and even to his associates he has never admitted that there were other children besides his half-sister, Angela. Very little more is said about his mother, either in writing or speaking. This concealment in itself would make us suspicious about the truth of the statement quoted above. We become even more suspicious when we find that not a single patient manifesting Hitler's character traits has grown up in such a well-ordered and peaceful home environment.

If we read on in *Mein Kampf* we find that Hitler gives us a description of a child's life in a lower-class family. He says:

> Among the five children there is a boy, let us say, of three.... When the parents fight almost daily, their brutality leaves nothing to the imagination; then the results of such visual education must slowly but inevitably become apparent to the little one. Those who are not familiar with such conditions can hardly imagine the results, especially when the mutual differences express themselves in the form of brutal attacks on the part of the father toward the mother or to assaults due to drunkenness. The poor little boy, at the age of six, senses things which would make even a grown-up person shudder.... The other things the little fellow hears at home do not tend to further his respect for his surroundings.[2]

In view of the fact that we now know that there were five children in the Hitler home and that his father liked to spend his spare time in the village tavern where he sometimes drank so heavily that he had to be brought home by his wife or children, we begin to suspect that in this passage Hitler is, in all probability, describing conditions in his own home as a child.

If we accept the hypothesis that Hitler is actually talking about his own home when he describes conditions in the average lower-class family, we can obtain further information concerning the nature of his home environment. We read:

> ... things end badly indeed when the man from the very start goes his own way and the wife, for the sake of the children, stands up against him. Quarreling and nagging set in, and in the same measure in which the husband becomes estranged from his wife, he becomes familiar with alcohol.... When he finally comes home ... drunk and brutal, but always without a last cent or penny, then God have mercy on the scenes which follow. I witnessed all of this personally in hundreds of scenes and at the beginning with both disgust and indignation.[3]

When we remember the few friends that Hitler has made in the course of his life, and not a single intimate friend, one wonders where he had the opportunity of observing these scenes personally, hundreds of times, if it was not in his own home. And then he continues:

> The other things the little fellow hears at home do not tend to further his respect for his surroundings. Not a single good shred is left for humanity, not a single institution is left unattacked; starting with the teacher, up to the head of the State, be it religion, or morality as such, be it the State or society, no matter which, everything is pulled down in the nastiest manner into the filth of a depraved mentality.[4]

All of this agrees with information obtained from other sources whose veracity might otherwise be open to question. With this as corroborating evidence, however, it seems safe to assume that the above passages are a fairly accurate picture of the Hitler household, and we may surmise that these scenes did arouse disgust and indignation in him at a very early age.

These feelings were aggravated by the fact that when his father was sober he tried to create an entirely different impression. At such times he stood very much on his dignity and prided himself on his position in the civil service. Even after he had retired from this service he always insisted on wearing his uniform when he appeared in public. He was scrupulous about his appearance and strode down the village street in his most dignified manner. When he spoke to his neighbors or acquaintances he did so in a very condescending manner and always demanded that they use his full title when they addressed him. If one of them happened to omit a part of it, he would call attention to their omission. He carried this to the point where, so informants tell us, he became a source of amusement to the other villagers and their children. At home he demanded that the children address him as Herr Vater instead of using one of the intimate abbreviations or nicknames that children commonly do.

Father's Influence on Hitler's Character

We know from our study of many cases that the character of the father is one of the major factors determining the character of the child, particularly that of a boy. In cases in which the father is a fairly well-integrated individual and presents a consistent pattern of behavior that the small boy can respect, he becomes a model that the child strives to emulate. The image the child has of his father becomes the cornerstone of his later character structure, and with its help he is able to integrate his own behavior along socially accepted lines. The importance of this first step in character development can scarcely be overestimated. It is almost a prerequisite for a stable, secure, and well-integrated personality in later life.

In Hitler's case, as in almost all other psychopaths of his type, this step was not feasible. Instead of presenting an image of a consistent, harmonious, socially adjusted, and admirable individual that the child could use as a guide and model, the father showed himself to be a mass of contradictions. At times he played the role of "a faithful civil servant," who respected his position and the society he served, and demanded that all others do likewise. At such times he was the soul of dignity, propriety, sternness, and justice. To the outside world he tried to appear as a pillar of society whom all should respect and obey. At home, on the other hand, particularly after he had been drinking he appeared the exact opposite. He was brutal, unjust, and inconsiderate. He had no respect for anybody or anything. The world was all wrong and an unfit place in which to live. At such times he also played the part of the bully and whipped his wife and children who were unable to defend themselves. Even the dog comes in for his share of this sadistic display.

Under such circumstances the child become̶
and is unable to identify himself with
that he can use as a guide for hi
Not only is this a severe handicap in its
the child is given a distorted picture of
him and the nature of the people in it. I
the home is his world, and later he ju
world in terms of it. In Hitler's case we v
the whole world would appear as extre

uncertain, and unjust, and the child's impulse would be to avoid it as far as possible because he felt unable to cope with it. His feelings of insecurity would be enhanced inasmuch as he could never predict beforehand how his father would behave when he came home or what he could expect from him. The person who should give him love, support, and a feeling of security fills him with anxiety, uneasiness, and uncertainty.

His Search for a Competent Guide

As a child Hitler must have felt his lack very keenly for throughout his later life we find him searching for a strong masculine figure whom he can respect and emulate. The men with whom he had contact during his childhood evidently could not fill the role of guide to his complete satisfaction. There is some evidence that he attempted to regard some of his teachers in this way, but whether it was the influence of his father's ranting or the shortcomings of the teachers themselves, his attempts always miscarried. Later he attempted to find great men in history who could fill this need. Caesar, Napoleon, and Frederick the Great are only a few of the legion to whom he became attached. Although historic figures serve an important role of this kind in the life of almost every child, they are in themselves inadequate. Unless a fairly solid foundation already exists in the mind of the child these heroes never become flesh and blood people inasmuch as the relationship is one-sided and lacks reciprocation. The same is also true of the political figures with which Hitler sought to identify himself during the Vienna period. For a time Schoenerer and Lueger became his heroes, and although they were instrumental in forming some of his political beliefs and channeling his feelings, they were still too far removed from him to play the role of permanent guides and models.

During his career in the army we have an excellent example of Hitler's willingness to submit to the leadership of strong males who were willing to guide him and protect him. Throughout his army life there is not a shred of evidence to show that Hitler was anything but the model soldier as far as submissiveness and obedience are concerned. From a psychological point of view his life in the army a kind of substitute for the home life he had always wanted but could never find, and he fulfilled his duties willingly and faithfully. He liked it so well that after he was wounded in 1916, he wrote to his commanding officer and requested that he be called back to front duty before his leave had expired.

After the close of the war he stayed in the army and continued to be docile to his officers. He was willing to do anything they asked, even to the point of spying on his own comrades and then condemning them to death. When his officers singled him out to do special propaganda work because they believed he had a talent for speaking, he was overjoyed. This was the beginning of his political career, and here, too, we can find many manifestations of his search for a leader. In the beginning he may well have thought of himself as the "drummer-boy" who was heralding the coming of the great leader. It is certain that during the early years of his career he was very submissive to a succession of important men to whom he looked for guidance—von Kahr, Ludendorff, and Hindenburg, to name only a few.

It is true that in the end he turned upon them one after another and treated them in a despicable fashion, but usually this change came after he discovered their personal shortcomings and inadequacies. As in many psychopathic people of Hitler's type who have a deep craving for guidance from an older man, their requirements grow with the years. By the time they reach maturity they are looking for, and can only submit to, a person who is perfect in every respect—literally a superman. The result is that they are always trying to come in contact with new persons of high status in the hope that each one, in turn, will prove to be the ideal. No sooner do they discover a single weakness or shortcoming than they depose him from the pedestal on which they have placed him. They then treat their fallen heroes badly for having failed to live up to their expectations. And so Hitler has spent his life looking for a competent guide but always ends with the discovery that the person he has chosen falls short of his requirements and is fundamentally no more capable than himself. That this tendency is a carryover from his early childhood is evidenced by the fact that throughout these years he has always laid great stress on addressing these persons by their full titles. Shades of his father's training during early childhood!

It may be of interest to note at this time that of all the titles that Hitler might have chosen for himself he is content with the simple one of "Fuehrer." To him this title is the greatest of them all. He has spent his life searching for a person worthy of the role but was unable to find one until he discovered himself. His goal now is to fulfill this role to millions of other people in a way in which he had hoped some person might do for him. The fact that the German people have submitted so readily to his leadership would indicate that a great many Germans were in a similar state of mind as Hitler himself and were not only willing, but anxious, to submit to anybody who could prove to them that he was competent to fill the role. There is some sociological evidence that this is probably so and that its origins lie in the structure of the German family and the dual role played by the father within the home as contrasted with the outside world. The duality, on the average is, of course, not nearly as marked as we have shown it to be in Hitler's case, but it may be this very fact that qualified him to identify the need and express it in terms that the others could understand and accept.

There is evidence that the only person in the world at the present time who might challenge Hitler in the role of leader is Roosevelt. Informants are agreed that he fears neither Churchill nor Stalin. He feels that they are sufficiently like himself so that he can understand their psychology and defeat them at the game. Roosevelt, however, seems to be an enigma to him. How a man can lead a nation of 130,000,000 people and keep them in line without a great deal of name-calling, shouting, abusing, and threatening is a mystery to him. He is unable to understand how a man can be the leader of a large group and still act like a gentleman. The result is that he secretly admires Roosevelt to a considerable degree, regardless of what he publicly says about him. Underneath he probably fears him inasmuch as he is unable to predict his actions.

Hitler's Mother and Her Influence

Hitler's father, however, was only a part of his early environment. There was also his mother who, from all reports, was a very decent type of woman. Hitler was written very little and said nothing about her publicly. Informants tell us, however, that she was an extremely conscientious and hard-working individual whose life centered around her home and children. She was an exemplary housekeeper, and there was never a spot or speck of dust to be found in the house—everything was very neat and orderly. She was a very devout Catholic, and the trials and tribulations that fell upon her home she accepted with Christian resignation. Even her last illness, which extended over many months and caused her great pain, she endured without a single complaint. We may assume that she had to put up with much from her irascible husband, and it may be that at times she did have to stand up against him for the welfare of her children. But all of this she probably accepted in the same spirit of abnegation. To her own children she was always extremely affectionate and generous although there is some reason to suppose that she was mean at times to her two stepchildren.

In any event every scrap of evidence indicates that there was an extremely strong attachment between herself and Adolf. As previously pointed out, this was due in part to the fact that she had lost two, or possibly three, children before Adolf was born. Since he, too, was frail as a child it is natural that a woman of her type would do everything within her power to guard against another recurrence of her earlier tragedies. The result was that she catered to his whims, even to the point of spoiling him, and that she was overprotective in her attitude toward him. We may assume that during the first five years of Adolf's life, he was the apple of his mother's eye and that she lavished affection on him. In view of her husband's conduct and the fact that he was twenty-three years her senior and far from having a loving disposition, we may suppose that much of the affection that normally would have gone to him also found its way to Adolf.

The result was a strong libidinal attachment between mother and son. It is almost certain that Adolf had temper tantrums during this time but that these were not of a serious nature. Their immediate purpose was to get his own way with his mother, and he undoubtedly succeeded in achieving this end. They were a technique by which he could dominate her whenever he wished, either out of fear that she would lose his love or out of fear that if he continued he might become like his father. There is reason suppose that she frequently condoned behavior of the father would have disapproved and may have a partner in forbidden activities during the father's absence. Life with his mother during these early years must have been a veritable Paradise for Adolf except for the fact that his father would intrude and disrupt the happy relationship. Even when his father did not make a scene or lift his whip, he would demand attention from his wife, which prevented her participation in pleasurable activities. It was natural, under these circumstances, that Adolf should resent this intrusion into his Paradise, and this undoubtedly aggravated the feelings of uncertainty and fear that his father's conduct aroused in him.

As he became older and the libidinal attachment to his mother became stronger, both the resentment and fear undoubtedly increased. Infantile sexual feelings were probably quite prominent in this relationship as well as fantasies of a childish nature. This is the Oedipus complex mentioned by psychologists and psychiatrists who have written about Hitler's personality. The great amount of affection lavished upon him by his mother and the undesirable character of his father served to develop this complex to an extraordinary degree. The more he hated his father the more dependent he became upon the affection and love of his mother, and the more he loved his mother the more afraid he became of his father's vengeance should his secret be discovered. Under these circumstances little boys frequently fantasize about ways and means of ridding the environment of the intruder. There is reason to suppose that this also happened in Hitler's early life.

Influences Determining His Attitude
toward Love, Women, Marriage

Two other factors entered into the situation and served to
accent???   ???nflict still further. One of these was the
                   brother when he was five years of age.
                   new rival onto the scene and undoubt-
                   of some of his mother's affection and
                   rly since the new child was also sickly.
                   ??at the newcomer in the family also be-
                   f Adolf's animosity and that he fan-
                   g rid of him as he had also contem-
                   his father. There is nothing abnormal
                   nsity of the emotions involved.

The other factor that served to intensify these feelings was the fact that as a child he must have discovered his parents during intercourse. An examination of the data makes this conclusion almost inescapable, and from our knowledge of his father's character and past history it is not at all impossible. It would seem that his feelings on this occasion were very mixed. On the one hand, he was indignant at his father for what he considered to be a brutal assault upon his mother. On the other hand, he was indignant with his mother because she submitted so willingly to the father, and he was indignant with himself because he was powerless to intervene. Later, as we shall see, there was a symbolic reliving of this experience that played an important part in shaping his future destinies.

Being a spectator to this early scene had many repercussions. One of the most important of these was the fact that he felt that his mother had betrayed him in submitting to his father, a feeling that became accentuated still further when his baby brother was born. He lost much of his respect for the female sex, and while in Vienna, Hanisch reports, he frequently spoke at length on the topic of love and marriage and "he had very austere ideas about relations between men and women." Even at that time he maintained that if men only wanted to they could adopt a strictly moral way of living. "He often said it was the woman's fault if a man went astray," and "He used to lecture us about this, saying every woman can be had." In other words, he regarded women as seductresses responsible for men's downfall, and he condemned them for their disloyalty. These attitudes are probably the outcome of his early experiences with his mother who first seduced him into a love relationship and then betrayed him by giving herself to his father. Nevertheless, he still continued to believe in an idealistic form of love and marriage that would be possible if a loyal woman could be found. As we know, Hitler never gave himself into the hands of a woman again with the possible exception of his niece, Geli Raubal; this also ended in disaster. Outside of that single exception he has lived a loveless life. His distrust of both men and women is so deep that in all his history there is no record of a really intimate and lasting friendship.

The outcome of these early experiences was probably a feeling of being very much alone in a hostile world. He hated his father for his brutality, he distrusted his mother for her lack of loyalty, and despised himself for his weakness. The immature child finds such a state of mind almost unendurable for any length of time, and in order to gain peace and security in his environment these feelings are gradually repressed from his memory.

This is a normal procedure that happens in the case of every child at a relatively early age. This process of repression enables the child to re-establish a more or less friendly relationship with his parents without the interference of disturbing memories and emotions. The early conflicts, however, are not solved or destroyed by such a process, and we must expect to find manifestations of them later on. When the early repression has been fairly adequate these conflicts lie dormant until adolescence when, due to the process of maturation, they are reawakened. In some cases they reappear in very much their original form, while in others they are expressed in a camouflaged or symbolic form.

In Hitler's case, however, the conflicting emotions and sentiments were so strong that they could not be held in complete abeyance during this entire period. Quite early in his school career we find his conflicts appearing again in a symbolic form. Unfortunately, the symbols he unconsciously chose to express his own inner conflicts were such that they have seriously affected the future of the world. And yet these symbols fit his peculiar situation so perfectly that it was almost inevitable that they would be chosen as vehicles of expression.

His Early Conflicts Expressed in Symbolic Form

Unconsciously, all the emotions he had once felt for his mother became transferred to Germany. This transfer of affect was relatively easy inasmuch as Germany, like his mother, was young and vigorous and held promise of a great future under suitable circumstances. Furthermore, he felt shut off from Germany as he now felt shut off from his mother, even though he secretly wished to be with her. Germany became a symbol of his ideal mother, and his sentiments are clearly expressed in his writings and speeches. A few excerpts will serve to illustrate the transfer of emotion:

> The longing grew stronger to go there (Germany) where since my early youth I have been drawn by secret wishes and secret love.

> What I first had looked upon as an impassable chasm now spurred me on to greater love for my country than ever before.

> An unnatural separation from the great common Motherland.

> I appeal to those who, severed from the Motherland, ... and who now in painful emotion long for the hour that will allow them to return to the arms of the beloved mother.

It is significant that although Germans, as a whole, invariably refer to Germany as the "Fatherland," Hitler almost always refers to it as the "Motherland."

Just as Germany was ideally suited to symbolize his mother, so Austria was ideally suited to symbolize his father. Like his father Austria was old, exhausted, and decaying from within. He therefore transferred all his unconscious hatred from his father to the Austrian state. He could now give vent to all his pent-up emotions without exposing himself to the dangers he believed he would have encountered had he expressed these same feelings toward the persons really involved. In *Mein Kampf* he frequently refers to the Austrian state in terms such as these:

> ... an intense love for my native German-Austrian country and a bitter hatred against the Austrian state.

> With proud admiration I compared the rise of the Reich with the decline of the Austrian state.

The alliance between Austria and Germany served to symbolize the marriage of his mother and father. Over and over again we find references to this alliance, and we can see clearly how deeply he resented the marriage of his parents because he felt that his father was a detriment to his mother, and only through the death of the former could the latter obtain her freedom and find her salvation. A few quotations will illustrate his sentiments:

And who could keep faith with an imperial dynasty which betrayed the cause of the German people for its own ignominious ends, a betrayal that occurred again and again.

What grieved us most was the fact that the whole system was morally protected by the alliance with Germany, and thus Germany herself ... walked by the side of the corpse.

It suffices to state here that from my earliest youth I came to a conviction which never deserted me, but on the contrary grew stronger and stronger: that the protection of the German race presumed the destruction of Austria ... that above all else, the Royal House of Hapsburg was destined to bring misfortune upon the German nation.

Since my heart had never beaten for an Austrian monarchy but only for a German Reich, I could only look upon the hour of the ruin of this state as the beginning of the salvation of the German nation.

When we have grasped the significance of this transference of affect we have made a long step in the direction of understanding Hitler's actions. Unconsciously, he is not dealing with nations composed of millions of individuals but is trying to solve his personal conflicts and rectify the injustices of his childhood. Unable to enter into a "give-and-take" relationship with other human beings that might afford him an opportunity of resolving his conflicts in a realistic manner, he projects his personal problems on great nations and then tries to solve them on this unrealistic level. His microcosm has been inflated into a macrocosm.

We can now understand why Hitler fell on his knees and thanked God when the last war broke out. To him it did not mean simply a war, as such, but an opportunity of fighting for his symbolic mother, of proving his manhood and of being accepted by her. It was inevitable that he would seek enlistment in the German Army rather than in the Austrian Army, and it was also inevitable, under these circumstances, that he would be a good and obedient soldier. Unconsciously, it was as though he were a little boy who was playing the part of a man while his mother stood by and watched him. Her future welfare was his great concern, and in order to prove his love he was willing, if need be, to sacrifice his own life for her. His relationship to Germany was, in effect, the sexless, idealistic marriage he longed for.

The Effects of Germany's Defeat

Everything went smoothly as long as he felt sure that all would turn out well in the end. He never complained about the hardships that were imposed on him and he never grumbled with the other men. He was happy in what he was doing and met the trials and tribulations of army life with his chin up until he discovered that things were going badly and that his symbolic mother was about to be degraded as he had imagined his real mother had been degraded in his childhood. To him it was as if his mother was again the victim of a sexual assault. This time it was the November Criminals and the Jews who were guilty of the foul deed, and he promptly transferred his repressed hate to these new perpetrators.

When he became fully aware of Germany's defeat he reacted in a typically hysterical manner. He refused to accept or adjust to the situation on a reality level. Instead, he reacted to this event as he probably reacted to the discovery of his parents in intercourse. He writes: "I stumbled and tottered rearwards with burning eyes. . . . Already a few hours later the eyes had turned into burning coals; it had become dark around me." In another place he writes: "While everything began to go black again before my eyes, stumbling, I groped my way back to the dormitory, threw myself on my cot and buried my burning head in the covers and pillows."

At the time this happened he had been exposed to a slight attack of mustard gas. He immediately believed that he was blinded and speechless. Although he spent several weeks in the hospital, neither his symptoms nor the development of the illness corresponded to those found in genuine gas cases. It had been definitely established that both the blindness and the mutism were of an hysterical nature. The physician who treated him at that time found his case so typical of hysterical symptoms in general that for years after the war he used it as an illustration in his courses given at a prominent German medical school. We know from a great many other cases that during the onset of such attacks the patient behaves in exactly the same manner as he did earlier in his life when confronted by a situation with the same emotional content. It is as though the individual were actually reliving the earlier experience over again. In Hitler's case this earlier experience was almost certainly the discovery of his parents in intercourse and his interpretation of this as a brutal assault in which he was powerless. He refused to believe what his eyes told him, and the experience left him speechless.

That this interpretation is correct is evidenced by his imagery in dealing with the event later on. Over and over again we find figures of speech that illustrate his sentiments very clearly: "... by what wiles the soul of the German nation has been raped," and "... our German pacifists will pass over in silence the most bloody rape of the nation."

The Origins of His Belief in His Mission and His Longing for Immortality

It was while he was in the hospital suffering from hysterical blindness and mutism that he had the vision that he would liberate the Germans from their bondage and make Germany great. It was this vision that set him on his present political career and that has had such a determining influence on the course of world events. More than anything else it was this vision that convinced him that he was chosen by Providence and that he had a great mission to perform. This is probably the most outstanding characteristic of Hitler's mature personality, and it is this that guides him with the "precision of a sleepwalker."

From an analysis of many other cases we know that such convictions never result from an adult experience alone. In order to carry conviction they must reawaken earlier beliefs that have their roots far back in childhood. It is, of course, nothing unusual for a child to believe that he is some special creation and is destined to do great things before he dies. One can almost say that every child passes through such a period on his way to growing up. In many people remnants of such early beliefs are observable inasmuch as they feel or believe that Fate, Luck, Providence, or some other extranatural power has chosen them for special favors. In most of these cases, however, the adult individual only half believes that this is really so even when a whole series of favorable events may make the hypothesis plausible. Only rarely do we find a firm conviction of this kind in adulthood and then only when there were extenuating circumstances in childhood that made such a belief necessary and convincing.

In Hitler's case the extenuating circumstances are relatively clear. Mention has already been made of the fact that his mother had given birth to at least two and possibly three children, all of whom had died prior to his own birth. He himself was a frail and rather sickly infant. Under these circumstances his mother undoubtedly exerted herself to the utmost to keep him alive. He was unquestionably spoiled during this period, and his survival was probably the great concern of the family. From his earliest days there was, no doubt, considerable talk in the household about the death of the other children and constant comparisons between their progress and his own.

Children first become aware of death as a phenomenon very early in life, and in view of these unusual circumstances it may have dawned on Hitler even earlier than with most children. The thought of death in itself is inconceivable to small children, and they usually are able to form only the vaguest conception of what it means or implies before they push it out of their minds. In Hitler's case, however, it was a living issue, and the fears of the mother were in all likelihood communicated to him. As he pondered the problem in his immature way, he probably wondered why the others died while he continued to live. The natural conclusion for a child to draw would be that he was favored in some way or that he was chosen to live for some particular purpose. The belief that he was the "chosen one" would have been reinforced by the fact that as far as his mother was concerned he was very much the chosen one in comparison with her two stepchildren who were also living in the home at that time.

This belief must have been strengthened considerably at the age of five when his baby brother was born. This baby brother has undoubtedly played a much more important role in Adolf's life than has been acknowledged by his biographers. The pertinent fact, at the moment, however, is that this brother, too, died before he was six years old. It was Adolf's first real experience with death, and it must have brought up the problem of death again in a much more vivid form. Again, we can surmise, he asked himself why they died while he continued to be saved. The only plausible answer to a child at that age would be that he must be under divine protection. This may seem far-fetched, yet as an adult Hitler tells us that he felt exactly this way when he was at the front during the war, even before he had the vision. Then, too, he speculated on why it is that comrades all around him are killed while he is saved, and again he comes to the conclusion that Providence must be protecting him. Perhaps the exemplary courage he displayed in carrying messages at the front was due to the feeling that some kindly Fate was watching over him. Throughout *Mein Kampf* we find this type of thinking. It was Fate that had him born so close to the German border; it was Fate that had sent him to Vienna to suffer with the masses; it was Fate that caused him to do many things. The experience he reports at the front, when a voice told him to pick up his plate and move to another section of the trench just in time to escape a shell that killed all his comrades, must certainly have strengthened this belief to a marked degree and paved the way for his vision later on.

The Messiah Complex

Another influence may have helped to solidify this system of belief. Among patients we very frequently find that children who are spoiled at an early age and establish a strong bond with their mother tend to question their paternity. Eldest children in particular are prone to such doubts, and it is most marked in cases where the father is much older than the mother. In Hitler's case the father was twenty-three years older, or almost twice the age of the mother. Just why this should be is not clear, from a psychological point of view, but in such cases there is a strong tendency to believe that their father is not their real father and to ascribe their birth to some kind of supernatural conception. Usually such beliefs are dropped as the child grows older. It can be observed in young children, however, and can often be recovered in adults under suitable conditions. Due to the unsympathetic and brutal nature of his father we may suppose that there was an added incentive in Hitler's case for rejecting him as his real father and postulating some other origin to himself.

The problem is not important in itself at the moment except insofar as it may help to throw some light on the origins of Hitler's conviction in his mission and his belief that he is guided by some extranatural power, which communicates to him what he should or should not do under varying circumstances. This hypothesis is tenable in view of the fact that during his stay in Vienna, when still in his early twenties, he grew a beard and directly after the war he again grew a Christlike beard. Then, too, when he was a student at the Benedictine school his ambition was to join the Church and become an abbot or priest. All of these give some indication of a Messiah complex long before he had started on his meteoric career and became an open competitor of Christ for the affection of the German people.

Fear of Death and Desire for Immortality

Although beliefs of this kind are common during childhood they are usually dropped or are modified as the individual becomes more experienced. In Hitler's case, however, the reverse has taken place. The conviction became stronger as he grew older until at the present time it is the core of his thinking. Under these circumstances we must suppose that some powerful psychological stream continued to nourish these infantile modes of thought. This psychological stream is probably, as it is in many other cases, a fear of death. It seems logical to suppose that in the course of his early deliberations on the deaths of his brothers his first conclusion was probably that all the others died and that consequently he, too, would die. His fear would not be allayed by his mother's constant concern over his well-being, which he may have interpreted as an indication that the danger was imminent. Such a conclusion would certainly be a valid one for a child to make under the circumstances. The thought of his own death, however, is almost unbearable to a small child. Nothing is quite so demoralizing as the constant dread of self-annihilation. It gnaws away day and night and prevents him from enjoying the good things that life affords.

To rid himself of this devastating fear becomes his major objective. This is not easily accomplished, especially when all available evidence seems to corroborate the validity of the fear. In order to offset its potency he is almost driven to deny its reality by adopting the belief that he is of divine origin and that Providence is protecting him from all harm. Only by use of such a technique is the child able to convince himself that he will not die. We must also remember that in Hitler's case there was not only the unusual succession of deaths of siblings, but there was also the constant menace of his father's brutality, which helped to make the fear more intense than in most children. This danger could easily be exaggerated in Hitler's mind due to a sense of guilt concerning his feelings toward his respective parents and what his father might do to him if he discovered his secret. These feelings would tend to increase his fear of death at the same time that they caused him to reject his father. Both tendencies would serve to nourish the belief that he was of divine origin and was under its protection.

It is my belief that this basic fear of death is still present and active in Hitler's character at the present time. As time goes on and he approaches the age when he might reasonably expect to die, this infantile fear asserts itself more strongly. As a mature, intelligent man he knows that the law of nature is such that his physical self is destined to die. He is still not able, however, to accept the fact that he as an individual, his psyche, will also die. It is this element in his psychological structure that demands that he become immortal. Most people are able to take the sting out of this fear of death through religious beliefs in life after death, or through the feeling that a part of them, at least, will continue to go on living in their children. In Hitler's case both of these normal channels have been closed, and he has been forced to seek immortality in a more direct form. He must arrange to go on living in the German people for at least a thousand years to come. In order to do this he must oust Christ as a competitor and usurp his place in the lives of the German people.

In addition to evidence drawn from experience with patients that would make this hypothesis tenable, we have the evidence afforded by Hitler's own fears and attitudes. We have discussed these in detail in Part IV. Fear of assassination, fear of poisoning, fear of premature death, and so forth, all deal with the problem of death in an uncamouflaged form. One can, of course, maintain that in view of his position all these fears are more or less justified. There is certainly some truth in this contention, but we also notice that as time goes on these fears have increased considerably until now they have reached the point where the precautions for his own safety far exceed those of any of his predecessors. As long as he could hold a plebescite every now and then and reassure himself that the German people loved him and wanted him, he felt better. Now that this is no longer possible, he has no easy way of curbing the fear and his uncertainty in the future becomes greater. There can be little doubt concerning his faith in the results of the plebescites. He was firmly convinced that the 98 percent vote, approving his actions, really represented the true feelings of the German people. He believed this because he needed such reassurance from time to time in order to carry on with a fairly easy mind and maintain his delusions.

When we turn to his fear of cancer we find no justification whatever for his belief, especially in view of the fact that several outstanding specialists in this disease have assured him that it is without foundation. Nevertheless, it is one of his oldest fears and he continues to adhere to it in spite of all the expert testimony to the contrary. This fear becomes intelligible when we remember that his mother died following an operation for cancer of the breast. In connection with his fear of death we must not forget his terrifying nightmares from which he awakes in a cold sweat and acts as though he were being suffocated. If our hypothesis is correct, namely, that a fear of death is one of the powerful unconscious streams that drive Hitler on in his mad career, then we can expect that as the war progresses and as he becomes older the fear will continue to increase. With the progress of events along their present course, it will be more and more difficult for him to feel that his mission is fulfilled and that he has successfully cheated death and achieved immortality in the German people. Nevertheless, we can expect him to keep on trying to the best of his ability as long as a ray of hope remains. The great danger is that if he feels that he cannot achieve immortality as the Great Redeemer he may seek it as the Great Destroyer who will live on in the minds of the German people for a thousand years to come. He intimated this in a conversation with Rauschning when he said: "We shall not capitulate—no, never. We may be destroyed, but if we are, we shall drag a world with us—a world in flames." With him, as with many others of his type, it may well be a case of immortality of any kind at any price.

Sexual Development

Closely interwoven with several of the themes that have already been elaborated is the development of his sexual life. From what we know about his mother's excessive cleanliness and tidiness we may assume that she employed rather stringent measures during the toilet training period of her children. This usually results in a residual tension in this area and is regarded by the child as a severe frustration that arouses feelings of hostility. This facilitates an alliance with his infantile aggression that finds an avenue for expression through anal activities and fantasies. These usually center around soiling, humiliation, and destruction, and form the basis of a sadistic character.

Here, again, we may assume that the experience was more intense in Hitler's case than in the average due to the strong attachment and spoiling of his mother in early infancy. Unaccustomed to minor frustrations that most children must learn to endure prior to the toilet training, he was poorly equipped to deal with this experience that plays an important role in the life of all infants. Even now, as an adult, Hitler is unable to cope with frustrating experiences on a mature level. That a residual tension from this period still exists in Hitler is evidenced by the frequency of imagery in his speaking and writing that deals with dung and dirt and smell. A few illustrations may help to clarify his unconscious preoccupation with these subjects:

> You don't understand: we are just passing a magnet over a dunghill, and we shall see presently how much iron was in the dunghill and has clung to the magnet. (By "dunghill" Hitler meant the German people.)

> And when he (the Jews) turns the treasures over in his hand they are transformed into dirt and dung.

> ... One's hands seize slimy jelly; it slips through one's fingers only to collect again in the next moment.

Charity is sometimes actually comparable to the manure which is spread on the field, not out of love for the latter, but out of precaution for one's own benefit later on.

... dragged into the dirt and filth of the lowest depths.

Later the smell of these caftan wearers made me ill. Added to this were their dirty clothes and their none too heroic appearance.

The rottenness of artificially nurtured conditions of peace has more than once stunk to high heaven.

His libidinal development, however, was not arrested at this point, but progressed to the genital level at which the Oedipus complex, already referred to, developed. This complex, as we have seen, was aggravated by his mother's pregnancy at precisely the age when the complex normally reaches its greatest intensity. In addition to accentuating his hatred for his father and estranging him from his mother, we can assume that this event at this particular time served to generate an abnormal curiosity in him. He, like all children at this age, must have wondered how the unborn child got into the mother's stomach and how it was going to get out.

These three reactions have all played an important part in Hitler's psychosexual development. It would seem from the evidence that his aggressive fantasies toward the father reached such a point that he became afraid of the possibility of retaliation if his secret desires were discovered. The retaliation he probably feared was that his father would castrate him or injure his genital capacity in some way—a fear that is later expressed in substitute form in his syphilophobia. Throughout *Mein Kampf* he comes back to the topic of syphilis again and again and spends almost an entire chapter describing its horrors. In almost all cases we find that fear of this sort is rooted in a fear of genital injury during childhood. In many cases this fear was so overpowering that the child abandoned his genital sexuality entirely and regressed to earlier stages of libidinal development. In order to maintain these repressions later in life he uses the horrors of syphilis as a justification for his unconscious fear that genital sexuality is dangerous for him, and also as a rationalization for his avoidance of situations in which his earlier desires might be aroused.

In abandoning the genital level of libidinal development the individual becomes impotent as far as heterosexual relations are concerned. It would appear, from the evidence, that some such process took place during Hitler's early childhood. Throughout his early adult life, in Vienna, in the Army, in Munich, in Landsberg, no informant has reported a heterosexual relationship. In fact, the informants of all these periods make a point of the fact that he had absolutely no interest in women or any contact with them. Since he has come to power his peculiar relationship to women has been so noticeable that many writers believe that he is completely asexual. Some have surmised that he suffered a genital injury during the last war, others that he is homosexual. The former hypothesis, for which there is not a shred of real evidence, is almost certainly false. The second hypothesis we will examine later on.

The Diffusion of the Sexual Instinct

When a regression of this kind takes place the sexual instinct usually becomes diffuse, and many organs that have yielded some sexual stimulation in the past become permanently invested with sexual significance. The eyes, for example, may become a substitute sexual organ and seeing then takes on a sexual significance. This seems to have happened in Hitler's case for a number of informants have commented on his delight in witnessing striptease and nude dancing numbers on the stage. On such occasions he can never see enough to satisfy him even though he uses opera glasses in order to observe more closely. Striptease artists are frequently invited to the Brown House, in Munich, to perform in private, and there is evidence that he often invites girls to Berchtesgaden for the purpose of exhibiting their bodies. On his walls are numerous pictures of obscene nudes that conceal nothing and he takes particular delight in looking through a collection of pornographic pictures that Hoffmann has made for him. We also know the extreme pleasure he derives from huge pageants, circus performances, opera, and particularly the movies of which he can never get enough. He has told informants that he gave up flying not only because of the danger involved but because he could not see enough of the country. For this reason automobile travel is his favorite form of transportation. From all of this it is evident that seeing has a special sexual significance for him. This probably accounts for his "hypnotic glance," which has been the subject of comment by so many writers. Some have reported that at their first meeting Hitler fixated them with his eyes as if "to bore through them." It is also interesting that when the other person meets his stare, Hitler turns his eyes to the ceiling and keeps them there during the interview. Then, too, we must not forget that in the moment of crisis his hysterical attack manifested itself in blindness.

In addition to the eyes, the anal region has also become highly sexualized, and both feces and buttocks become sexual objects. Due to early toilet training, certain inhibitions have been set up that prevent their direct expression. However, we find so many instances of imagery of this kind, particularly in connection with sexual topics, that we must assume that this area has taken on a sexual significance. The nature of this significance we will consider in a moment.

The mouth, too, seems to have become invested as an erogenous zone of great importance. Few authors or informants have neglected to mention Hitler's peculiar dietary habits. He consumes tremendous quantities of sweets, candies, cakes, whipped cream, and the like, in the course of a day in addition to his vegetable diet. On the other hand, he refuses to eat meat, drink beer or smoke, all of which suggest certain unconscious inhibitions in this area. In addition, he has a pathological fear of poisoning by mouth and has shown an obsessional preoccupation at times with mouth washing. These suggest a reaction formation or defense against an unacceptable tendency to take something into his mouth or get something out that from one point of view appears to be disgusting. In this connection we must not forget his resolve to starve himself to death after the failure of the Beer Hall Putsch, his hysterical mutism at the end of the last war, and his love of speaking. The significance of these we shall consider later on.

Disturbance of Love Relations

The second effect of his mother's pregnancy was his estrangement from her. The direct result of this was, on the one hand, an idealization of love but without sexual component and, on the other hand, the setting up of a barrier against intimate relationships with other people, particularly women. Having been hurt once, he unconsciously guards himself against a similar hurt in the future. In his relationship to his niece, Geli, he tried to overcome this barrier, but he was again disappointed and since then has not exposed himself to a really intimate relationship either with man or woman. He has cut himself off from the world in which love plays any part for fear of being hurt, and what love he can experience is fixated on the abstract entity—Germany, which, as we have seen, is a symbol of his ideal mother. This is a love relationship in which sex plays no direct part.

Origins of His Perversion

The third outcome of his mother's pregnancy was to arouse an excessive curiosity. The great mystery to children of this age, who find themselves in this situation, is how the unborn child got into the mother's stomach and how it is going to get out. Even in cases where the children have witnessed parental intercourse, this event is rarely linked with the ensuing pregnancy. Since in their limited experience everything that gets into their stomach enters by way of the mouth and everything that comes out usually does so by way of the rectum, they are prone to believe that conception somehow takes place through the mouth and that the child will be born via the anus. Hitler, as a child, undoubtedly adhered to this belief, but this did not satisfy his curiosity. He evidently wanted to see for himself how it came out and exactly what happened.

This curiosity laid the foundation for his strange perversion, which brought all three of his sexualized zones into play. In her description of sexual experiences with Hitler, Geli stressed the fact that it was of utmost importance to him that she squat over him in such a way that he could see everything. It is interesting that Roehm, in an entirely different connection, once said:

He (Hitler) is thinking about the peasant girls. When they stand in the fields and bend down at their work so that you can see their behinds, that's what he likes, especially when they've got big round ones. That's Hitler's sex life. What a man.

Hitler, who was present, did not stir a muscle but only stared at Roehm with compressed lips.

From a consideration of all the evidence it would seem that Hitler's perversion is as Geli has described it. The great danger in gratifying it, however, is that the individual might get feces or urine into his mouth. It is this danger that requires that suitable inhibitions be instituted.

Return to the Womb

Another possibility in infantile thinking presents itself in this connection. When the home environment is harsh and brutal, as it was in Hitler's case, the small child very frequently envies the position of passivity and security the unborn child enjoys within the mother. This, in turn, gives rise to fantasies of finding a way in to the longed-for claustrum and ousting his rival in order that he may take his place. These fantasies are usually of very brief duration because the child believes that if he succeeded he would have nothing to eat or drink except feces and urine. The thought of such a diet arouses feelings of disgust, and consequently he abandons his fantasies in order to avoid these unpleasant feelings. In many psychotics, however, these fantasies continue and strive to express themselves overtly. The outstanding bit of evidence in Hitler's case that such fantasies were present is to be found in the Kehlstein or Eagle's Nest that he has built for himself near Berchtesgaden. Interestingly enough, many people have commented that only a madman would conceive of such a place, let alone try to build it. From a symbolic point of view one can easily imagine that this is a materialization of a child's conception of the return to the womb. First there is a long hard road, then a heavily guarded entrance, a trip through a long tunnel to an extremely inaccessible place. There one can be alone, safe and undisturbed, and revel in the joys that Mother Nature bestows. It is also interesting to note that very few people have ever been invited there, and many of Hitler's closest associates are either unaware of its existence or have only seen it from a distance. Extraordinarily enough, Francois-Poncet is one of the few people who was ever invited to visit there. In the French Yellow Book he gives us an extremely vivid description of the place, a part of which may be worthwhile quoting:

> The approach is by a winding road about nine miles long, boldly cut out of the rock.... the road comes to an end in front of a long underground passage leading into the mountains, enclosed by a heavy double door of bronze. At the far end of the underground passage a wide lift, panelled with sheets of copper, awaits the visitor. Through a vertical shaft of 330 feet cut right through the rock, it rises up to the level of the Chancellor's dwelling place. Here is reached the astonishing climax. The visitor finds himself in a strong and massive building containing a gallery with Roman pillars, an immense circular hall with windows all around.... It gives the impression of being suspended in space, an almost overhanging wall of bare rock rises abruptly. The whole, bathed in the twilight of the autumn evening, is grandiose, wild, almost hallucinating. The visitor wonders whether he is awake or dreaming.[5]

If one were asked to plan something that represented a return to the womb, one could not possibly surpass the Kehlstein. It is also significant that Hitler often retires to this strange place to await instructions concerning the course he is to pursue.

Vegetarianism

We can surmise from the psychological defenses Hitler has set up that there was a period during which he struggled against these tendencies. In terms of unconscious symbolism meat is almost synonymous with feces and beer with urine. The fact that there is a strict taboo on both would indicate that these desires are still present and that it is only by refraining from everything symbolizing them that he can avoid arousing anxieties. Rauschning reports that Hitler, following Wagner, attributed much of the decay of our civilization to meat eating. He believed that the decadence "had its origin in the abdomen—chronic constipation, poisoning of the juices, and the results of drinking to excess." This assertion suggests decay (contamination, corruption, pollution, and death) as the resultant of constipation, that is, feces in the gastrointestinal tract, and if this is so, decay might be avoided both by not eating anything resembling feces and by taking purges or ejecting as frequently as possible. It has been reported that Hitler once said that he was confident that all nations would arrive at the point where they would not feed any more on dead animals. It is interesting to note that according to one of our most reliable informants Hitler only became a real vegetarian after the death of his niece, Geli. In clinical practice one frequently finds compulsive vegetarianism setting in after the death of a loved object.

We may, therefore, regard Hitler's perversion as a compromise between psychotic tendencies to eat feces and drink urine on the one hand, and to live a normal, socially adjusted life on the other. The compromise is not, however, satisfactory to either side of his nature, and the struggle between these two diverse tendencies continues to rage unconsciously. We must not suppose that Hitler gratifies his strange perversion frequently. Patients of this type rarely do, and in Hitler's case it is highly probable that he had permitted himself to go this far only with his niece, Geli, and possibly with Henny Hoffmann. The practice of this perversion represents an extreme form of masochistic degradation.

Masochistic Gratifications

In most patients suffering from this perversion the unconscious forces only get out of control to this degree when a fairly strong love relationship is established and sexuality makes decisive demands. In other relationships where the love component is less strong the individual contents himself with less degrading activities. This is brought out clearly in the case of Rene Mueller who confided to her director, Zeissler, who had asked her what was troubling her after spending an evening at the Chancellory, "that the evening before she had been with Hitler and that she had been sure that he was going to have intercourse with her; that they had both undressed and were apparently getting ready for bed when Hitler fell on the floor and begged her to kick him. She demurred, but he pleaded with her and condemned himself as unworthy, heaped all kinds of accusations on his own head, and just groveled in an agonizing manner. The scene became intolerable to her, and she finally acceded to his wishes and kicked him. This excited him greatly, and he begged for more and more, always saying that it was even better than he deserved and that he was not worthy to be in the same room with her. As she continued to kick him he became more and more excited."[6] Rene Mueller committed suicide shortly after this experience. At this place it might be well to note that Eva Braun, his present female companion, has twice attempted suicide, Geli was either murdered or committed suicide, and Unity Mitford has attempted suicide. Rather an unusual record for a man who has had so few affairs with women.

Hanfstaengl, Strasser, and Rauschning, as well as several other informants, have reported that even in company when Hitler is smitten with a girl he tends to grovel at her feet in a most disgusting manner. Here, too, he insists on telling the girl that he is unworthy to kiss her hand or to sit near her and that he hopes she will be kind to him, and the like. From all of this we see the constant struggle against complete degradation whenever any affectionate components enter into the picture. It now becomes clear that the only way in which Hitler can control these coprophagic tendencies or their milder manifestations is to isolate himself from any intimate relationships in which warm feelings of affection or love might assert themselves. As soon as such feelings are aroused, he feels compelled to degrade himself in the eyes of the loved object and eat their dirt figuratively, if not literally. These tendencies disgust him just as much as they disgust us, but under these circumstances they get out of control and he despises himself and condemns himself for his weakness. Before considering further the effects of this struggle on his manifest behavior, we must pause for a moment to pick up another thread.

Femininity

We noticed that in all of these activities Hitler plays the passive role. His behavior is masochistic in the extreme inasmuch as he derives sexual pleasure from punishment inflicted on his own body. There is every reason to suppose that during his early years, instead of identifying himself with his father as most boys do, he identified himself with his mother. This was perhaps easier for him than for most boys since, as we have seen, there is a large feminine component in his physical makeup. His mother, too, must have been an extremely masochistic individual, or she never would have entered into this marriage nor would she have endured the brutal treatment from her husband. An emotional identification with his mother would, therefore, carry him in the direction of a passive, sentimental, abased, and submissive form of adjustment. Many writers and informants have commented on his feminine characteristics—his gait, his hands, his mannerisms, and his ways of thinking. Hanfstaengl reports that when he showed Dr. Jung a specimen of Hitler's handwriting, the latter immediately exclaimed that it was a typically feminine hand. His choice of art as a profession might also be interpreted as a manifestation of a basic feminine identification.

There are definite indications of such an emotional adjustment later in life. The outstanding of these is perhaps his behavior toward his officers during the last war. His comrades report that during the four years he was in service he was not only oversubmissive to all his officers but frequently volunteered to do their washing and take care of their clothes. This would certainly indicate a strong tendency to assume the feminine role in the presence of a masculine figure whenever this was feasible and could be duly rationalized. His extreme sentimentality, his emotionality, his occasional softness, and his weeping, even after he became Chancellor, may be regarded as manifestations of a fundamental feminine pattern that undoubtedly had its origin in his relationship to his mother. His persistent fear of cancer, which was the illness from which his mother died, may also be considered as an expression of his early identification with her.

Although we cannot enter into a discussion concerning the frequency of this phenomenon in Germany, it may be well to note that there is sociological evidence that would indicate that it is probably extremely common. If further research on the subject should corroborate this evidence, it might prove of extreme value to our psychological warfare program insofar as it would give us a key to the understanding of the basic nature of the German male character and the role that the Nazi organization plays in their inner life.

Homosexuality

The great difficulty is that this form of identification early in life carries the individual in the direction of passive homosexuality. Hitler has for years been suspected of being a homosexual, although there is no reliable evidence that he has actually engaged in a relationship of this kind. Rauschning reports that he has met two boys who claimed that they were Hitler's homosexual partners, but their testimony can scarcely be taken at its face value. More condemning would be the remarks dropped by Foerster, the Danzig gauleiter, in conversations with Rauschning. Even here, however, the remarks deal only with Hitler's impotence as far as heterosexual relations go without actually implying that he indulges in homosexuality. It is probably true that Hitler calls Foerster "Bubi," which is a common nickname employed by homosexuals in addressing their partners. This alone, however, is not adequate proof that he has actually indulged in homosexual practices with Foerster, who is known to be a homosexual.

The belief that Hitler is homosexual has probably arisen because he does show so many feminine characteristics and because there were so many homosexuals in the Party during the early days and many continue to occupy important positions. It does seem that Hitler feels much more at ease with homosexuals than with normal persons, but this may be because they are all fundamentally social outcasts and consequently have a community of interests that tends to make them think and feel more or less alike. In this connection it is interesting to note that homosexuals, too, frequently regard themselves as a special form of creation or as chosen ones whose destiny it is to initiate a new order. The fact that underneath they feel themselves to be different and ostracized from normal social contacts usually makes them easy converts to a new social philosophy that does not discriminate against them. Being among civilization's discontents, they are always willing to take a chance on something new that holds any promise of improving their lot, even though their chances of success may be small and the risk great. Having little to lose to begin with, they can afford to take chances that others would refrain from taking. The early Nazi Party certainly contained many members who could be regarded in this light. Even today Hitler derives sexual pleasure from looking at men's bodies and associating with homosexuals. Strasser tells us that his personal bodyguard is almost always 100 percent homosexuals. He also derives considerable pleasure from being with his Hitler Youth, and his attitude toward them frequently tends to be more that of a woman than that of a man.

There is a possibility that Hitler has participated in a homosexual relationship at some time in his life. The evidence is such that we can only say there is a strong tendency in this direction that, in addition to the manifestations already enumerated, often finds expression in imagery about being attacked from behind or being stabbed in the back. His nightmares, which frequently deal with being attacked by a man and being suffocated, also suggest strong homosexual tendencies and a fear of them. From these indications, however, we would conclude that for the most part these tendencies have been repressed, which would speak against the probability of their being expressed in overt form. On the other hand, persons suffering from his perversion sometimes do indulge in homosexual practices in the hope that they might find some sexual gratification. Even this perversion would be more acceptable to them than the one with which they are afflicted.

Early School Years

The foundations of all the diverse patterns we have been considering were laid during the first years of Hitler's life. Many of them, as we have seen, were due primarily to the peculiar structure of the home, while others developed from constitutional factors or false interpretations of events. Whatever their origins may have been, they did set up antisocial tendencies and tensions that disturbed the child to a high degree. From his earliest days it would seem he must have felt that the world was a pretty bad place in which to live. To him it must have seemed as though the world was filled with insurmountable hazards and obstacles that prevented him from obtaining adequate gratifications, and dangers that would menace his well-being if he attempted to obtain them in a direct manner. The result was that he felt an unusual amount of bitterness against the world and the people in it for which he could find no suitable outlets. As a young child he must have been filled with intense feelings of inadequacy, anxiety, and guilt that made him anything but a happy child.

It would seem, however, that he managed to repress most of his troublesome tendencies and make a temporary adjustment to a difficult environment before he was six years old, because at that time he entered school and for the next several years he was an unusually good student. All of the report cards that have been found from the time he entered school until he was eleven years old show an almost unbroken line of "A's" in all his school subjects. At the age of eleven the bottom dropped right out of his academic career. From an "A" student he suddenly dropped to a point where he failed in almost all his subjects and had to repeat the year. This amazing about-face only becomes intelligible when we realize that his baby brother died at that time. We can only surmise that this event served to reawaken his earlier conflicts and disrupt his psychological equilibrium.

In Hitler's case we may suppose that this event affected him in at least two important ways. First, it must have reawakened fears of his own death, which, in turn, strengthened still further the conviction that he was the "chosen one" and under divine protection. Second, it would seem that he connected the death of his brother with his own thinking and wishing on the subject. Unquestionably, he hated this intruder and frequently thought of how nice it would be if he were removed from the scene. Unconsciously, if not consciously, he probably felt that the brother's death was the result of his own thinking on the subject. This accentuated his feelings of guilt on the one hand, while it strengthened still further his belief in special powers of Divine origin on the other. To think about these things was almost synonymous with having them come true. In order to avoid further guilt feelings he had to put a curb on his thinking processes. The result of this inhibition on thinking was that Hitler the good student was transformed into Hitler the poor student. Not only did he have to repeat the school year during which the brother died, but ever after his academic performance was mediocre, to say the least. When we examine his later report cards we find that he does well only in such subjects as drawing and gymnastics, which require no thinking. In all the other subjects such as mathematics, languages, or history that require some thinking his work is on the borderline—sometimes satisfactory and sometimes unsatisfactory.

We can easily imagine that it was during this period that the father's ire was aroused and he began to bring pressure on the boy to apply himself in his schoolwork and threatened dire consequences if he failed to do so. From sociological evidence it would seem that this is about the age at which most German fathers first take a real interest in their sons and their education. If Hitler's father followed this general pattern, we can assume that he had cause to be irate at his son's performance. The constant struggle between himself and his father, which he describes in *Mein Kampf*, is probably true although the motivations underlying his actions were in all likelihood quite different from those he describes. He was approaching the adolescent period, and this, together with his little brother's death, served to bring many dormant attitudes nearer the surface of consciousness.

Many of these attitudes now found expression in the father-son relationship. Briefly enumerated these would be (1) rejection of the father as a model; (2) an inhibition against following a career that demanded thinking; (3) the anal tendencies that found an outlet of expression in smearing; (4) his passive, feminine tendencies; and (5) his masochistic tendencies and his desire to be dominated by a strong masculine figure. He was not, however, ready for an open revolt, for he tells us in his autobiography that he believed passive resistance and obstinacy were the best course and that if he followed them long enough his father would eventually relent and allow him to leave school and follow an artist's career. As a matter of fact, his brother Alois, in 1930, before the Hitler myth was well established, reported that his father never had any objections to Adolf's becoming an artist but that he did demand that Adolf do well in school. From this we might surmise that the friction between father and son was not determined so much by his choice of a career as by unconscious demands that were deriving satisfaction from the antagonism.

Later School Career

He carried the same pattern into the schools where he was forever antagonizing his teachers and the other boys. He has tried to create the impression that he was a leader among his classmates, which is almost certainly false. More reliable evidence indicates that he was unpopular among his classmates as well as among his teachers, who considered him lazy, uncooperative, and a troublemaker. The only teacher during these years with whom he was able to get along was Ludwig Poetsch, an ardent German Nationalist. It would be an error, however, to suppose that Poetsch inculcated these nationalist feelings in Hitler. It is much more logical to assume that all these feelings were present in Hitler before he came in contact with Poetsch and that his nationalist teachings only offered Hitler a new outlet for the expression of his repressed emotions. It was probably during this period that he discovered a resemblance between the young state of Germany and his mother, and between the old Austrian monarchy and his father. At this discovery he promptly joined the Nationalist group of students who were defying the authority of the Austrian state. In this way he was able to proclaim openly his love for his mother and advocate the death of his father. These were feelings he had had for a long time but was unable to express. Now he was able to obtain partial gratification through the use of symbols.

The Death of His Father

This probably served to increase the friction between father and son, for in spite of what Hitler says the best evidence seems to indicate that the father was anti-German in his sentiments. This again placed father and son on opposite sides of the fence and gave them new cause for hostility. There is no telling how this would have worked out in the long run because while the struggle between the two was at its height, the father fell dead on the street. The repercussions of this event must have been severe and reinforced all those feelings that we have described in connection with the brother's death. Again, it must have seemed like a fulfillment of a wish and again, there must have been severe feelings of guilt, with an additional inhibition on thinking processes.

His school work continued to decline, and it seems that in order to avoid another complete failure, he was taken from the school at Linz and sent to school in Steyr. However, he managed to complete the year, with marks that were barely satisfactory. It was while he was there that the doctor told him that he had a disease from which he would never recover. His reaction to this was severe since it brought the possibility of his own death very much into the foreground and aggravated all his childhood fears. The result was that he did not return to school and finish his course, but stayed at home where he lived a life that was marked by passivity. He neither studied nor worked but spent most of his time in bed where he was again spoiled by his mother who catered to his every need despite her poor financial circumstances.

One could suppose that this was the materialization of his conception of Paradise inasmuch as it reinstated an earlier childhood situation that he had always longed for. It would seem from his own account, however, that things did not go too smoothly, for he writes in *Mein Kampf:*

> When at the age of fourteen, the young man is dismissed from school, it is difficult to say which is worse; his unbelievable ignorance as far as knowledge and ability are concerned, or the biting impudence of his behavior combined with an immorality which makes one's hair stand on end.... The three-year-old child has now become a youth of fifteen who despises all authority ... now he loiters about, and God only knows when he comes home.

We can imagine the deaths of his brother and his father in rapid succession had filled him with such guilt that he could not enjoy this idyllic situation to the full. Perhaps the situation aroused desires in him that he could no longer face on a conscious level, and he could only keep these in check by either remaining in bed and playing the part of a helpless child or absenting himself from the situation entirely. In any case he must have been a considerable problem to his mother who died four years after his father. Dr. Bloch informs us that her great concern in dying was: "What would become of poor Adolf, he is still

so young." At this time Adolf was eighteen years of age.
He had failed at school and had not gone to work. He describes himself at this time as a milksop, which he undoubtedly was.

Admission Examinations to the Academy of Art

Two months before his mother's death he had gone to Vienna to take the entrance examinations for admission to
the Academy of Art. At this time he knew that his mother
was in a critical condition and that it was only a matter of
a few months before death would overtake her. He knew,
therefore, that his easy existence at home would shortly
come to an end and that he would then have to face the
cold, hard world on his own. It is sometimes extraordinary
how events in the lifetime of an individual fall together.
The first day's assignment on the examination was to draw
a picture depicting "The Expulsion from Paradise." It
must have seemed to him that Fate had chosen this topic
to fit his personal situation. On the second day he must
have felt that Fate was rubbing it in when he found the
assignment to be a picture depicting "An Episode of the
Great Flood." These particular topics in his situation must
have aroused such intense emotional reactions within him
that he could hardly be expected to do his best. Art critics
seem to feel that he had some artistic talent even though
it was not outstanding. The comment of the examiners
was: "Too few heads." We can understand this in view of
the circumstances under which he had taken the examination.

Vienna Days

He returned home shortly after the examinations. He
helped to look after his mother, who was rapidly failing
and in extreme pain. She died on December 21, 1907, and
was buried on Christmas Eve. Adolf was completely broken and stood for a long time at her grave after the remainder of the family had left. His world had come to an
end. Not long after the funeral he left for Vienna. There
he seems to have dropped out of sight for a time. The
next thing we know is that in October, following his
mother's death, he was again refused admission to the

Academy of Art and subsequently rejected by the School of Architecture. What happened during this ten-month stay in Vienna is a complete mystery on which history sheds no light. This is probably due to the generally accepted fact that his mother died in December 1908 instead of 1907. On this basis, it was assumed that Adolf remained at home up until this time. Since this was not the case it would be interesting to know where and with whom and on what he lived for these first ten months in Vienna. We know that he had little money when he left Linz, certainly not enough to live on for almost a year without working or getting additional support from some outside source. There is no evidence that he worked during this time. Instead he seems to have spent his time painting and preparing himself for the upcoming examinations in October. How was this possible? We do not know. There is a possibility, of course, that the distortion of his mother's death was not accidental. Sometimes dates are deliberately changed in order to cover up certain happenings. This may have taken place in the present instance. It may be that Hitler's Jewish godparents, who were living in Vienna at this time, had taken him into their home and supported him while he was preparing work for the Academy. When he failed a second time, and having become acquainted with his working habits, they may have felt that he was a poor investment and put him out to earn his own living. There is one piece of evidence that favors this hypothesis. In his book Hanisch mentions, in passing, that later on, when they were particularly destitute, he went with Hitler to seek help from a well-to-do Jew whom Hitler said was his father. Hanisch, in all probability, mistook father for godfather. This would make sense and would indicate that Hitler had had previous contact with his Jewish godparents and that they were fed up with him and refused to give him any additional help. In any event, after his second rejection by the Academy of Art, Hitler did go to work. He was, however, unsuccessful in holding down a job for any length of time. He gradually sank lower and lower on the social scale, until he was finally compelled to live with the dregs of society.

As he writes about these experiences in *Mein Kampf* one gets the impression that it was a terrific struggle against overwhelming odds. From what we now know of Adolf Hitler it would seem more likely that this existence yielded him considerable gratification in spite of its hardships. It is perfectly clear from what Hanisch writes that with a very small amount of effort he could have made a fair living and improved his condition by painting watercolors. He refused to make this effort and preferred to live in the filth and poverty that surrounded him. There must have been something in this that he liked, consciously or unconsciously. When we examine Hanisch's book carefully, we find the answer. Hitler's life in Vienna was one of extreme passivity in which activity was held at the lowest level consistent with survival. He seemed to enjoy being dirty and even filthy in his appearance and personal cleanliness. This can mean only one thing from a psychological point of view, namely, that his perversion was in the process of maturation and was finding gratification in a more or less symbolic form. His attitude during this period could be summarized in the following terms: "I enjoy nothing more than to lie around while the world defecates on me." And he probably delighted in being covered with dirt, which was tangible proof of the fact. Even in these days he lived in a flophouse that was known to be inhabited by men who lent themselves to homosexual practices, and it was probably for this reason that he was listed on the Vienna police record as a "sexual pervert."

Nobody has ever offered an explanation of why he remained in Vienna for over five years if his life there was so distasteful and if the city disgusted him to the degree that he claims in his autobiography. He was free to leave whenever he wished and could have gone to his beloved Germany years earlier if he had so desired. The fact of the matter is that he probably derived great masochistic satisfaction from his miserable life in Vienna, and it was not until his perversion became full-blown and he realized its implications that he fled to Munich at the beginning of 1913.

Projection

Hitler's outstanding defense mechanism is one commonly called *projection*. It is a technique by which the ego of an individual defends itself against unpleasant impulses, tendencies, or characteristics by denying their existence in himself while he attributes them to others. Innumerable examples of this mechanism could be cited in Hitler's case, but a few will suffice for purposes of illustration:

> In the last six years I had to stand intolerable things from states like Poland.

> It must be possible that the German nation can live its life ... without being constantly molested.

> Social democracy ... directs a bombardment of lies and calumnies toward the adversary who seemed most dangerous, till finally the nerves of those who have been attacked give out and they, for the sake of peace, bow down to the hated enemy.

> For this peace proposal of mine I was abused, and personally insulted. Mr. Chamberlain in fact spat upon me before the eyes of the world.

> It was in keeping with our own harmlessness that England took the liberty of one day meeting our peaceful activity with the brutality of the violent egoist.

> The outstanding features of Polish character were cruelty and lack of moral restraint.

From a psychological point of view it is not too far-fetched to suppose that as the perversion developed and became more disgusting to Hitler's ego, its demands were disowned and projected upon the Jew. By this process, the Jew became a symbol of everything that Hitler hated in himself. Again, his own personal problems and conflicts were transferred from within himself to the external world where they assumed the proportions of racial and national conflicts.

Forgetting entirely that for years he not only looked like a lower class Jew but was as dirty as the dirtiest and as great a social outcast, he now began to see the Jew as a source of all evil. The teachings of Schoenerer and Lueger helped to solidify and rationalize his feelings and inner convictions. More and more he became convinced that the Jew was a great parasite on humanity who sucked its life-

blood and if a nation was to become great it must rid itself of this pestilence. Translated back into personal terms
this would read: "My perversion is a parasite that sucks
my lifeblood and if I am to become great I must rid myself of this pestilence." When we see the connection between his sexual perversion and anti-Semitism, we can understand another aspect of his constant linking of syphilis
with the Jew. Syphilis is a disease that can destroy nations
as a perversion or infection destroys an individual.

The greater the demands of his perversion became, the
more he hated the Jews and the more he talked against
them. Everything that was bad was attributed to them.
Here was his political career in an embryo state. He now
spent most of his time reading books, attending political
talks, and reading newspapers in cafés. He himself tells
us in so many words that he skipped through this material
and only took out those parts that were useful to him. In
other words, he was not reading and listening in order to
become educated sufficiently to form a rational judgment
of the problem. This would have been a violation of his
earlier inhibition on thinking. He read only in order to
find additional justification for his own inner feelings and
convictions and to rationalize his projections. He has continued this technique up to the present time. He does a
great deal of reading on many diverse subjects, but he
never forms a rational opinion in the light of the information but only pays attention to those parts that convince
him that he was right to begin with.

In the evening he would return to his flophouse and
harangue his associates with political and anti-Semitic
speeches until he became a joke. This, however, did not
disturb him too much. On the contrary, it seemed to act
as a stimulant for further reading and the gathering of
more arguments to prove his point of view. It was as
though in trying to convince others of the dangers of
Jewish domination, he was really trying to convince himself of the dangers of being dominated by his perversion.
Perhaps Hitler is really referring to his perversion when he
writes: "During the long pre-war years of peace certain
pathological features had certainly appeared. . . . There
were many signs of decay which ought to have stimulated
serious reflection."[7] The same may also be true when he
says:

How could the German people's political instincts become so morbid? The question involved here was not that of a single symptom, but instances of decay which flared up now in legion ... which like poisonous ulcers ate into the nation now here, now there. It seemed as though a continuous flow of poison was driven into the farthest blood vessels of this one-time heroic body by a mysterious power, so as to lead to ever more severe paralysis of sound reason and of the simple instinct of self-preservation.[8]

As time went on the sexual stimulation of the Viennese environment seemed to aggravate the demands of his perversion. He suddenly became overwhelmed by the role that sex plays in the life of the lower classes and the Jews. Vienna became for him "the symbol of incest," and he suddenly left it to seek refuge with his ideal mother, Germany. But his prewar days in Munich were not different from those he left behind in Vienna. His life was still one of extreme passivity, and although we know little about them we can surmise that his days were filled with inner troubles.

The First World War

Under these circumstances, we can understand why he thanked God for the First World War. For him it represented an opportunity of giving up his individual war against himself in exchange for a national war in which he would have the help of others. It also represented to him, on an unconscious level, an opportunity of redeeming his mother and assuming a masculine role for himself. Even at that time, we may suppose, he had inklings that he was destined to be a Great Redeemer. It was not only his mother he was going to redeem, but also himself.

His entering the German Army was really his first step in attempting to redeem himself as a social human being. No longer was he to be the underdog, for he was joining forces with those who were determined to conquer and become great. Activity replaced his earlier passivity to a large degree. Dirt, filth, and poverty were left behind, and he could mingle with the chosen people on an equal footing. But for him this was not enough. As we have pointed out in an earlier section, he was not content to be as clean as the average soldier. He had to go to the other extreme and become exceedingly clean. Whenever he returned from the front he immediately sat down and scrupulously removed every speck of mud from his person, much to the amusement of his comrades. Mend, his comrade during this time, relates an experience at the front when Hitler upbraided one of the other men for not keeping himself clean and called him a "manure pile," which sounds very much like a memory of himself in Vienna.

During this period, as previously mentioned, his passive feminine tendencies were finding an outlet in his abased conduct toward his officers. It looks as though he had not progressed sufficiently far in his conquest of himself to maintain a wholly masculine role. But with the help of others and the guidance of his respected officers he was making some progress toward what appeared to be a social adjustment. The final defeat of Germany, however, upset his well-laid plans and shattered his hopes and ambitions.

The Defeat of Germany

Nevertheless, it was this event that proved to be the turning point in his life and determined that he would be an outstanding success rather than a total failure. Unconscious forces, some of which had been dormant for years, were now reawakened and upset his whole psychological equilibrium. His reaction to this event was an hysterical attack that manifested itself in blindness and mutism. Although the hysterical blindness saved him from witnessing what he regarded as an intolerable spectacle, it did not save him from the violent emotional reactions it aroused. These emotions, we may assume, were similar to those that he had experienced as a child when he witnessed his parents in intercourse. It seems logical to suppose that at that time he felt his mother was being defiled before his eyes, but in view of his father's power and brutality he felt himself utterly helpless to redeem her honor or to save her from future assaults. If this is true, we would expect that he swore secret vengeance against his father, and, as has been shown, there is evidence to this effect.

Now the same thing was happening again, but instead of his real mother it was his ideal mother, Germany, who was being betrayed, corrupted, and humiliated, and again he was unable to come to her rescue. A deep depression set in of which he writes: "What now followed were terrible days and even worse nights. Now I knew that everything was lost. ... In those nights my hatred arose, the hatred against the originators of this deed." But again he was weak and helpless—a blind cripple lying in a hospital. He struggled with the problem: "How shall our nation be freed from the chains of this poisonous embrace?" It would seem that the more he thought about it, the more his intellect told him that all was lost. He probably despised and condemned himself for his weakness, and as his hatred continued to rise in the face of this frustrating experience he vowed then and there: "To know neither rest nor peace until the November Criminals had been overthrown. . . ."

Undoubtedly his emotions were extremely violent and would serve as a powerful motive for much of the retaliation that becomes so prominent in his later behavior. There are, however, many ways of retaliating that do not involve a complete upheaval and transformation of character such as we find in Hitler at this time.

From our experience with patients we know that complete transformations of this kind usually take place only under circumstances of extreme duress that demonstrate to the individual that his present character structure is no longer tenable. Naturally, we do not know exactly what went on in Hitler's mind during this period or how he regarded his own position. We do know, however, that under such circumstances very strange thoughts and fantasies pass through the minds of relatively normal people and that in the case of neurotics, particularly when they have strong masochistic tendencies, these fantasies can become extremely absurd. Whatever the nature of these fantasies might have been, we may be reasonably sure that they involve his own safety or well-being. Only a danger of this magnitude would ordinarily cause an individual to abandon or revolutionize his character structure.

It may be that his nightmares will yield a clue. These, it may be remembered, center on the theme of his being attacked or subjected to indignities by another man. It is not his mother who is being attacked, but himself. When he wakes from these nightmares he acts as though he were choking. He gasps for breath and breaks out in a cold sweat. It is only with great difficulty that he can be quieted because frequently there is an hallucinatory aftereffect, and he believes he sees the man in his bedroom.

Under ordinary circumstances we would be inclined to interpret this as the result of an unconscious wish for homosexual relations together with an ego revulsion against the latent tendency. This interpretation might apply to Hitler, too, for to some extent it seems as though he reacted to the defeat of Germany as to a rape of himself as well as of his symbolic mother. Furthermore, while he was lying helpless in the hospital, unable to see or to speak, he could well have considered himself an easy object for a homosexual attack. When we remember, however, that for years he chose to live in a Vienna flophouse that was known to be inhabited by many homosexuals and later on associated with several notorious homosexuals, such as Hess and Roehm, we cannot feel that this form of attack alone would be sufficient to threaten his integrity to such an extent that he would repudiate his former self.

A further clue to his thoughts during this period may be found in his great preoccupation with propaganda, which in his imagery is almost synonymous with poison.

> Slogan after slogan rained down on our people.
> ... the front was flooded with this poison.
> ... for the effect of its language on me was like that of spiritual vitriol.... I sometimes had to fight down the rage rising in me because of this concentrated solution of lies.

This type of imagery probably has a double significance. There is considerable evidence to show that as a child he believed that the man during intercourse injected poison into the woman that gradually destroyed her from within and finally brought about her death. This is not an uncommon belief in childhood, and in view of the fact that his mother died from a cancer of the breast after a long illness, the belief may have been more vivid and persisted longer in Hitler than in most children. On the other hand, the importance of poison in connection with his perversion has already been considered. We know about his inhibitions against taking certain substances into his mouth. These were not present during the early days of his career, but developed much later in connection with his transformed character.

In view of all this it may not be too farfetched to suppose that while he was fantasizing about what the victors might do to the vanquished when they arrived, his masochistic and perverse tendencies conjured up the thought that they might attack him and force him to eat dung and drink urine (a practice that, it is alleged, is fairly common in Nazi concentration camps). Interestingly enough, this idea is incorporated in the colloquial expression "to eat the dirt of the victors." And in his weakened and helpless condition he would be unable to ward off such an attack. Such an hypothesis gains credence when we review the behavior of Nazi troops in the role of conquerors.

Transformation of Character

Although a thought of this kind would have certain pleasurable aspects to a masochistic person, it would also arouse fear of consequences together with violent feelings of guilt and disgust. If the thought kept recurring at frequent intervals and refused to be suppressed, we can easily imagine that it might drive an individual into such depths of despair that death would appear as the only solution. Hitler's fear of death has already been reviewed, and it is possible that it was this alternative that shocked him out of his former self. It is certain that in his public utterances, as well as in his actions, he attributes extraordinary powers to the fear of death. "I shall spread terror by the surprise employment of my measures. The important thing is the sudden shock of an overwhelming fear of death." And in *Mein Kampf* he tells us that:

> In the end, only the urge for self-preservation will eternally succeed. Under its pressure so-called "humanity," as the expression of a mixture of stupidity, cowardice, and imaginary superior intelligence, will melt like snow under the March sun.

Sentiments of this sort suggest rather strongly that he was brought face to face with the prospect of his own death and that in order to save himself he had to rid himself of a bad conscience as well as the dictates of the intellect. The following quotations illustrate his attitude toward conscience and the need of rendering it inactive:

Only when the time comes when the race is no longer overshadowed by the consciousness of its own
guilt, then it will find internal peace and external energy to cut down regardlessly and brutally the wild
shoots, and to pull up the weeds.

Conscience is a Jewish invention. It is a blemish
like circumcision.

I am freeing men from the restraints of an intelligence that has taken charge; from the dirty and degrading modifications of a chimera called conscience
and morality. . . .

And of the intellect he says:

The intellect has grown autocratic and has become
a disease of life.

We must distrust the intelligence and the conscience and must place our faith in our instincts.

Having repudiated these two important human functions, he was left almost entirely at the mercy of his pas-
sions, instincts, and unconscious desires. At the crucial moment these forces surged to the fore in the form of an
hallucination in which an inner voice informed him that he
was destined to redeem the German people and lead them
to greatness. This, for him, was a new view of life. It
opened new vistas to him particularly in connection with
himself. Not only did it confirm the vague feeling he had
had since childhood, namely, that he was the "Chosen One"
and under the protection of Providence, but also it revealed that he had been saved for a divine mission. This
revelation served to crystallize his personality on a new
pattern. He writes:

In the hours of distress, when others despair, out
of apparently harmless children, there shoots suddenly heroes of death-defying determination and icy
coolness of reflection. If this hour of trial had never
come, then hardly anyone would ever have been able
to guess that a young hero is hidden in the beardless
boy. Nearly always such an impetus is needed in or-

der to call genius into action. Fate's hammer-stroke, which then throws the one to the ground, suddenly strikes steel into another, and while now the shell of everyday life is broken, the erstwhile nucleus lies open to the eyes of the astonished world.

In another place he writes: "A fire had been lighted, and out of its flames there was bound to come some day the sword which was to regain the freedom of the Germanic Siegfried and the life of the German nation."

How, one may ask, was it possible for a person with Hitler's past life and abnormal tendencies to take this seriously? The answer is relatively simple. He believed it because he wanted to believe it—in fact, had to believe it in order to save himself. All the unpleasantness of the past he now interpreted as part of a great design. Just as it was Fate that ordained he should be born on the Austrian side of the border, so it was Fate that sent him to Vienna to suffer hardships in order to take the "milksop out of him by giving him Dame Sorrow as a foster mother" and that "kept him at the front where any Negro could shoot him down when he could have rendered a much more worthwhile service elsewhere," and so it was probably Fate that decreed his present plight. These were the crosses he had to bear in order to prove his mettle. He might have been speaking about himself when he said of Germany:

> ... if this battle should not come, never would Germany win peace. Germany would decay and at the best would sink to ruin like a rotting corpse. But that is not our destiny. We do not believe that this misfortune which today our God sends over Germany has no meaning: it is surely the scourge which should and shall drive us to new greatness, to a new power and glory. ...

Before this new greatness, power, and glory could be achieved, however, it was necessary to conquer the misfortune. The misfortune in Hitler's case, so he probably thought, was the emotional identification he had made with his mother during childhood. He had used this as a cornerstone for his personality, and it was responsible for his "humanity." But it also carried with it a passive, masochistic form of adjustment that, instead of leading to greatness as he had hoped, had carried him to the brink of degradation, humiliation, and self-destruction. It exposed him to untold dangers that were no longer compatible with self-preservation. Consequently, if he were to survive he must rid himself not only of his conscience and intellect but of all the traits that were associated with false "humanity." In its place he must set a personality that was in keeping with the "Law of Nature." Only after he had achieved this transformation could he feel safe from attack. To overcome his weakness and to grow strong became the dominant motive of his life.

> ... feels the obligation in accordance with the Eternal Will that dominates this universe to promote the victory of the better and stronger, and to demand the submission of the worse and weaker.

> A stronger generation will drive out the weaklings because in its ultimate form the urge to live will again and again break the ridiculous fetters of so-called "humanity" of the individual, so that its place will be taken by the "humanity of nature," which destroys weakness in order to give its place to strength.

If our hypothesis concerning his mental processes while he lay helpless in Pasewalk Hospital is correct, we may assume that in order to quiet his fears he sometimes imagined himself as a person who far surpassed his enemies in all the "virile" qualities. Under these circumstances he could conquer his enemies and do to them what he now feared they would do to him. This is, of course, pure wishful thinking, but evidently this play of imagery yielded him so much pleasure and so subdued his fear that he unconsciously identified himself with this superman image. We would guess that it was at the moment when this mechanism, which is known as "Identification with the Aggressor," operated that the aforementioned hallucination was produced. He was no longer the weak and puny individual who was exposed to all kinds of attacks and indignities. On the contrary, he was fundamentally more powerful than all the others. Instead of his being afraid of them, they should be afraid of him. The "Aggressor" image was undoubtedly that of his father as he envisioned him in early childhood.

The image Hitler created was a form of compensation for his own inferiorities, insecurities, and guilts. Consequently, the image negated all his former qualities and turned them into their opposites and to the same degree. All the human qualities of love, pity, sympathy, and compassion were interpreted as weaknesses and disappeared in the transformation.

> All passivity, all inertia ... (became) senseless, inimical to life.

> The Jewish Christ-creed with its effeminate pity-ethics.

> Unless you are prepared to be pitiless you will get nowhere.

In their place we find what Hitler's warped mind conceived the supermasculine to be:

> ... if a people is to become free it needs pride and will-power, defiance, hate, hate and once again hate.

> Brutality is respected. Brutality and physical strength. The plain man in the street respects nothing but brutal strength and ruthlessness.

> We want to be the supporters of the dictatorship of national reason, of national energy, of national—brutality and resolution.

Significance of Hitler's Anti-Semitism

When the "Identification with the Aggressor" mechanism is used, however, there is no conscious struggle within the personality in which the new personality gradually overcomes the old one. The identification takes place outside the realm of consciousness, and the individual suddenly feels that he is this new person. There is no process of integration or assimilation. The old personality is automatically suppressed, and its characteristics are projected onto some external object against which the new personality can carry on the struggle. In Hitler's case all his undesirable characteristics were projected onto the Jew. To Hitler the Jew became Evil incarnate and responsible for all the world's difficulties, just as Hitler's earlier femininity now appeared to him to be the source of all his personal difficulties. This projection was relatively easy for him to make inasmuch as in his Vienna days the Jew had become for him the symbol of sex, disease, and his perversion. Now another load of undesirable qualities was poured upon his head with the result that Hitler now hated and despised the Jew with the same intensity as he hated his former self.

Obviously, Hitler could not rationalize his projection as long as he stood by himself as a single individual, nor could he combat the Jew single-handed. For this he needed a large group that would fit the picture he had created. He found this in defeated Germany as a whole. At the close of the war it was in a position almost identical with his own before the transformation had taken place. It, too, was weak and exposed to further attack and humiliation. It, too, had to be prepared to eat the dirt of the conquerors, and during the inflation period it, too, was confused, passive, and helpless. It, therefore, made an excellent symbol of his earlier self, and Hitler again shifted his personal problems to a national and racial scale where he could deal with them more objectively. Providence had "given" him the spark that transformed him overnight. It was now his mission to transform the remainder of the German people by winning them to his view of life and the New Order. The Jews now played the same role in the life of Germany as his effeminate, masochistic, and perverse adjustment had played in his own life. He now resolved to become a politician.

Many writers have expressed the opinion that Hitler's anti-Semitism is motivated primarily by its great propaganda value. Undoubtedly, anti-Semitism is the most powerful weapon in his propaganda arsenal, and Hitler is well aware of it. He has even expressed the opinion on several occasions that the Jews would make Germany rich. All our informants who knew him well, however, agree that this is superficial and that underneath he has a sincere hatred for the Jews and everything Jewish. This is in complete agreement with our hypothesis. We do not deny that he often uses anti-Semitism propagandistically when it suits his purpose. We do maintain, however, that behind this superficial motivation is a much deeper one that is largely unconscious. Just as Hitler had to exterminate his former self in order to get the feeling of being great and strong, so must Germany exterminate the Jews if it is to attain its new glory. Both are poisons that slowly destroy the respective bodies and bring about death.

> All the great cultures of the past perished only because the originally creative race died off through blood poisoning.

> ... alone the loss of purity of the blood destroys the inner happiness forever; it eternally lowers man, and never again can its consequences be removed from body and mind.

The symbolism in these quotations is obvious, and the frequency with which they recur in his speaking and writing bears testimony to their great importance in his thinking and feeling processes. It would seem from this that unconsciously he felt that if he succeeded in ridding himself of his personal poison, his effeminate and perverse tendencies as symbolized in the Jew, then he would achieve personal immortality.

In his treatment of the Jews we see the "Identification with the Aggressor" mechanism at work. He is now practicing on the Jews in reality the things he feared the victors might do to him in fantasy. From this he derives a manifold satisfaction. First, it affords him an opportunity of appearing before the world as the pitiless brute he imagines himself to be; second, it affords him an opportunity of proving to himself that he is as heartless and brutal as he wants to be (that he can really take it); third, in eliminating the Jews he unconsciously feels that he is ridding himself, and Germany, of the poison that is responsible for all difficulties; fourth, as the masochist he really is, he derives a vicarious pleasure from the suffering of others in whom he can see himself; fifth, he can give vent to his bitter hatred and contempt of the world in general by using the Jew as a scapegoat; and sixth, it pays heavy material and propagandistic dividends.

Early Political Career

Armed with this new view of life Hitler sought for opportunities to put his resolve to become a politician into effect and start on the long road that would redeem Germany and lead her to new greatness and glory. This was not easy in postwar Germany, which was now engaged in violent internal strife. He remained in the Reserve Army for a time where he engaged in his "first political activity"— that of spying on his comrades. His duties were to mingle with the men in his barracks and engage them in political discussions. Those who voiced opinions with a Communistic flavor he reported to his superior officers. Later, when the offenders were brought to trial, it was his job to take the witness stand and give the testimony that would send these comrades to their death. This was a severe trial for his new character, but he carried it off in a brazen and unflinching manner. It must have given him tremendous satisfaction to find that he actually could play this new role in such an admirable fashion. Not long afterward it was discovered that he had a talent for oratory, and he was rewarded for his services by being promoted to instructor. The new Hitler, the embryo Fuehrer, was beginning to pay dividends.

"Identification with the Aggressor" is, at best, an unstable form of adjustment. The individual always has a vague feeling that something is not just as it should be, although he is not aware of its origins. Nevertheless, he feels insecure in his new role, and in order to rid himself of his uneasiness he must prove to himself, over and over again, that he is really the type of person he believes himself to be. The result is a snowball effect. Every brutality must be followed by a greater brutality, every violence by a greater violence, every atrocity by a greater atrocity, every gain in power by a greater gain in power, and so on down the line. Unless this is achieved successfully, the individual begins to feel insecure, and doubts concerning his borrowed character begin to creep in together with feelings of guilt regarding his shortcomings. This is the key to an understanding of Hitler's actions since the beginning of his political activities to the present day. This effect has not escaped the attention of nonpsychological observers. Francois-Poncet, for example, writes in the French *Yellow Book*:

> The Chancellor chafes against all these disappointments with indignant impatience. Far from conducing him to moderation, these obstacles irritate him. He is

aware of the enormous blunder which the anti-Jewish persecutions of last November have proved to be; yet, by a contradiction which is part of the dictator's psychological make-up, he is said to be preparing to enter upon a merciless struggle against the Church and Catholicism. Perhaps he thus wishes to wipe out the memory of past violence with fresh violence. . . .[9]

The mechanism feeds on itself and must continue to grow in order to maintain itself. Since it has no real foundations to support it, the individual can never quite convince himself that he is secure and need fear no longer. The result is that he can brook no delays but must plunge ahead on his mad career.

Hitler's political career shows these tendencies to a marked degree. Scarcely had he affiliated himself with the group that had founded the Party than he connived to get control over it. Then followed a rapid expansion of membership, the introduction of terror, a series of broken promises, collusions, and betrayals. Each brought him fresh gains and new power, but the pace was still too slow to satisfy him. In 1923 he believed himself to be strong enough to undertake a Putsch and seize the reins of government. The Putsch failed and Hitler's conduct during it has been the subject of much comment. There are a number of versions concerning what happened. Some report that when the troops fired on them Hitler fell to the ground and crawled through an alley that carried him to safety while Ludendorff, Roehm, and Goering marched ahead. Some claim that he stumbled, others that he was knocked down by his bodyguard, who was killed. The Nazi version is that he stopped to pick up a small child who had run out into the street and been knocked down. Years later they produced a child on the anniversary of the event to prove the story!

From a psychological point of view it would appear that he turned coward on this occasion and that he did fall down and crawl away from the scene of activities. Although he had usurped considerable power and had reason to have some faith in his new character, it seems unlikely that it was sufficient for him to actually engage the recognized authority in physical combat. His attitude toward recognized superiors and authority in general would make such a direct attack improbable. Furthermore, his reactions after his escape would seem to indicate that his new role had temporarily failed. He went into a deep depression and was restrained from committing suicide only by constant reassurances. When he was taken to Landsberg prison he went on a hunger strike and refused to eat for three weeks. This was his response to being placed again in the position of the vanquished. Perhaps memories of his fantasies in the hospital were returning to harass him! It was only after he discovered that his jailers were not unkindly disposed to him that he permitted himself to be persuaded to take food.

During his stay in Landsberg he became much quieter. Ludecke says: "Landsberg had done him a world of good. Gone from his manner was the nervous intensity which formerly had been his most unpleasant characteristic."[10] It was during this period that he wrote *Mein Kampf,* and we may suppose that his failure in the Putsch made it necessary for him to take a fresh inventory and integrate his new character more firmly. He resolved at this time not to try another Putsch in the future but to gain the power by legal means alone. In other words, he would not participate again in an open conflict with the recognized authority.

His Rise to Power

It is scarcely necessary for us to trace the history of his rise to power and his actions after he achieved it. They all follow along the same general pattern we have outlined. Each successful step served to convince him that he was the person he believed himself to be, but brought no real sense of security. In order to attain this he had to go a step higher and give additional proof that he was not deluding himself. Terror, violence, and ruthlessness grew with each advance, and every recognized virtue was turned into a vice—a sign of weakness. Even after he became the undisputed leader of the nation he could not rest in peace. He projected his own insecurities onto the neighboring states and then demanded that they bow to his power. As long as there was a nation or a combination of nations more powerful than Germany, he could never find the peace and security he longed for. It was inevitable that this course would lead to war because only by that means could he crush the threat and prove to himself that he need no longer be afraid. It was also inevitable that the war would be as brutal and pitiless as possible, for only in this way could he prove to himself that he was not weakening in his chosen course, but was made of stuff becoming to his conception of what a victor should be.

Rages

Although space will not permit a detailed analysis of the operation of the various psychological streams we have enumerated in the determination of his everyday behavior, a few have aroused sufficient speculation to warrant a place in our study. One of the outstanding of these is his rages. Most writers have regarded these as temper tantrums, his reaction to minor frustrations and deprivations. On the surface they appear to be of this nature, and yet when we study his behavior carefully we find that when he is confronted by a real frustration or deprivation, such as failure to be elected to the Presidency or being refused the Chancellorship, his behavior is exactly the opposite. He is very cool and quiet. He is disappointed but not enraged. Instead of carrying on like a spoiled child, he begins immediately to lay plans for a new assault. Heiden, his biographer, describes his characteristic pattern as follows:

> When others after a defeat would have gone home despondently, consoling themselves with the philosophical reflection that it was no use contending against adverse circumstances, Hitler delivered a second and third assault with sullen defiance. When others after a success would have become more cautious, because they would not dare put fortune to the proof too often and perhaps exhaust it, Hitler persisted and staked a bigger claim on Destiny with every throw.[11]

This does not sound like a person who would fly into a rage at a trifle.

Nevertheless, we know that he does fly into these rages and launches into tirades on very slight provocation. If we examine the causes of these outbursts, we almost invariably find that the trigger that sets them off is something that he considers to be a challenge of his superman personality. It may be a contradiction, a criticism, or even a doubt concerning the truth or wisdom of something he has said or done, or it might be a slight or the anticipation of opposition. Even though the subject may be trifling or the challenge only by implication, or even wholly imagined, he feels called upon to display his primitive character. Francois-Poncet has also detected and described this reaction. He writes:

> Those who surround him are the first to admit that he now thinks himself infallible and invincible. That explains why he can no longer bear either criticism or contradiction. To contradict him is in his eyes a crime of "lese-majeste"; opposition to his plans, from whatever side it may come, is a definite sacrilege, to which the only reply is an immediate and striking display of his omnipotence.[12]

As soon as his display has served its purpose and cowed his listeners into submission, it is turned off as suddenly as it was turned on. How great is the insecurity that demands such constant vigilance and apprehension!

Fear of Domination

We find this same insecurity at work when he is meeting new people and particularly those to whom he secretly feels inferior in some way. Earlier in our study we had occasion to point out that his eyes had taken over a diffuse sexual function. When he meets persons for the first time he fixates his eyes on them as though to bore through them. There is a peculiar glint in them on these occasions that many have interpreted as a hypnotic quality. To be sure, he uses them in such a way and tries to overpower the other person with them. If he turns his eyes away, Hitler keeps his fixed directly on him or her, but if the other person returns his gaze Hitler turns his away and looks up at the ceiling as long as the interview continues. It is as though he were matching his power against theirs. If he succeeds in overpowering the other person, he rudely follows up his advantage. If, however, the other person refuses to succumb to his glance, he avoids the possibility of succumbing to theirs. Likewise, he is unable to match wits with another person in a straightforward argument. He will express his opinion at length, but he will not defend it on logical grounds. Strasser says: "He is afraid of logic.

Like a woman he evades the issue and ends by throwing in your face an argument entirely remote from what you were talking about." We might suspect that even on this territory he cannot expose himself to a possible defeat that would mar the image he has of himself. He is, in fact, unable to face real opposition on any ground. He cannot speak to a group in which he senses opposition, but walks out on his audience. He has run out of meetings with Ludendorff, Gregor Strasser, Bavarian Industrialists, and many others because he could not risk the possibility of appearing in an inferior light or exposing himself to a possible domination by another person. There is reason to suppose that his procrastination is not so much a matter of laziness as it is a fear of coming to grips with a difficult problem. Consequently, he avoids it as long as possible, and it is only when the situation has become dangerous and disaster lies ahead that his "inner voice" or intuition communicates with him and tells him what course he should follow. Most of his thinking is carried on subconsciously, which probably accounts for his ability to penetrate difficult problems and time his moves. Psychological experiments in this field seem to indicate that on this level the individual is often able to solve very complex problems that are impossible for him on the level of consciousness. Wherever we turn in studying Hitler's behavior patterns we find the specter of possible defeat and humiliation as one of his dominant motivations.

Monuments

His passion for constructing huge buildings, stadia, bridges, roads, and the like, can only be interpreted as attempts to compensate for his lack of confidence. These are tangible proofs of his greatness that are designed to impress himself as well as others. Just as he must be the greatest man in all the world, so he has a tendency to build the greatest and biggest of everything. Most of the structures he has erected he regards as temporary buildings. They are, to his way of thinking, on a par with ordinary mortals. The permanent buildings he plans to construct later on. They will be much larger and grander and will be designed to last at least a thousand years. In other words, these are befitting monuments to himself who plans on ruling the German people for that period of time through his new view of life.

It is also interesting to note the frequency with which he uses gigantic pillars in all his buildings. Most of the buildings are almost surrounded by them, and he places them in every conceivable place. Since pillars of this sort are almost universally considered to be phallic symbols, we may regard the size and frequency as an unconscious attempt to impress upon the world, in symbolic form at least, not only the masculinity of his visionary projections but their potency as well. His love of pageantry and spectaculars may serve a similar subconscious purpose.

Oratory

No study of Hitler would be complete without mentioning his oratory talents. His extraordinary gift for swaying large audiences has contributed, perhaps more than any other single factor, to his success and the partial realization of his dream. In order to understand the power of his appeal, we must be cognizant of the fact that for him the masses are fundamentally feminine in character. To Hanfstaengl and other informants he has frequently said: "The masses are like a woman," and in *Mein Kampf* he writes: "The people, in an overwhelming majority, are so feminine in their nature and attitude that their activities and thoughts are motivated less by sober consideration than by feeling and sentiment." In other words, his unconscious frame of reference, when addressing a huge audience, is fundamentally that of talking to a woman.

In spite of this his insecurities assert themselves. He never is the first speaker on the program. He must always have a speaker precede him who warms up the audience for him. Even then he is nervous and jittery when he gets up to speak. Frequently he has difficulty in finding words with which to begin. He is trying to get the "feel" of the audience. If it "feels" favorable he starts in a rather cautious manner. His tone of voice is quite normal, and he deals with his material in a fairly objective manner. But as he proceeds his voice begins to rise and his tempo increases. If the response of the audience is good, his voice becomes louder and louder and the tempo faster and faster. By this time all objectivity has disappeared, and passion has taken complete possession of him. The mouth

that can never utter a fragment of profanity off the
speaker's platform now pours forth a veritable stream of
curses, foul names, vilification, and hatred. Hanfstaengl
compares the development of a Hitlerian speech with the
development of a Wagnerian theme, which may account
for Hitler's love for Wagnerian music and the inspiration
he derives from it.

This steady stream of filth continues to pour forth until
both he and the audiences are in a frenzy. When he stops
he is on the verge of exhaustion. His breathing is heavy
and uncontrolled, and he is wringing wet with perspira-
tion. Many writers have commented on the sexual components in his speaking, and some have described the climax as a veritable orgasm. Heyst writes:

> In his speeches we hear the suppressed voice of pas-
> sion and wooing which is taken from the language of
> love; he utters a cry of hate and voluptuousness, a
> spasm of violence and cruelty. All those tones and
> sounds are taken from the backstreets of the instincts;
> they remind us of dark impulses repressed too long.[13]

And Hitler himself says: "Passion alone will give to him,
who is chosen by her, the words that, like beats of a ham-
mer, are able to open the doors to the heart of a people."
Undoubtedly, he uses speaking as a means of talking himself into the superman role and of living out the role of
"Identification with the Aggressor." He carefully builds up
imposing enemies—Jews, Bolsheviks, capitalists, and democracies in order to demolish them without mercy (these
are all inventions of the Jews to his way of thinking, and
consequently in attacking any one of them he is fundamentally attacking the Jews). Under these circumstances
he appears to the naive and unsophisticated listener as the
Great Redeemer of Germany.

But this is only one side of the picture. On the other
side we have the sexual attack, which in his case is of a
perverse nature. It finds expression in his speaking, but
due to the transformation of character everything appears
in the reverse. The steady stream of filth he pours on the
heads of his "feminine" audience is the reverse of his
masochistic perversion that finds gratification in having
women pour their "filth" on him. Even the function of the
physical organs is reversed. The mouth, which under ordi-

nary circumstances is an organ of injection and is surrounded with inhibitions and prohibitions, now becomes the
organ through which filth is ejected. Hitler's speaking has
been aptly described as a "verbal diarrhea." Rauschning
describes it as an oral enema. It is probably this unconscious sexual element in his speaking that holds such a fascination for many people.

His Appeal

A word may be added in connection with the content of
his speeches. Strasser summed this up very concisely as
follows:

> Hitler responds to the vibrations of the human
> heart with the delicacy of a seismograph ... enabling
> him, with a certainty with which no conscious gift
> could endow him, to act as a loudspeaker proclaiming
> the most secret desires, the least permissible instincts,
> the sufferings, and personal revolts of a whole nation.

We are now in a position to understand how this is possible for him. In regarding his audience as fundamentally
feminine in character, his appeal is directed at a repressed
part of their personalities. In many of the German men
there seems to be a strong feminine-masochistic tendency
that is usually covered over by more "virile" characteristics but which finds partial gratification in submissive behavior, discipline, sacrifice, and so forth. Nevertheless, it
does seem to disturb them, and they try to compensate for
it by going to the other extreme of courage, pugnacious-
ness, and determination. Most Germans are unaware of
this hidden part of their personalities and would deny its
existence vehemently if such an insinuation is made. Hitler, however, appeals to it directly, and he is in an excellent position to know what goes on in that region because
in him this side of his personality was not only conscious
but dominant throughout his earlier life. Furthermore,
these tendencies were far more intense in him than in the
average person, and he had a better opportunity of observing their operation. In addressing an audience in this way
he need only dwell on the longings, ambitions, hopes, and
desires of his earlier life in order to awaken these hidden
tendencies in his listeners. This he does with inordinate

skill. In this way he is able to arouse the same attitudes and emotions in his listeners that he himself experienced earlier in life and is able to redirect them into the channels that he has found useful. Thus he is able to win them to his new view of life, which sets a premium on brutality, ruthlessness, dominance, and determination and which frowns upon all the established human qualities. The key is always to strive to be what you are not and to do your best to exterminate that which you are. The behavior of the German armies has been an outstanding manifestation of this contradiction. To the psychologist it seems as though the brutality expressed toward the people of the occupied countries is motivated not only by a desire to prove to themselves that they are what they are not, but also by a vicarious masochistic gratification that they derive from an identification with their victims. On the whole one could say of many of the German troops what Rauschning said of Hitler:

> ... there lies behind Hitler's emphasis on brutality and ruthlessness the desolation of a forced and artificial inhumanity, not the amorality of the genuine brute, which has after all something of the power of a natural force.

It is Hitler's ability to play upon the unconscious tendencies of the German people and to act as their spokesman that has enabled him to mobilize their energies and direct them into the same channels through which he believed he had found a solution to his own personal conflicts. The result has been an extraordinary similarity in thinking, feeling, and acting in the German people. It is as though Hitler had paralyzed the critical functions of the individual Germans and had assumed the role for himself. As such he has been incorporated as a part of the personalities of his individual supporters and is able to dominate their mental processes. This phenomenon lies at the very root of the peculiar bond that exists between Hitler, as a person, and the German people and places it beyond the control of any purely rational, logical, or intellectual appeal. In fighting for Hitler these persons are now unconsciously fighting for what appears to them to be their own psychological integrity.

All of this throws a very interesting light on the underlying psychology of a large part of the German people both in war and in peace, and one is forced to suspect that fundamental changes within the German culture itself must be effected before the German people are ready to play a constructive role in a family of nations. A consideration of these aspects of the problem, however, lies beyond the scope of the present study.

PART VI

卐

HITLER

His Probable Behavior in the Future

As the tide of battle turns against Hitler it may be well to consider very briefly the possibilities of his future behavior and the effect that each would have on the German people as well as on ourselves.

1. *Hitler may die of natural causes*. This is only a remote possibility since, as far as we know, he is in fairly good health except for his stomach ailment, which is in all probability a psychosomatic disturbance. The effect such an event would have on the German people would depend on the nature of the illness that brought about his death. If he should die from whooping cough, mumps, or some other ridiculous disease it would be a material help in breaking the myth of his supernatural origins.

2. *Hitler might seek refuge in a neutral country*. This is extremely unlikely in view of his great concern about his immortality. Nothing would break the myth more effectively than to have the leader run away at the critical moment. Hitler knows this and has frequently condemned the Kaiser for his flight to Holland at the close of the last war. Hitler might want to escape as he has escaped from other unpleasant situations, but it seems almost certain that he would restrain himself.

3. *Hitler may get killed in battle*. This is a real possibility. When he is convinced that he cannot win, he may lead his troops into battle and expose himself as the fearless and fanatical leader. This would be most undesirable from our point of view because his death would serve as an example to his followers to fight on with fanatical, death-defying determination to the bitter end. This would be what Hitler would want for he has predicted that:

> We shall not capitulate . . . no, never. We may be destroyed, but if we are, we shall drag a world with us . . . a world in flames.

213

But even if we could not conquer them, we should drag half the world into destruction with us and leave no one to triumph over Germany. There will not be another 1918.

At a certain point he could do more toward the achievement of this goal by dying heroically than he could by living. Furthermore, death of this kind would do more to bind the German people to the Hitler legend and insure his immortality than any other course he could pursue.

4. *Hitler may be assassinated.* Although Hitler is extremely well protected there is a possibility that someone may assassinate him. Hitler is afraid of this possibility and has expressed the opinion that:

> His own friends would one day stab him mortally in the back. . . . And it would be just before the last and greatest victory, at the moment of supreme tension. Once more Hagen would slay Siegfried. Once more Hermann the Liberator would be murdered by his own kinsmen. The eternal destiny of the German nation must be fulfilled yet again, for the last time.

This possibility, too, would be undesirable from our point of view inasmuch as it would make a martyr of him and strengthen the legend.

It would be even more undesirable if the assassin were a Jew, for this would convince the German people of Hitler's infallibility and strengthen the fanaticism of the German troops and people. Needless to say, it would be followed by the complete extermination of all Jews in Germany and the occupied countries.

5. *Hitler may go insane.* Hitler has many characteristics that border on the schizophrenic. It is possible that when faced with defeat his psychological structure may collapse and leave him at the mercy of his unconscious forces. The possibilities of such an outcome diminish as he becomes older, but they should not be entirely excluded. This would not be an undesirable eventuality from our point of view since it would do much to undermine the Hitler legend in the minds of the German people.

6. *German military might revolt and seize him.* This seems unlikely in view of the unique position Hitler holds

in the minds of the German people. From all the evidence it would seem that Hitler alone is able to rouse the troops, as well as the people, to greater efforts, and as the road becomes more difficult this should be an important factor. One could imagine, however, that as defeat approaches Hitler's behavior may become more and more neurotic and reach a point where it would be well for the military to confine him. In this case, however, the German people would probably never know about it. If they discovered it, it would be a desirable end from our point of view because it would puncture the myth of the loved and invincible leader.

The only other possibility in this connection would be that the German military should decide, in the face of defeat, that it might be wiser to dethrone Hitler and set up a puppet government to sue for peace. This would probably cause great internal strife in Germany. What the ultimate outcome might be would depend largely on the manner in which it was handled and what was done with Hitler. At the present time the possibility seems rather remote.

7. *Hitler may fall into our hands.* This is the most unlikely possibility of all. Knowing his fear of being placed in the role of the vanquished, we can imagine that he would do his utmost to avoid such a fate. It should, however, be considered as a possibility if for no other reason than that we have a precedent for such behavior in the case of Jan Bockelsson. His early life, character, and career bear an uncanny resemblance to that of Hitler. In the final stages of his mad career his masochistic tendencies got the upper hand, and he surrendered to his enemies and proposed to them that they confine him in a cage and exhibit him throughout the country in order that the people, for a small admission fee, might look at him and express their contempt. In Hitler's case such an outcome seems remote, but it is difficult to estimate the extent to which an extreme masochist will go in order to gratify these tendencies. From our point of view it would be most desirable to have Hitler fall into our hands, and in the long run it would probably be of benefit to the German people as well.

8. *Hitler might commit suicide.* This is the most plausible outcome. Not only has he frequently threatened to commit suicide, but from what we know of his psychology

it is the most likely possibility. It is probably true that he has an inordinate fear of death, but being a psychopath he could undoubtedly screw himself up into the superman character and perform the deed. In all probability, however, it would not be a simple suicide. He has much too much of the dramatic for that, and since immortality is one of his dominant motives we can imagine that he would stage the most dramatic and effective death scene he could possibly think of. He knows how to bind the people to him, and if he cannot have the bond in life he will certainly do his utmost to achieve it in death. He might even engage some other fanatic to do the final killing at his orders.

Hitler has already envisaged a death of this kind, for he has said to Rauschning: "Yes, in the hour of supreme peril I must sacrifice myself for the people." This would be extremely undesirable from our point of view because if it is cleverly done it would establish the Hitler legend so firmly in the minds of the German people that it might take generations to eradicate it.

Whatever else happens, we may be reasonably sure that as Germany suffers successive defeats Hitler will become more and more neurotic. Each defeat will shake his confidence still further and limit his opportunities for proving his own greatness to himself. In consequence he will feel himself more and more vulnerable to attack from his associates, and his rages will increase in frequency. He will probably try to compensate for his vulnerability by continually stressing his brutality and ruthlessness.

His public appearances will become less and less, for, as we have seen, he is unable to face a critical audience. He will probably seek solace in his Eagle's Nest on the Kehlstein near Berchtesgaden. There among the ice-capped peaks he will wait for his "inner voice" to guide him. Meanwhile, his nightmares will probably increase in frequency and intensity and drive him closer to a nervous collapse. It is not wholly improbable that in the end he might lock himself into this symbolic womb and defy the world to get him.

In any case his mental condition will continue to deteriorate. He will fight as long as he can with any weapon or technique that can be conjured up to meet the emergency.

The course he will follow will almost certainly be the one that seems to him to be the surest road to immortality and that at the same time wreaks the greatest vengeance on a world he despises.

AFTERWORD

by Robert G. L. Waite

IT was neither the exigencies of war nor training as a psychoanalyst that brought me as a professional consultant to the study of Adolf Hitler. Indeed, during the war I do not recall being consulted about anything. My military career was not unlike that of Alexander Woollcott: only the Armistice prevented me from becoming a corporal.

I came to Hitler along a different path. Initially, as a schoolboy in the late 1930's, I was fascinated by a phenomenon that seemed so incomprehensible: the bizarre little man with the Charlie Chaplin mustache who bestrode Europe like a Colossus and decided the fate of men and nations. After the war, requirements for a doctorate and an academic career led me to study the political, social, and military conditions which helped him into power.[1] Years of teaching German history and research on the Fuehrer of the Germans convinced me that, as a professional historian dealing with this problem, I needed psychiatric help.

For in my research I had come across literally hundreds of facts that my training had not equipped me to interpret. I found, to take a few examples, that the dread dictator was a highly vulnerable person beset by fears of horses, microbes, and moonlight; that he sucked his little finger in moments of agitation; that he longed to create and lusted to destroy; that he ordered the massacre of the innocents but worried about the most humane way to cook lobsters; that, while he saw himself as the veritable Messiah of his people and spoke, often without knowing it, the very words of Jesus, he also referred to himself as a shithead (*Scheisskerl*); that the three favorite riding whips with which he was wont to strike his hand or thigh were given him by three female intimates who were the age of his mother; that he was intrigued by wolves. At the start of his political career he chose as his cover name, "Herr Wolf." His favorite dogs—and the only ones he allowed

221

himself to be photographed with—were Alsatians, that is in German, *Wolfhuende*. He called his headquarters in France *Wolfschlucht* (Wolf's Gulch). In the Ukraine, his headquarters were *Werwolf* and, in East Prussia, *Wolfschanze* (Wolf's Lair)—saying to a servant "I am the wolf and this is my den." After the *Anschluss* with Austria in 1938, he asked his sister Paula to change her name to Frau Wolf. The name of the secretary he kept for twenty years was Johanna Wolf. One of the tunes from a favorite Walt Disney movie that he whistled often and absent-mindedly was "Who's Afraid of the Big Bad Wolf?"

He played childish guessing games, seeing how fast he could get dressed or how quickly his valet could tie his tie for him. He held his breath and counted to ten anxiously waiting until the knot was pulled tight.

He liked to think about heads, particularly when they were severed. They were his favorite doodle. Asked what he would do upon first landing in England, he replied without hesitation he wanted most to see the place where Henry VIII chopped off the heads of his wives. When he flipped a coin to see if he should go on another picnic, heads never won. His definition of politics was one that does not seem to have occurred to Jefferson, Gladstone, or Adenauer: "Politics is like a whore; if you love her unsuccessfully she bites your head off." He was infatuated with the head of the Medusa, once remarking that in von Stuck's painting the flashing eyes that turned men to stone and impotency reminded him of the eyes of his mother. He was reputed to have taken great pleasure in having young ladies defecate on his head.

Confronted with facts such as these, an historian of Hitler has at least three choices. First, he can decide to join his traditionally trained colleagues and ignore facts, telling himself that they are probably unimportant and certainly beneath his professional dignity—if not beyond his professional competence. Secondly, he can insert a few of them into his biography as "human interest material," adding little touches and sidelights which, he hopes, will titillate the reader's interest. Or, he can attempt seriously to interpret these facts and try to discover their meaning.

Interpretation is the problem. For history is not a collection of facts. If it were, the local telephone book or dentist's appointment register would be history—they contain a great number of indisputable facts. As Carl Becker pointed out long ago, historical facts are neither "hard" nor "cold," and they do not "speak for themselves."[2] They take on vitality and meaning only when the historian begins to use them, to say something about them; in a word, when he starts to interpret them. But which facts to choose? And how should they be interpreted? Since the number of facts about Hitler is very large, historians select for interpretation those that they feel competent to handle. I suspect they may be disposed to ignore the kind of facts cited above not because the private behavior of a world-historical personage is not significant, but because historians may not feel confident that they can correctly interpret such behavior. How can one discuss facts about Hitler when one does not really understand their meaning, indeed may not be able to tell whether they are trivial or important?

At this point in my researches I sought the aid of psychoanalysts. First I received help at the Austin Riggs Center in Stockbridge, Massachusetts. I also profited enormously from conversations with Gertrud Kurth and Erik Erikson and from my collaboration with Norbert Bromberg. In the course of my inquiries, I discovered that, during World War II, Dr. Walter C. Langer had written for the OSS a psychological analysis of Hitler. I first read his study several years ago and have used it extensively.[3]

An historian's evaluation of Langer's book will depend on what Jacques Barzun has recently called his "working notion of history."[4] My own notion about this matter can be simply stated. I welcome any methodological approach to Hitler that gives me a better understanding of him. Where psychoanalysis is helpful, I believe it should be used; where other methods seem more appropriate in investigating other aspects of his remarkable career, they too should be used.

Since the evidence convinced me that Hitler was pathological, it seemed sensible to use the work of competent pathologists. I was not disappointed. Langer gave me insights into that strange and twisted personality that no historian using traditional methods had been able to give. And in Hitler's case, knowing the personality is of the very essence. For the political system he established was dependent ultimately upon the power of his person, the efficacy of his charisma. He *was* Nazism. Since he was the sole source of final authority, he alone could legitimize Party decisions and determine public policy. His personal whim became the law of the land; his will decided war or peace in the world. Seldom in the history of Western civilization since Jesus has so much depended on one man's personality. It is important to study it in depth.

The Limitations of Traditional Approaches

The inadequacy of traditional historical methods and the need for studies like Langer's in dealing with so patently pathological a subject as Adolf Hitler have been poignantly illustrated in the best-known books on Hitler and his Third Reich. These volumes have been written by distinguished historians with solid and well-deserved reputations. In different ways, they have made important contributions to our understanding or—as in the case of A. J. P. Taylor—they have been so clever and perverse that they have forced us to rethink many an important issue. Yet all these books have one thing in common. They ignore one historical fact of overriding importance about their subject: he was mentally ill.

Mr. Taylor does not think so. He prefers to believe that Hitler was really a normal person: a "traditional" German leader who was "no more wicked and unscrupulous than many other contemporary statesmen," and whose ideas were "commonplace." Hitler's single most striking personal characteristic, Mr. Taylor thinks, was his patience.[5]

Professor Hugh Trevor-Roper of Oxford, who disagrees with Taylor on nearly everything historical, joins him in this: he too refuses to come to grips with Hitler's pathological personality. In his exciting and largely accurate thriller, devoted to finding out what happened during Hitler's last days, Trevor-Roper gingerly approaches the problem of Hitler's psychological condition, then quickly backs off saying with conspicuous caution, "Whatever Hitler's psychological condition may have been—and on such a subject, and in so unique a character, it would be imprudent to speculate—there can be no doubt that his physical stamina was exceptionally strong."[6] The sense of relief is palpable as the author, having disposed of the irrational, hurries on to describe in loving detail how well the Fuehrer's body withstood Dr. Morell's quack nostrums, thereby demonstrating once again that it is easier—if less helpful in understanding "so unique a character"—to describe a man's body than it is to wrestle with his psyche. To speculate on Hitler's psychological condition may or may not be "imprudent"; it is certainly necessary. To refuse to discuss it is not unlike failing to mention in a biography of Jack the Ripper that he had homicidal tendencies, or in a profile of Caruso to ignore his voice.

Nor does Alan Bullock, in his standard biography, really face basic problems of his subject's personality. To Mr. Bullock, Hitler is reminiscent of a classical Greek tyrant: an evil man, goaded by ambition and felled by *hubris*. So far so good, but it is not nearly enough. Hitler was certainly a Study in Tyranny;[7] but he was also a problem in psychopathology. As such, he baffles Mr. Bullock, who has admitted with refreshing candor that he finds Hitler's strange behavior "offensive" both to his reason and to his historical training: "For my part, the more I learn about Adolf Hitler, the harder I find it to explain and accept what followed. Somehow the causes are inadequate to account for the size of the effects. It is offensive to both our reason and to our experience to be asked to believe that [the youthful Hitler] was the stuff of which ... the Caesars and Bonapartes were made. Yet the record is there to prove us wrong."[8]

The late German authority on Hitler, Professor Percy Ernst Schramm, manifested a similar confusion about his specialty. In the generally useful essay on Hitler's personality with which he introduced his excellent edition of Picker's *Tischgespraeche*—those long soliloquies that Hitler inflicted on captive audiences—Schramm quite rightly noticed that throughout Hitler's monologues the theme of anti-Semitism runs "like a red thread." But he was unable to explain Hitler's all-consuming hatred for the Jews and concluded despairingly, "We must be satisfied with the realization that there is about Hitler's ... anti-Semitism an unknown factor." Apparently, without bothering to consult journals on abnormal psychology or to confer with specialists, Schramm was confident that "psychology and psychiatry, in spite of all their refinements, must ... also confess that they are confronted by an 'X'." He himself finally reached the intriguing conclusion that Hitler's anti-Semitism resulted from nameless "demons" that plagued him.[9]

The greatest historian of the Third Reich has a similar

problem. Karl Dietrich Bracher's monumental studies will remain absolutely basic to an understanding of Hitler's seizure and consolidation of power and the functioning of his dictatorship.[10] But the personality of Hitler remains pretty much a mystery to Professor Bracher. He prefers to describe in measured and judicious prose what Hitler did and to avoid the more difficult question of personal motivation. A few examples from his most recent and immensely valuable book, now happily available in English, illustrate his difficulties.

Bracher raises fleetingly the question of whether Hitler may have feared that his paternal grandfather was Jewish, but he dismisses such speculations quickly by saying "such digressions [sic] are as sensational as they are questionable and pointless for, though well-meaning, they are rooted in racist superstitions." One might well ask: Pointless and of questionable importance to whom? Certainly not to Adolf Hitler himself. For, throughout his life, he showed that he was haunted by the fear that he himself might have "Jewish blood." And what is meant here by racist superstition? Is it not legitimate for a nonracist and nonsuperstitious historian to ask if Hitler believed he might be Jewish and, if so, concern himself with the enormous psychological and historic consequences of that belief?

Although he shows that Hitler's childhood was spent not in penury but in relative comfort, and that he was in general an incomprehensible and spoiled youth, Bracher displays no other interest in Hitler's boyhood. He dismisses the whole period with a clumsy slap at psychoanalysis, a subject about which he is apparently ignorant: "It is pointless to speculate about possible breakdowns suffered during his adolescence, Oedipal complexes, unrequited love, etc."

Pointless to speculate? Dr. Langer's enlightening analysis and probing questions about the crucially important years of Hitler's childhood are the answer to such naiveté.

The limitations of Bracher's methodology are shown most clearly in his inability to understand Hitler's hatred of the Jews. He emphasizes that racist anti-Semitism was the very core of Nazi theory and that it was "probably the only 'genuine' fanatically held and realized conviction of [Hitler's] entire life." But in the same paragraph Mr.

Bracher reaches the interesting conclusion that since it is impossible to explain this fanatic conviction in rational terms it is not worth trying to explain it at all. He writes: "Hitler's fanatical hatred of the Jews defies all rational explanation; it cannot be measured by political and practical gauges." He concludes roundly that what we have here is "the inexplicable dynamics of one man."[11]

These eminent historians of Hitler persuade me less of the unimportance of understanding his mental illness than of their inability to help me to do so.

Of course traditional historians may be right in saying that the personality of Adolf Hitler will ultimately remain "inexplicable." This will certainly be the case as long as we dismiss important evidence about his personality and brand attempts to interpret it as sensational, questionable, or pointless. We are not likely to find out why Hitler did the things he did if we continue to ignore the insights that psychoanalysis may be able to give us. At any rate, it behooves us to try, for historians profess to follow Ranke's categorical imperative to seek the full truth about the past.

Should we fail in our efforts to understand Klara Hitler's son, it will be neither the first nor the last time that answers to historical questions have escaped us. It is probably a little subversive to admit it, but historians can never give final and definitive answers to any of the more interesting questions asked of history.

But we need not despair. Let us take seriously Trevelyan's trenchant admonition to those who would try to force our lady Clio to become a scientist: "In the most important part of its business history is . . . an imaginative guess."[12] Let us hope that we can guess as imaginatively and well as has Langer in this study of Hitler. And let us rejoice in the pursuit of answers to questions that may continually elude us. The question, for example, of *why?* Now here we have the question that is at once the most obvious and the most subtle—and ultimately unanswerable—that historians can ask about about the past. *"Why* did the French Revolution happen?" *"Why* did an historical person—Gandhi, George III, Hitler—do what he did?"

At the very point the question is asked, the historian is probing the complex realm of motivation. And at that point, whether he likes it or not—and he may not like it very much—he is becoming some sort of psychologist. At least he is dealing with the kinds of questions psychoanalysts are well equipped to handle. They are not able to give all the answers either, but they generally do better in this area than historians for their knowledge of human personality is deeper. Most of us have assumed that since "man is a rational animal" he behaves as he intends to behave. Upon occasion, it is true, he may act on a sudden and inexplicable whim or momentary aberration or fit of pique. But, in general, we have been accustomed to think that man acts rationally and is consciously aware of what he is doing. We like to believe this is true because we have been trained to hunt for human motivation within the boundaries of the rational. Whatever psychological insights that have been brought to our endeavor have generally come from "common sense." But we begin to feel helpless when the subject with whom we are dealing just doesn't behave sensibly. Most of us are "not equipped to make even a conjecture about motives that are irrational and hence unconscious."[13] Simply to conclude that such conduct is strange and irrational and inexplicable—or that the man seemeth beset by unknown Demons—is not really very useful.

Understanding Hitler's Behavior: Langer's Probing Eye

It is precisely here, in the professional analysis of abnormal personality, that Walter Langer's study is most helpful in explaining *why* that strange person, Adolf Hitler, acted the way he did. His contribution is not so much that he has given a medical diagnosis. For to term Hitler a "neurotic, bordering on schizophrenia" may or may not be accurate; certainly it does not tell us very much. There were hundreds of other such neurotics who never came to power in Germany in 1933, plunged the world into war, or deliberately set out to kill all the Jews of Europe. The value of Langer's analysis is rather that he shows the *patterns of behavior* of his subject patient. When he concludes that Hitler's actions and modes of conduct are strikingly similar to clinical cases, we can test his diagnosis by examining our evidence on Hitler and checking it with literature on similar cases; in so doing, we can gain new insight into Hitler's actions; we can learn to recognize patterns of behavior; and we can become alerted to the significance of psychologically important facts which previously escaped our attention.

Another contribution made by Langer's study, and that of other psychoanalysts, is that they have shown us how to read historical documents differently. A personal example may help here. Like everyone else interested in Hitler, I had read *Mein Kampf* many times. But never had it occurred to me, until Erik Erikson pointed it out, that in the book Hitler displays in disguised form his highly ambivalent attitude to his mother and hence to all other women. He does it by the curious way he feminizes certain German neuter nouns. He changes them into female deities and these Goddesses of Fate, or Destiny, or Fortune are kind but also cruel; helpful but fickle; beneficent but capricious. They are never to be trusted. No one, Erikson feels, could have talked about women the way Hitler did who had not been deeply disappointed and disillusioned with his own mother.[14]

It will be noted that Langer's sources are not particularly new. With the exception of a few live interviews with subjects now dead, or otherwise unavailable for comment, his reliance is on materials familiar to historians. For a long time, we have had the writings of Ernst Roehm, Otto Strasser, Ernst Hanfstaengl, Hermann Rauschning, Konrad Heiden, Friedelinde Wagner, and the others. And all of us, alas, have had to read Langer's chief source, Hitler's *Mein Kampf*. But no one, I think, with so probing an eye as his. Historians have read it to discover "facts" about Hitler's career and have been unimpressed with its value. Langer has studied it for insight into Hitler's unconscious, and has found it indispensable. He also uses it to find out about Hitler's childhood. He does so by indirection and retrospective reconstruction on the basis of close textural analysis. First, he warns us in reading these memoirs to distrust Hitler's idyllic description of harmonious family life. It does not ring true psychologically: "We find that not a single patient manifesting Hitler's character traits has grown up in such a well-ordered and peaceful home environment." Then, Langer proceeds to compensate for the data he misses from Adolf's childhood. And in so doing he shows us a method. Even when we lack other evidence, we can get at childhood experience by examining adult behavior patterns closely and imaginatively. This is a valid approach because since childhood experience shapes the adult personality, adult behavior reveals to us childhood crises and trauma. In the case at hand, Langer's well-trained guess is that Adolf's childhood family life must have been fraught with tension, discord, and trauma. He is correct.

New evidence and interviews with neighbors still alive in the 1950's, who knew the Hitler family well in Passau and Leonding, substantiate Langer's professional hunches. Even an old crony and mayor of the village of Leonding admitted that Alois Hitler was "awfully rough" (*Saugrob*) with his wife and "hardly ever spoke a word to her at home." He concluded with deliberate understatement that "Frau Klara had nothing to smile about."[15]

A particularly revealing example of the psychoanalytic method of reading historical documents is Langer's brilliant, and to me thoroughly convincing, reconstruction of one episode in Hitler's past: at the age of three, young Adolf saw—or just as important, he fantasied that he saw—his drunken father rape his dear mother. (See above, p. 161.) The biographer should follow this suggestive lead and investigate other childhood traumas to discover how crucial these early years actually were.

There is one critically important fact about Hitler's childhood that Langer did not know anything about. It was only discovered when Russian doctors, who performed an autopsy on Hitler's body in May 1945, found that he was sexually malformed. The report reads, in part, as follows: "The left testicle could not be found either in the scrotum or on the spermatic cord inside the inguinal canal, nor in the small pelvis."[16]

Since to this day it is often impossible, without surgery, to determine whether a testicle missing from the scrotum is due to its total absence or its failure to descend, it is likely that Adolf as well as his parents and the family doctor hopefully thought of his missing testicle as undescended.

The condition of monorchism (the lack of a testicle) or cryptorchism (undescended testicle) is of course neither uncommon nor, in itself, pathogenic. But it may become so if, as in Hitler's case, there are other infantile disorders and a badly disturbed parent-child relationship. Psychological studies of prepubertal boys with a history of behavioral disturbances combined with a missing testicle show a common pattern of symptoms. What is particularly interesting to a student of Hitler is how closely his behav-

ior resembles theirs. Indeed, in reading the clinical literature on the subject, I had to keep reminding myself that
the studies were concerned with American boys and not
with young Adolf Hitler, for sooner or later he exhibited
every one of their symptoms: impatience and hyperactiv-
ity; sudden development of learning difficulties and lack of
concentration; distinct feelings of social inadequacy;
chronic indecision; tendency to exaggerate, to lie and to
fantasize; identification of the mother as the person responsible for the defect. All patients exhibit body damage
anxiety such as concern about bowel training or castration
fantasies. When confronted by criticism all are defensive,
insisting they are special people with an unusual mission to
perform or that they are "magical persons." There is a
pattern of preoccupation with time and death; further preoccupation with eyes and breasts as substitutes for the testicle; prevalence of revenge fantasies and eroticized megal-
omanic daydreams, conscious or semi-conscious aspirations
to greatness or immortality. Patients have a passion for
creativity, redesigning and reconstruction of almost feverish
intensity.[17]

To be sure, as Langer has noted, the sudden death of
his younger brother Edmond when Adolf was eleven was
certainly important to Hitler's psychological development.
Here his speculations are supported by Robert Jay Lifton's
impressive work on the behavior patterns of those who
have survived death.[18] But Hitler's sexual malformation, of
which Langer was unaware, also fills in the picture. For it
is at the prepubertal age of eleven or twelve that pathological symptoms appear most vividly. Thus Hitler's failure
in school at the age of eleven was not only the result of
"survivor guilt." Probably more important was the psychological consequence of his defective genitals. This condition and its lifelong consequence also help explain why
the Fuehrer concept as developed by Hitler took the form
of exaggerated masculinity, a self-image which did indeed
have, as Langer has observed, "all the earmarks of reaction formation."

Langer contributes not only a different way of reading
historical documents; he supplies a method of testing hypotheses that may be new to many of us. Take for example his hypothesis about Hitler's masochistic perversion.
Many historians will be dubious because they may conclude that the "hard" external evidence for the perversion

is not impressive. They may wish to question the testimony of such congenital gossips as Otto Strasser and Putzi Hanfstaengl. But Langer does not depend completely on this testimony. Basically, he is convinced that the perversion existed because he knows as an experienced analyst widely read in the literature of abnormal psychology that many patients with the same patterns of behavior as Hitler have exhibited a penchant for the same perversion. And here again clinical and theoretical advances, made years after he wrote his report, support his conclusion. Clinical studies have demonstrated that, against a background of disturbed infant-mother relations which surely existed between Adolf and his mother, a trauma such as a primal scene experience can have very important, disturbing effects on ego development and functioning in many areas. When this is compounded by another traumatic phenomenon such as the existence of monorchism, the effects on many aspects of the personality can be shattering. All of this in the setting of Hitler's special relationship with his mother and with his father and his siblings, conspired to create a personality structure in which his perversion was one of the many psychologically appropriate consequences.[19]

Criticisms

I agreed to write a critical appreciation of this book as an historian interested in Hitler. Appreciative I have been and remain, for it is a very valuable work. Let me now be critical.

In a sense, the criticisms I am about to make are not quite fair. Langer's purpose was not to give a full account of Hitler as an historical phenomenon, but to provide American military policy makers with a psychological profile that might make some practical contribution to the defeat of a wartime enemy. Dr. Langer fulfilled that assignment admirably and thus contributed new insights to the study of historical biography. But to the extent that the analysis is restricted in purpose and scope, its value remains limited.

First, Langer made no effort to investigate the sources of Hitler's ideas. He demonstrates convincingly that irrational and unconscious urges helped to shape Hitler's life.

But so did rational and conscious ideas. Shoddy as they were, these ideas were important to Hitler. He was an intellectual, Bullock has noticed, "in a double sense that he lived intensely in a world of his own thought and that words and ideas were the instrument of his power."[20] Hitler believed his ideas. More important, they formed the foundation upon which he reordered society. Indeed never in human history has a political theory been so ruthlessly carried out in practice. His ideas on race determined the law, the art, the education, the medicine of the Third Reich. They dictated that physics be taught without Einstein and psychology without Freud. Hitler's ideas shaped the lives and determined the deaths of millions of people. Karl Dietrich Bracher is right in emphasizing the importance of Hitler's ideas and concluding that their history "is the history of their underestimation."[21] A study devoted to the analysis of Hitler's personality should have considered more thoroughly the ideas that helped shape it.

The emphasis in this book, perhaps inevitably, is on the pathological aspects of Hitler's life. And it is a side, I have been insisting, that needs very much to be emphasized. But the unwary reader may get the notion—certainly not intended by Langer—that Hitler was so mentally disturbed he could not have functioned effectively. On the contrary. Hitler could act with high rationality and paralyzing effectiveness. The paradox of the irrational fanatic who was a master of calculated maneuver needs more thorough probing. Hitler was a consummately able political and military tactician. David Lloyd George, no mean judge of these matters, was enormously impressed with Hitler's political acumen and called him one of the most effective statesmen of all history. The late military historian Sir Basil Liddell Hart considered him one of the greatest of all strategists. Hitler was also highly effective in social situations. He had the charm and intelligence to captivate and impress philosophers and farmers; architects and laborers; artists and housewives; generals, ambassadors and American co-eds. He was a perceptive, capable and many-sided person. Indeed he was far more complex than this analysis suggests.

Having said that Langer has not done enough with so complicated a personality, let me now complain that too many other things have been neglected. This report is so sharply focused on the individual that we see very little of the historic setting, and thus get a distorted picture of Hitler and his times. Of course, Langer, had no intention of providing such a broad picture, which would have been inappropriate to his purposes, but today the approach of his work needs to be expanded and assimilated into a much broader and more comprehensive study. We need to consider not only Hitler's unconscious mind, but his conscious ideas, as well as the historic setting for his movement, with all the manifold social, political and cultural forces which helped push him toward power. In short, we need a far broader study of the man and the period than Langer and his associates had the intent or the time to provide.

A second limitation of Langer's work, again not one for which he can be blamed, is that the source materials on Hitler's life available in 1943 were much less plentiful than they are today. Since this study was written, vast quantities of new evidence have become available to historians—only a hint can be given here. Fresh light, for example, on the important childhood years has come from interviews with family neighbors, documents, and affidavits in the Upper Austrian Archives in Linz, and the immense Nazi Party archives now largely on microfilm in the Hoover Institution in California. We also have the very valuable memoirs of Hitler's only boyhood friend in Linz, and roommate in Vienna, August Kubizek, as well as the careful researches of the Linz archivist, Franz Jetzinger, and a fine book by the American historian, Bradley Smith.[22] Of first-rate importance, too, is the special file on Hitler's family collected by the Gestapo.

It is one of history's many ironies that while General Donovan's OSS was investigating the Fuehrer, Hitler's Gestapo was doing precisely the same thing. We now have the Gestapo reports of these investigations made in 1935, 1938, 1941, 1942, 1943, and 1944. They were made, most probably, on Hitler's orders because he wanted desperately to prove to himself what no one then or now could possibly prove: that his paternal grandfather was not a Jew—of which more in a moment. Also available to us, and denied to Langer, is the vast document collection gathered for purposes of the Nuremberg trials, and the invaluable, stream-of-consciousness monologues of Hitler's *Tischgespraeche*. A new book written by Hitler has also been discovered,[23] and there has now appeared a spate of memoirs of people who knew Hitler personally: his architect, his lawyer, secretaries, valets, chauffeurs, personal pilots as well as—it might seem—most of the generals of the *Wehrmacht*. Almost every month new monographs or articles in professional journals appear.

In addition to a great expansion of our historical knowledge about Hitler and his times, there has also been significant advance made in the fields of abnormal psychology and personality development during the thirty years that have gone by since Langer wrote. To take a few examples: we now know a great deal more about child psychology; Erik Erikson has notably increased our understanding of the stages of personality development; the work and writings of Robert Knight, Otto Kernberg, and Norbert Bromberg have given us new insight into "borderline personality"—a type of mental illness showing close parallels to the behavorial patterns of Hitler.[24]

It is high compliment to the quality of the work done by Dr. Langer and his associates that their psychological profile of Hitler's personality does not suffer great damage from this veritable avalanche of new testimony. True, some of Langer's evidence is faulty, some of his conclusions need modifying; much more needs to be done on other aspects of Hitler's personality and the role of psychopathology in his political leadership. But the point to emphasize is that this book stands the test of time remarkably well. It will remain a significant and suggestive interpretation which no serious student of Hitler will ignore. It is, in its own right, a fascinating historical document.

There are, as Langer suspected there would be, factual errors. And, in reading his pages, historians will no doubt indulge their professional penchant for pointing out mistakes. Here are a few, none of which strike me as being horrendous: Klara Hitler was buried on December 23 not December 24, 1907; Hitler had no taboo about beer, he drank a special low-alcoholic type, brewed especially for him in the Holzkirchen Brewery; he seldom used the Kehlstein retreat since he was frightened by elevator shafts; he did not have "long dirty fingernails": he scrubbed his hands often and compulsively; he never wore a Christ-like beard; his report cards in school were neither as good nor as bad as described here; he was never charged with perversion in the courts; his godfather was not a Jew; and he did not secretly admire Franklin Roosevelt. To a small gathering of intimates he said, "Neither of the two Anglo-Saxons is any better than the other . . . Churchill and Roosevelt, what imposters! . . . Roosevelt, who both in his handling of political issues and in his general attitudes, behaves like a tortuous petty-fogging Jew, himself boasted recently that he had 'noble' Jewish blood in his veins. The completely Negroid appearance of his wife is also a clear indication that she too is a half-caste." He wrote Roosevelt off as having a "sick brain"; he saw Winston Churchill as "the undisciplined swine who is drunk for eight hours of every twenty-four." His greatest praise was preserved for Joseph Stalin, a rival worthy of his steel. He spoke admiringly of the "cunning Caucasian" who commanded "unconditional respect" and who was "in his own way, just one hell of a fellow."[25]

Langer is also incorrect in thinking that Hitler did not become an anti-Semite during his first years in Vienna (1908–1913). The inception of his anti-Semitism came, and was directly associated with the death of his mother. An unpublished memoir of Kubizek's preserved in the Upper Austrian Archives in Linz tells us that Hitler joined an anti-Semitic society in April of 1908. Quite possibly the precise date was Easter Monday which fell that year on Hitler's birthday.[26]

Langer's assertion that Hitler could not have been an anti-Semite because he showed that he was grateful to the family doctor, the Jewish Dr. Bloch, raises a more interesting question than it answers. It is a curious fact that throughout his life Hitler had reason to be grateful to Jews who had helped him in his direst need. His hatred of the Jews may have been intensified precisely *because* he had reason to be grateful to them for befriending him or rendering him important services. Their number includes the kindly family Dr. Bloch to whom Hitler sent handpainted postcards signed "Your eternally grateful patient, Adolf Hitler." His landlady in Vienna who charged him minimum rent and obligingly moved out of her own room to accommodate him and his friend is reported to have been a Jew. Antonescu, the Rumanian dictator who suffered from stomach trouble, as did Hitler, sent him his Jewish cook, Fraulein Kunde. When Himmler raised questions about the propriety of having a Jew prepare the Fuehrer's food, Hitler turned furiously to an aide and said "Aryanize the Kunde family!" When the youthful Hitler was really up against it in Vienna, Jewish art dealers be-friended him and paid generously for his mediocre water colors—as the Gestapo files make clear. The most impor-tant military honor Hitler ever received was the unusual distinction of earning the Iron Cross First and Second Class as a Lance Corporal in World War I. He wore the decoration constantly, for it substantiated his claim to be the unknown hero of the war and was of enormous politi-cal value to him. He would not have received it without the persistent efforts of the regimental adjutant, Hugo Gutmann, a Jew.[27]

But even when Langer is mistaken and his guesses prove incorrect, he is often on the right track. Consider his hint that Hitler's grandfather might have been a Jew. There is no reason to believe the unlikely story told by Langer's informant that Hitler's grandmother Maria Anna Schicklgruber, a peasant woman in her forties from the *Waldviertel* of rural Austria, had had an intimate liaison with a Baron Rothschild in Vienna. But Hitler had wor-ried that he might be blackmailed over a Jewish grandfa-ther and ordered his private lawyer, Hans Frank, to inves-tigate his paternal lineage. Frank did so and told the Fuehrer that his grandmother had become pregnant while working as a domestic servant in a Jewish household in Graz.[28] The facts of this matter are in dispute—and a very lengthy dispute it has been. The point of overriding psy-chological and historical importance is not whether it is true that Hitler had a Jewish grandfather; but whether he *believed* that it might be true. He did so believe and that fact shaped both his personality and his public policy.[29]

Prognoses and Predictions

We turn now to Langer's prognoses for his patient. His first guess, it will be recalled, was that "Hitler may die of natu-ral causes" though this was deemed unlikely because "as far as we know, he is in fairly good health." On the con-trary, we now know that by the end of the war the Fuehrer was in very bad health indeed. He was suffering, among other things, either from advanced Parkinson's Syndrome (*paralysis agitans*) or localized degenerative brain damage to lower brain centers. He also suffered from the medicines prescribed to him by Dr. Theodore

Morell. Since Hitler feared body odors and was particularly troubled by his propensity to flatulate, Morell prescribed huge quantities of "Dr. Koester's Anti-Gas Pills," which contained strychnine and atrophene; since he feared obesity, he was given reducing pills of various sorts; since he suffered from nightmares and insomnia, he took at least a dozen different kinds of sleeping pills; because he feared impotency, Morell prescribed injections of pulverized bull testicles in grape sugar. He was also given massive doses of dexedrene, pervatin, caffeine, cocaine, prozymen and ultraseptyl as well as huge amounts of vitamins.[30] Partly as a consequence of these medications, we have the following picture of the Fuehrer as he appeared about the time Langer was writing his report:

> The external evidences of his illness became increasingly apparent ... not only his left hand but the entire left side of his body shook. In sitting he had to hold his right hand over his left, his right leg crossed over his left in order to make the constant shaking less noticeable. His gait became shuffling, and his posture bent, his movements slow as in a slow-motion film. He had to have a chair placed under him when he wanted to seat himself. His mind, to be sure, remained active—but there was often something weird [unheiliches] about this activity for it was dominated by constant wanderings, a mistrust of humanity and dictated by the efforts to conceal his physical, mental, political and military collapse.... With the tenacity of a fanatic he grabbed at the last straw which, he imagined, would save him ... from disaster.[31]

And a few months before the end, an adjutant recalls:

> There is an indescribable flickering stare in his eyes that is at the same time shocking and completely unnatural. His face, particularly the area around the eyes, gives the impression of a man who is totally and completely washed up. He shuffles slowly forward ... his movements are those of a very sick old man....[32]

Langer's basic prediction about Hitler's last days, however, is uncannily accurate. It is in itself dramatic and convincing evidence of the validity of his approach to an

understanding of Hitler's personality. Indeed, his prediction, made in the Autumn of 1943, is a description of
what happened two years later in the Spring of 1945. Let
us be reminded of what Langer wrote:

> Whatever else happens, we may be reasonably sure
> that as Germany suffers successive defeats Hitler will
> become more and more neurotic. Each defeat will
> shake his confidence still further and limit his oppor-
> tunities for proving his own greatness to himself. In
> consequence he will feel himself more and more vul-
> nerable to attack from his associates and his rages
> will increase in frequency. He will probably try to
> compensate for his vulnerability by continually stress-
> ing his brutality and ruthlessness.

Hitler had indeed always imagined himself to be a totally masculine, infallible and brutal leader whose ideal for
German youth expressed his own self-idealization: "They
must be lithe and taut, swift as greyhounds, tough as
leather and hard as Krupp steel." But now, during the
period after 1943, it was increasingly apparent that the
soft-muscled, slightly paunchy man with the shuffling gait,
grey skin, and trembling, effeminate hands did not at all fit
his own picture of the powerful, all-conquering Fuehrer.
Each military defeat unnerved him further and required
more and more proof that he was the ice-cold, steel-hard,
ruthless victor of his fantasies. Since he could not play
that role by conquering Russia or the Western Allies, he
now manufactured ruthless "victories" over the Jews. He
conquered his unarmed and helpless enemy in the gas
ovens of the Greater German Reich. While destroying the
"Jewish Peril" he sought also to destroy the Germany
which, he yelled in a voice cracking with fury, was no longer worthy of him. Everything was to be smashed, everything essential to life: not only industrial plants but gas,
water, and electrical works; ration card files, files of marriage and death and residence registries; records of bank
accounts, of food supplies. Hospitals, farms, and wood-
lands were to be burned, cattle slaughtered. Works of art,
monuments, palaces, castles, churches, theatres—everything Hitler had once loved—were to be destroyed. The
idea is conveyed clearly in an editorial which, at the
Fuehrer's express command, appeared in the Party organ,

Voelkischer Beobachter: "Not a German stock of wheat is to feed the enemy, not a German mouth to give him information, not a German hand to offer him help. He is to find nothing but death, annihilation and hatred. . . ."

Hitler's Death

"Hitler might commit suicide. This is the most plausible outcome." It certainly was. Again Langer's prediction of 1943 was accurate. And now, on the basis of evidence unavailable to him, let me try to reconstruct what actually happened and finish the story of Hitler's life. Having decided to kill himself, he poisoned his favorite dog Wolf and, on the afternoon of 30 April 1945, entered his private rooms in the air-raid shelter of the Chancellory in Berlin with his bride. It had now become of the utmost importance to him that his death be absolutely assured, that he avoid the intolerable ignominy his friend Mussolini had suffered; and that he never be "exhibited by the Russians like a circus freak." But he had no confidence in the death pills prepared for him by the SS doctors. The SS was no longer to be trusted; it was shot through with treason, duplicity, and betrayal. Himmler ("The Loyal Heinrich") was a traitor treating with the English. Even Linge, his valet of many years, was suspect, and the motto on his SS belt a mockery: "Loyalty is my Honor." He needed someone else to make absolutely sure of his death in case the poison were not potent. He could no longer trust his own shaking hands.

In the whirling world of his paranoiac suspicions there was only one person left he could rely upon: Eva Braun. She had proven her courage and determination by flying into doomed Berlin to die with him; she had loved him selflessly for years; she was a sportswoman who knew how to handle pistols; she had proven her obedience in complying with his unusual sexual demands; she would now carry out his last request.

The death scene was taken from a bad novel written by a person with no taste.

As the Soviet Army advanced on Berlin that Monday afternoon Hitler sat in trembling confusion on a sofa with his bride next to him. In front of them was a coffee table with a vial of cyanide capsules, his 7.65 Walther automatic pistol, and a vase of roses. Roses were his favorite flowers, they had always reminded him of his mother's funeral. The pistol would not be disturbed; the flowers would soon be knocked over.

At 3:30 he swallowed cyanide. It worked efficiently. His puffy face contorted and turned blue as he strangled and gasped for breath; he thrashed about and kicked the coffee table. The bride put the muzzle of her 6.35 Walther to his left temple and pulled the trigger. She then poisoned herself. The shot brought aides who wrapped the bodies in gray army blankets and carried them out to the courtyard of the Chancellory.

The grand, all-consuming Wagnerian funeral he had promised himself was denied him. His chauffeur and others, it is true, had succeeded in collecting 220 liters of petrol but they had not planned on a proper place for burning the bodies. With the Russians coming ever closer, they dumped the corpses in a slight indentation in the ground next to a cement mixer and set them on fire. The location left something to be desired as a setting for the *Goetter-daemmerung*—most notably, the sandy soil absorbed too much of the precious petrol.

When it became apparent that the bodies would not be consumed, hurried orders were given to bury them. Again the job was bungled. No one had thought to bring appropriate digging tools. And, with Russian shells zeroing in on the courtyard, the men showed little desire to risk their lives any further for their now dead Fuehrer. Hastily and ineffectively, they covered the smoking, stinking corpses with loose earth and rubble. The charred remains were found four days later by a searching patrol of Soviet soldiers.

Identification at the autopsy was made by a careful examination of Hitler's rotting teeth.

NOTES

The numbers within brackets refer to the pages of "The Hitler Source-Book" on which the material can be found. The "Source-Book" is available in the National Archives. Wherever translations have been supplied in the text, the original German has been included in a footnote.

PART I: HITLER—AS HE BELIEVES HIMSELF TO BE

1. Hermann Rauschning. *Gespraeche mit Hitler* (New York: Europa Verlag, 1940), p. 161.

"Aber ich brauche Sie nicht, um mir von Ihnen meine geschichtiche Groesse bestaetigen zu lassen." [717]

2. Otto Strasser, *Hitler and I* (Boston: Houghton, 1940), p 67. [378]

3. Frederick Oechsner, *This Is the Enemy* (Boston: Little, Brown, 1942), p. 73. [699]

4. Rauschning, *Gespraeche mit Hitler*, p. 16.

Ich spiele nicht Krieg. Ich lasse mich nicht von "Feldherrn" Kommandieren. Den Krieg fuehre *Ich*. Den eigentlichen Zeitpunkt zum Angriff bestimme *Ich*. Es gibt nur einen guenstigen und ich werde auf ihn warten mit eiserner Entschlossenheit. Und ich werde ihn nicht verpassen.... [701]

5. George Ward Price, *I Know These Dictators* (London: Harrap, 1937), p. 144. [255]

6. Adolf Hitler, *My New Order.*

7. Francois-Poncet, French Ambassador in Berlin, to Georges Bonnet, Minister of Foreign Affairs, Berlin, October 20, 1938, *The French Yellow Book—Diplomatic Documents, 1938–1939*, no. 18. [945]

8. Sir Neville Henderson, *Failure of a Mission* (New York: Putnam's, 1940), p. 177. [129]

9. State Department, January 18, 1940. Confidential Memorandum concerning Hitler Prepared by the Dutch

Legation in Berlin for the Secretary of the Foreign Office,
the Hague. [654]

10. Karl von Wiegand, "Hitler Foresees His End," *Cosmopolitan* (April 1939), p. 28. [490]

11. Pierre J. Huss, *The Foe We Face* (New York: Doubleday, 1942), p. 281. [413]

12. Rauschning, *Gespraeche.* [714]

13. Hans Mend, *Adolf Hitler im Felde* (Diessen: Huber Verlag, 1931), p. 172.

An eine eigenartige Propheseiung errinere ich mich
noch in diesem Zusammenhang: Kurz vor Weihnachten
(1915) aeusserte er sich, dass wir noch vieles von ihm
hoeren werden. Wir sollen nur abwarten, bis seine Zeit
gekommen ist. [208]

14. George Ward Price, *I Know These Dictators* (London: Harrap, 1937), p. 40. [241]

15. Quoted in *Pariser Tages Zeitung,* "Vom Wahne Besessen," no. 1212 (January 23, 1940).

Als ich im Bett lag kam mir der Gedanke, dass ich
Deutschland befreien wuerde, dass ich es gross machen
wuerde, und ich habe sofort gewusst, dass das verwirklicht
werden wuerde. [429]

16. Nehmen Sie die Ueberzeugung him, dass ich die Erringung eines Ministerpostens nicht als erstrebenswert ansehe. Ich halte es einen grossen Mannes nicht fuer wuerdig
sienen Namen der Geschichte nur dadurch ueberliefern zu
wollen, dass er Minister wird. Was mir vor Augen stand,
das war vom ersten Tage tausendmal mehr: ich wollte der
Zerbrecher der Marxismus werden. Ich werde die Aufgabe
loesen, und wenn ich sie loese, dann waere der Titel eines
Ministers fuer mich eine Laecherlichkeit. Als ich zum ersten Mal vor Richard Wagners Grab stand, da quoll mir
das Herz ueber vor Stolz, dass hier ein Mann ruht, der es
sich verbeten hat, hinaufzuschreiben: Hier ruht Geheimrat
Musikdirektor Excellenz Baron Richard von Wagner. Ich
war stolz darauf, dass dieser Mann und so viele Maenner
der deutschen Geschichte sich damit begnuegten, ihren
Namen der Nachwelt zu ueberliefern, nicht ihren Titel.
Nicht aus Bescheidenheit wollte ich "Trommler" sein. Das
ist das Hoechste, das andere ist eine Kleinigkeit.

17. Information Obtained from Ernst Hanfstaengl.

18. Ibid. [903]

19. Hitler, *My New Order,* p. 26.

20. W. C. White, "Hail Hitler," *Scribner* 9 (April 1932): 229-231. [664]

21. Karl von Wiegand, "Hitler Foresees His End," *Cosmopolitan*, April 1939, pp. 28 ff., May 1939, pp. 48 ff. [493]

22. S. Haffner, *Germany: Jekyll and Hyde* (New York: Dutton, 1941) [418]: Huss, *The Foe We Face* [401]; Ludwig Wagner, *Hitler, Man of Strife* (New York: Norton, 1942). [489]

23. Huss, *The Foe We Face*, p. 210. [410]

24. Ibid., p. 212 [410]

25. Interview with Friedelinde Wagner, New York City. [936]

26. Will D. Bayles, *Caesars in Goose Step* (New York: Harper Bros., 1940). [3]

27. Quoted in Rauschning, *Gespraeche*, p. 144. "Am liebsten taet er Heute schon in den Bergen sitzen und den lieben Gott spielen." [715]

28. Dr. E. Bloch, as told to J. D. Ratcliffe, "My Patient, Hitler," *Collier's*, March 15, 1941. [146]

29. Howard K. Smith, *Last Train from Berlin* (New York: 1942), p. 59. [290]

PART II: HITLER—AS THE GERMAN PEOPLE KNOW HIM

1. William L. Shirer, *Berlin Diary* (New York: Knopf, 1941), p. 13. [279]

2. Karl Trossman, *Hitler und Rom* (Nuremberg: Sebaldus Verlag, 1931), p. 152. [483]

3. Edgar Ansell Mowrer, *Germany Puts the Clock Back* (London: Penguin, 1938), pp. 193-194. [642]

4. Dorothy Thompson, "Good Bye to Germany," *Harper's Magazine*, December 1934, pp. 12-14. [307]

5. Howard K. Smith, *Last Train from Berlin* (New York: 1942), pp. 29-31. [289]

6. Emil Ludwig, *Three Portraits: Hitler, Mussolini, Stalin* (New York: 1940), p. 11. [575]

7. Bella Fromm, *Blood and Banquets* (New York: Harper Bros., 1942), p. 36. [369]

8. Hermann Rauschning, *The Voice of Destruction*, p. 12. This is the same as *Gespraeche mit Hitler*. [257]

9. Karl Tschuppik, "Hitler spricht," *Das Tagebuch*, 8, no. 13 (March 26, 1927): 498-500. [317]

10. Otto Strasser, *Hitler and I* (Boston: Houghton, 1940), p. 62. [376]

11. Konrad Heiden, *Adolf Hitler* (Zurich: Europa Verlag, 1936), p. 100. [499]

12. George Ward Price, *I Know These Dictators* (London: Harrap, 1937), pp. 39-40. [241]

13. *Newsweek*, "Cocksure Dictator Takes Timid Soul Precautions," 5 (April 6, 1935): 16. [572]

14. Janet Flanner, *An American in Paris* (New York: Simon & Schuster, 1940), pp. 414-415. [558]

15. F. Yeates-Brown, "A Tory Looks at Hitler," *Living Age*, August 1938, pp. 512-514. [592]

16. Lilian T. Mowrer, *Rip Tide of Aggression* (New York: Morrow, 1942), p. 179. [216]

17. Michael Fry, *Hitler's Wonderland* (London: Murray, 1934). p. 106. [577]

18. Kurt Georg W. Ludecke, *I Knew Hitler* (New York: Scribner's, 1937), p. 13. [164]

19. Stanley High, "The Man Who Leads Germany," *Literary Digest*, October 21, 1933, p. 42. [453]

20. Otto Strasser, *Flight from Terror*, pp. 24-25. [295]

21. Karl von Wiegand, "Hitler Foresees His End," *Cosmopolitan*, May 1939, p. 158. [494]

22. Price, *I Know These Dictators*, pp. 222-223. [236]

23. Ignatius Phayre, "Holiday with Hitler," *Current History*, July 1936, pp. 50-58. [225]

24. Pierre J. Huss, *The Foe We Face* (New York: Doubleday, 1942). [405]

25. Frederick Oechsner, *This Is the Enemy* (Boston: Little, Brown, 1942), p. 69. [668]

26. Henry Albert Phillips, *Germany Today and Tomorrow* (New York: Dodd), pp. 40-41. [868]

27. Erich Czech-Jochberg, *Adolf Hitler und sein Stab* (Oldenburg: G. Stalling, 1933), pp. 30-34.

Zunaechst Hitler selbst: Hitler ist der Mann ohne Kompromiss. Vor allem kennt er keinen Kompromiss mit sich selbst. Er hat einen einzigen Gedanken, der ihn leitet: Deutschland wieder aufzurichten. Diese Odee verdraengt alles um ihn. Er kennt kein Privatleben. Er kennt Familienleben ebensowenig, wie er ein Laster kennt. Er ist die Verkoerperung des nationalen Willens.

Die Ritterschaft eines heiligen Zieles, das sich kein

Mensch hoeher steken kann: Deutschland! ... Hitler ... ueberracht (durch) seine warme Liebenswuerdigkeit. Ueber die Ruhe und Kraft, die beinahe physisch von diesem Mann ausstraht. Man waechst in der Naehe dieses Menschen ... Wie er auf alle Dinge reagiert! ... Eisern werden die Zuege und die Worte fallen wie Bein ... Der klassische Ernst, mit dem Hitler und seine um den Fuehrer gescharten Mitarbeiter ihre Sendung nehmen, hat in der Geschichte dieser Welt nur wenige Paralellen. [861]

28. Heinrich Hoffman, *Hitler, wie ihn keiner kennt* (Berlin: 1932), pp. x-xiv.

... auch in den privaten Dingen des Lebens Vorbildlichkeit und menschliche Groesse ... ob Hitler ... umbraust wird vom jubelnden Zuruf der Strassenarbeiter, oder aufgewuehlt und erschuettert am Lager seine ermordeten Kameraden steht, immer ist um ihn diese Hoheit und tiefste Menschlichkeit ... dieser einzigartigen Perseonlichkeit ... ein grosser und guter Mensch. Hitler ist ein universaler Geist. Es ist unmoeglich der Mannigfaltigkeit seines Wesens mit 100 Aufnahmen gerecht zu werden. Auch auf diesen beiden Gebieten (Architecture and History) ist Hitler eine unangreifbare Autoritaet. Unsere Zeit wird diesen Ueberragenden vielleicht verehren und lieben, aber wird ihn nicht in seiner grossen Tief ermessen koennen. [899]

29. Phillips, *Germany Today and Tomorrow*, pp. 40-41. [868]

30. High, "The Man Who Leads Germany," p. 43. [453]

31. Patsy Ziemer, *2010 Days of Hitler* (New York: Harper Bros., 1940). p. 84. [763]

32. Stephen H. Roberts, *The House That Hitler Built* (New York: 1938), p. 11. [876]

33. William Teeling, *Know Thy Enemy!* (London: Nicholson, 1939), pp. 2, 7, 28. [565]

34. Hermann Rauschning, *Revolution of Nihilism* (New York: Alliance Book Corp. 1939).

"Wir alle glauben auf dieser Erde an Adolph Hitler, unseren Fuehrer, und wir bekennen, dass der National-sozialismus der allein seligmachende Glaube fuer unser Volk ist." [552]

35. Reveille Thomas, *The Spoil of Europe*. [550]

36. Hans Kerrl, quoted in Emily D. Lorrimer, *What Hitler Wants* (London: Penguin, 1939), p. 6. [749]

37. Thompson, "Good Bye to Germany," p. 46. [568]

PART III: HITLER—AS HIS ASSOCIATES KNOW HIM

1. William Russell, Berlin Embassy, 1941, p. 283. [747]
2. Adolf Hitler, *Mein Kampf.*
3. Information Obtained from Ernst Hanfstaengl. [902]
4. Hitler, *Mein Kampf*, p. 237.
5. Ibid., p. 222.
6. Ibid., p. 223.
7. Louis P. Lochner, *What about Germany?* (New York: Dodd, 1942), p. 99. [157]
8. Information Obtained from Hanfstaengl. [899]
9. Kurt Georg W. Ludecke, *I Knew Hitler* (New York: Scribner's, 1937), p. 97. [169]
10. Joseph Goebbels, *Vom Kaiserhof zur Reichskanzlei* (Munich: NSDAP, 1934), p. 27. [385]
11. R. Billing, *Rund um Hitler* (Munich: B. Funck, 1931), p. 69.

"Die inneren Schwierigkeiten einer Regierung Hitlers werden in der Person Hitler selbst liegen. Hitler wird nicht umhin koennen, sich an eine geregelte Giestige Taetigkeit zu gewoehnen." [588]

12. Ludecke, *I Knew Hitler*, p. 96. [168]
13. Ibid., p. 97. [168]
14. Shirer, *Berlin Diary* (New York: Knopf, 1941), p. 247. [280]
15. Hermann Rauschning, *The Voice of Destruction*, p. 261. [275]
16. Ludecke, *I Knew Hitler*, p. 58. [165]
17. Information Obtained from Hanfstaengl. [899]
18. State Department, January 18, 1940, Confidential Memorandum concerning Hitler prepared by the Dutch Legation in Berlin for the Secretary General of the Foreign Office, the Hague. [656]
19. Rauschning, *The Voice of Destruction*, pp. 183-184. [269]
20. Ibid., p. 260. [275]
21. Ernst Roehm, quoted in Ludecke, *I Knew Hitler*, p. 287. [176]
22. Rauschning, *The Voice of Destruction*, p. 181. [268]
23. State Department, Report by the Dutch Legation. [654]
24. Ibid. [654]

25. Otto Strasser, *Flight from Terror.* [297]

26. Roehm, quoted in Ludecke, *I Knew Hitler*, p. 287. [176]

27. Louis P. Lochner, *What about Germany?* (New York: Dodd, 1942), p. 47. [154]

28. Shirer, *Berlin Diary*, p. 137. [279]

29. State Department, Report by the Dutch Legation.

30. Hermann Rauschning, *Gespraeche mit Hitler* (New York: Europa Verlag, 1940), p. 80. [710]

31. Karl von Wiegand, "Hitler Foresees His End," *Cosmopolitan*, May 1939, p. 48. [492]

32. F. A. Voigt, *Unto Caesar* (New York: Putnam, 1938), p. 261, n. 50. [591]

33. Rauschning, *The Voice of Destruction*, pp. 66-67. [261]

34. Otto Strasser, *Hitler and I* (Boston: Houghton, 1940), pp. 66-67. [377]

35. Will D. Bayles, *Caesars in Goose Step* (New York: Harper Bros., 1940). [2]

36. Strasser, *Hitler and I*, p. 68. [378]

37. Konrad Heiden, *Adolf Hitler* (Zurich: Europa Verlag, 1936), pp. 347-348. [527]

38. "... Er stockt, sieht auf den Tisch. Schweigen alles sieht sich verbluefft an. Peinliche Minuten. Ploetzlich dreht sich Hitler auf dem Absatz um und geht ohne ein Wort an die Tuer."

39. Rudolf Olden, *Hitler* (Amsterdam: Querido, 1935), p. 168. [611]
"Das ist ein Trick, den der Fuehrer noch oft anwenden wird: wenn die Situation peinlich wird, versteckt er sich." [611]

40. Rauschning, *The Voice of Destruction*, p. 163. [267]

41. Strasser, *Hitler and I*, p. 105. [381]

42. Heiden, *Adolf Hitler*, p. 280. [280]

43. George Ward Price, *I Know These Dictators* (London: Harrap, 1937), p. 79. [253]

44. Strasser, *Flight from Terror*, p. 134. [302]

45. Heiden, *Adolf Hitler*, pp. 279-280. [98]

46. Friedelinde Wagner, unpublished manuscript. [630]

47. Price, *I Know These Dictators*, pp. 119-120. [255]

48. Reinhold Hanisch, "I Was Hitler's Buddy," *The New Republic*, April 5, 1939, p. 240. [64]

49. Hans Mend, *Adolf Hitler im Felde* (Diessen: Huber Verlag, 1931), p. 79. [199]

50. Otto Strasser, *Flight from Terror*, p. 134. [302]

51. Interview with Friedelinde Wagner, New York City. [937]

52. Rauschning, *Gespraeche*, pp. 159-160.

Aber zunaechst machte auch er nicht den Eindruck des Siegers. Mit gedunsenen, verzerrten Zuegen sass er mir gegenueber, als ich ihm Vortrag hielt. Seine Augen waren erloschen, er sah mich nicht an. Er spielte mit seien Fingern. Ich hatte nicht den Eindruck, dass er mir zuhoerte.... Waehrend der ganzen Ziet hatte ich den Eindruck, dass Ekel, Ueberdruss und Verachtung in ihm herumstritten, und dass er mit seinen Gedanken ganz wo anders war.... Ich hatte gehoert, er sollte nur noch stundenweise schlafen koennen. . . . Nachts irrte er ruhelos umher. Schlafmittel halfen nicht.... Mit Weinkraempfen sollte er aus dem kurzen Schlaf aufwachen. Er haette sich wiederholt erbrochen. Mit Schuettelfrost habe er in Decken gehuellt im Sessel gesessen.... Einmal wollte er alles erleuchtet und Menschen, viel Menschen um sich haben; im gleichen Augenblick haette er wieder niemanden sehem wollen.... [716]

53. Ludecke, *I Knew Hitler*, p. 81. [166]

54. Bella Fromm, *Blood and Banquets* (New York: Harper Bros., 1942), pp. 96-97. [371]

55. Pierre J. Huss, *The Foe We Face* (New York: Doubleday, 1942). [406]

56. Harry W. Flannery, *Assignment to Berlin* (New York: 1942), p. 96. [698]

57. Information Obtained from Ernst Hanfstaengl. [902]

58. Leo Lania, *Today We Are Brothers* (New York: Putnam's, 1940), p. 234. [149]

59. Fromm, *Blood and Banquets*, p. 75. [369]

60. Sir Neville Henderson, *Failure of a Mission* (New York: Putnam's, 1940), p. 42. [124]

61. Frederick Oechsner, *This Is the Enemy* (Boston: Little, Brown, 1942), p. 59. [665]

62. Ludwig Wagner, *Hitler, Man of Strife* (New York: Norton, 1942), p. 59. [487]

63. Ludecke, *I Knew Hitler*, pp. 489-490. [180]

64. Michael Fry, *Hitler's Wonderland* (London: Murray, 1934), p. 107. [577]

65. Strasser, *Flight from Terror*, pp. 43-44. [297]

66. Information Obtained from Hanfstaengl. [898]

67. George Ward Price, *I Know These Dictators* (London: Harrap, 1937), p. 5. [230]

68. Information Obtained from Hanfstaengl. [914]

69. Rauschning, *The Voice of Destruction*, pp. 135-136. [266]

70. Roehm, quoted in Ludecke, *I Knew Hitler*, p. 287. [176]

71. Rauschning, *The Voice of Destruction*, pp. 135-136. [266]

72. Axel Heyst, *After Hitler* (London: Minerva Publishing Co., 1940), p. 53. [600]

73. Von Wiegand, "Hitler Foresees His End," pp. 48, 151. [492]

74. Huss, *The Foe We Face*, p. 104. [408]

75. Information Obtained from Hanfstaengl. [910]

76. Friedelinde Wagner, unpublished manuscript. [632]

77. Strasser, *Flight from Terror*. [301]

78. Interview with Friedelinde Wagner, New York City. [939]

79. Information Obtained from Hanfstaengl. [904]

80. Interview with Friedelinde Wagner, New York City, [939]

81. Janet Flanner, *An American in Paris* (New York: Simon & Schuster, 1940), pp. 382-383. [554]

82. Ludecke, *I Knew Hitler*, p. 419. [177]

83. Ibid., pp. 476-477. [178]

84. R. Norburt, "Is Hitler Married?" *Saturday Evening Post*, December 16, 1939, pp. 14-15. [605]

85. Lochner, *What about Germany?* p. 94. [157]

86. Ludecke, *I Knew Hitler*, pp. 477-478. [179]

87. Rauschning, *The Voice of Destruction*, pp. 91-92. [264]

88. Rudolf Olden, *Hitler* (Amsterdam: Querido, 1935), pp. 180-181.

"Die Voelkische Partei ist nicht mehr die Partei der anstaendigen Leute, sie ist herunter gekommen und korrupt. Kurz, das ist ein Saustall." [614]

89. Hermann Rauschning, *The Voice of Destruction*, p. 263. [276]

90. Interview with Princess Stephanie von Hohenlohe at

the Alien Detention Camp, Seagoville, Texas, June 28, 1943 [658]; and Rauschning, ibid., p. 60. [261]

91. Oechsner, *This Is the Enemy*, pp. 86-87. [675]

92. Information Obtained from Ernst Hanfstaengl. [895]

93. Ernest Pope, *Munich Playground* (New York: Putnam's 1941), pp. 5-9. [229]

94. Rauschning, *Gespraeche*, p. 207. [718]

95. Interview with Princess Stephanie von Hohenlohe. [661]

96. S. Morrell, "Hitler's Hiding Place," *Living Age*, no. 352 (August 1937), pp. 486-488. [462]

97. Interview with Friedelinde Wagner, New York City. [934]

98. Lochner, *What about Germany?* p. 77. [156]

PART IV: HITLER—AS HE KNOWS HIMSELF

1. Hermann Rauschning, *The Voice of Destruction*, p. 255. [273] This is the same as *Gespraeche*.

2. E. Bloch, as told to J. D. Ratcliffe, "My Patient Hitler," *The New Republic*, April 5, 1939, p. 240. [29]

3. Resumé of Interview with Dr. Eduard Bloch, March 5, 1943. [21]

4. Reinhold Hanisch, "I Was Hitler's Buddy," *The New Republic*, April 5, 1939, p. 240. [64]

5. Ibid., p. 241. [65]

6. Ibid., April 12, 1939, p. 272. [73]

7. Andre Simone, *Men of Europe* (New York: Modern Age, 1941), p. 46. [467]

8. Hanisch, "I Was Hitler's Buddy," April 5, 1939, p. 241. [66]

9. Adolf Hitler, *Mein Kampf*.

10. Ibid., p. 30.

11. Interview with Hermann Rauschning, Hollywood, California, June 24, 1943. [947]

12. Hans Mend, *Adolf Hitler im Felde* (Diessen: Huber Verlag, 1931), p. 179. [209]

13. Karl Trossman, *Hitler und Rom* (Nuremberg: Sebaldus Verlag, 1931), p. 158. [483]

14. William Russell, *Berlin Embassy*, 1941, pp. 276-277. [746]

15. Kurt Georg W. Ludecke, *I Knew Hitler* (New York: Scribner's, 1937), p. 91. [166]

16. Rauschning, *The Voice of Destruction*, p. 85. [263]

17. Sisley Huddleston, *In My Time* (London: J. Cape, 1938). [759]

18. F. A. Voigt, *Unto Caesar* (New York: Putnam's, 1938), p. 261, n. 50. [591]

19. Rauschning, *The Voice of Destruction*, p. 173. [268]

20. Ibid., p. 216. [269]

21. Ibid., p. 78. [262]

22. F. Thyssen, *I Paid Hitler* (New York: Farrar, 1931), pp. 137-138. [308]

23. State Department, November 11, 1942, report by Frank. [652]

24. Rauschning, *The Voice of Destruction*, pp. 256-257. [274]

25. Interview with A. Zeissler, Hollywood, California, June 24, 1943. [923]

26. Information Obtained from Ernst Hanfstaengl. [914]

27. Michael Fry, *Hitler's Wonderland* (London: Murray, 1934), p. 107. [577]

28. Karl von Wiegand, "Hitler Foresees His End," *Cosmopolitan*, April 1939, p. 154. [491]

29. Interview with Otto Strasser, Montreal, Canada, May 13, 1943. [919] Also see the interview with Mrs. Shephard Morgan, New York City [939], and the interview with Dr. Raymond Saussure, September 11, 1943, New York City. [932]

PART V: HITLER—PSYCHOLOGICAL ANALYSIS AND RECONSTRUCTION

1. Adolf Hitler, *Mein Kampf.*

2. Ibid.

3. Ibid., p. 38.

4. Ibid., p. 43.

5. Francois-Poncet, French Ambassador in Berlin, to Georges Bonnet, Minister of Foreign Affairs, Berlin, October 20, 1938, *The Yellow Book—Diplomatic Documents 1938-1939*, no. 18, pp. 20, 21, 22. [943]

6. Interview with A. Zeissler, Hollywood, California, June 24, 1943. [921]

7. Hitler, *Mein Kampf.* p. 315.

8. Ibid., p. 201.

9. Francois-Poncet, *The Yellow Book*, p. 49. [946]

10. Kurt Georg W. Ludecke, *I Knew Hitler* (New York: Scribner's, 1937), pp. 233-234. [173]

11. Konrad Heiden, *Adolf Hitler* (Zurich: Europa Verlag, 1936), p. 106. [89]

12. Francois-Poncet, *The Yellow Book*, p. 49. [945-946]

13. Axel Heyst, *After Hitler* (London: Minerva Publishing Co., 1940), pp. 78-80.

AFTERWORD

1. Robert G. L. Waite, *Vanguard of Nazism: The Free Corps Movement in Postwar Germany, 1918-1923* (Cambridge, 1952, and Norton paperback, 1969); cotranslator with Harlan P. Hanson of Erich Eyck's *A History of the Weimar Republic*, 2 volumes (Cambridge, 1962-1963; New York, paper, 1970); editor and contributor, *Hitler and Nazi Germany*, (New York, 1965 and 1969).

2. Carl L. Becker, *Everyman His Own Historian: Essays on History and Politics* (New York, 1935).

3. I have incorporated several of his findings in the following: "Adolf Hitler's Guilt Feelings: A Problem in History and Psychology," *The Journal of Interdisciplinary History*, I, no. 2 (Winter 1971): 229-249; the chapter "Adolf Hitler's Anti-Semitism: A Study in History and Psychoanalysis" in *The Psychoanalytic Interpretation of History*, edited by Benjamin B. Wolman, foreword by William L. Langer (New York, 1971) and in the forthcoming full length study, *The Psychopathic God: A Biography of Adolf Hitler*.

4. Jacques Barzun, "History: The Muse and Her Doctors," *American Historical Review*, 77, no. 1 (February 1972): 55.

5. A. J. P. Taylor, *The Origins of the Second World War* (New York, 1961), pp. 67-72 and *passim*.

6. H. R. Trevor-Roper, *The Last Days of Hitler* (New York, 1947), p. 58.

7. Alan Bullock, *Hitler a Study in Tyranny*, completely revised edition (New York, 1962).

8. Alan Bullock, "Foreword" to the English edition of Franz Jetzinger, *Hitler's Youth* (London, 1958).

9. Percy E. Schramm, "Introduction," in Henry Picker, *Hitlers Tischgespraeche im Fuehrerhauptquartier, 1941-1942* (Stuttgart, 1965), pp. 51-52, 119.

10. Karl Dietrich Bracher, *Die Aufloesung der Weimarer Republik: Eine Studie zum Problem des Machtverfalls der Demokratie* (Stuttgart, 1957); *Deutschland zwischen Demokratie und Diktatur: Beitraege zur neueren Politik und Geschichte* (Bern, 1964) and, with Wolfgang Sauer and Gerhard Schultz, *Die Nationalsozialistische Machtergreifung: Studien zur Errichtung des totalitaeren Herrschaftssystem in Deutschland* (Koeln, 1960).

11. Karl Dietrich Bracher, *The German Dictatorship: The Origins, Structure, and Effects of National Socialism*, translated from the German by Jean Steinberg, Introduction by Peter Gay (New York, 1970), pp. 58, 60, 63.

12. G. M. Trevelyan, *Clio, A Muse and Other Essays Literary and Pedestrian* (London, 1913), p. 9.

13. William B. Willcox, "The Psychiatrist, the Historian, and General Clinton: The Excitement of Historical Research," *Michigan Quarterly Review*, 4 (Spring 1967): 123-130.

14. Conversation with Erik Erikson, April 1968.

15. Former Mayor Josef Mayerhofer as interviewed by *Revue*, no. 39 (27 September 1952) and by Franz Jetzinger, Hitler File, Oberoesterreichisches Landesarchiv, Linz, Folder 159.

16. The full autopsy report is given in Leo Bezymenski, *The Death of Adolf Hitler: Unknown Documents from Soviet Archives* (New York, 1968).

17. Peter Blos, "Comments on the Psychological Consequences of Cryptorchism," *Psychoanalytic Study of the Child*, 15, (1960): 395-429; William G. Niederland, "Narcissistic Ego Impairment with Early Physical Malformations," *Psychoanalytic Study of the Child*, 20 (1965): 518-534. For an excellent study of cryptorchism as it applied specifically to Adolf Hitler see Norbert Bromberg, "Hitler's Character and Its Development: Further Observations," *American Imago*, 28, no. 4 (Winter 1971): 289-303; see also his collaborative chapter on Hitler's childhood in my forthcoming biography, *The Psychopathic God*.

18. Robert Jay Lifton, *Death in Life: Survivors of Hiroshima* (New York, 1967); *History and Human Survival: Essays on the Young and Old, Survivors and the Dead, Peace and War and on Contemporary Psycho-History* (New York, 1970).

19. See especially Norbert Bromberg, "Hitler's Child-

hood" (unpublished paper) and his forthcoming collaborative chapter in *Psychopathic God.*

20. Alan Bullock, "The Political Ideas of Adolf Hitler," *The Third Reich*, edited by Maurice Baumont, John H. E. Fried, and Edmond Vermeil (New York, 1955), p. 351.

21. Bracher, *Dictatorship*, p. 199.

22. August Kubizek, *Adolf Hitler, mein Jugenfreund*, English Translation, *The Young Hitler I Knew* (Cambridge, Mass., 1955); Franz Jetzinger, *Hitlers Jugend: Phantasien, Luegen und die Wahrheit*, English translation, *Hitler's Youth* (London, 1958); Bradley F. Smith, *Adolf Hitler: His Family, Childhood and Youth* (Stanford, 1967).

23. *Hitlers Zeites Buch: Ein Dokument aus dem Jahr 1928*, edited by Gerhard L. Weinberg, English translation, *Hitler's Secret Book* (New York, 1961).

24. Robert P. Knight, "Boderline States," *Psychoanalytic Psychiatry and Psychology* (New York, 1954); Otto Kernberg, "Structural Derivatives of Object Relationships," *International Journal of Psychoanalysis* (1966), pp. 236-253, and unpublished papers by Norbert Bromberg.

25. *Hitler's Secret Conversations, 1941–1944*, edited by H. R. Trevor-Roper (New York, 1953), pp. 442, 476, *passim*.

26. August Kubizek, unpublished memoir, "Erinnerungen an die mit dem Fuehrer gemeinsam verlebte Juenglingsjahre 1904-1908 Linz und Wien," Oberoesterreichisches Landesarchiv, Folder 63. The importance of Easter Monday to the genesis of Hitler's anti-Semitism is shown in a fine piece of psychoanalytic sleuthing by Norbert Bromberg, *American Imago* (Winter 1971), p. 299.

27. Robert G. L. Waite, "Hitler's Anti-Semitism," *The Psychoanalytic Interpretation of History*, p. 195.

28. Hans Frank, *Im Angesicht des Galgens: Deutung Hitlers und seiner Zeit auf grundeigener Erlebnisse und Erkentnisse* (Munich, 1953), pp. 320-321.

29. Waite, "Hitler's Anti-Semitism," p. 195.

30. Military Intelligence: "Report of Hitler's Doctors," (Unclassified Army Documents, National Archives); Karl Brandt, "Theo. Morell," memoir dated 19 September 1945 (Bundesarchiv Bestand 441-443); Anton Braunmuehl, "War Hitler Krank?" *Stimmen der Zeit*, 79 (May 1954): 94-102; Johann Recktenwald, *Woran hat Adolf Hitler*

gelitten? Eine neuropsychiatrische Deutung (Munich, 1963); H. D. Roehrs, *Die Zerstoerung einer Persoenlichkeit* (Neckargemuend, 1965); Wilhelm Treue, *Mit den Augen Ihrer Leibaertzte: Von bedeutenden Medizinern und ihren grossen Patienten* (Dusseldorf, 1955).

31. Feldmarschall Heinz Guderian, *Erinnerungen eines Soldaten* (Heidelberg, 1951), p. 402.

32. Gerhard Boldt, *Die letzten Tage der Reichskanzlei* (Hamburg, 1947), pp. 15, 63–64. Similar testimony is given by the loyal Hitler supporters, Karl Wahl, " . . . *es ist das deutsche Herz": Erlebnisse und Erkenntnisse eines ehemaliges Gauleiters* (Privately Published, Augsburg, 1954), pp. 390–391.

BIBLIOGRAPHY

Abel, Theodor. *Why Hitler Came into Power?* Englewood Cliffs, N.J.: Prentice-Hall, 1938.

Adam, Adela M. *Philip alias Hitler.* Oxford: Oxford University Press, 1941. 10:105–113.

Agha Khan. "Faith in Hitler." *Living Age* 355 (1938): 299–302.

Albert, E. "Hitler and Mussolini." *Contemporary Review* 159 (1941):155–161.

Allard, Paul. *Quand Hitler espionne la France.* Paris: Les editions de France, 1939.

Allen, J. "Directors of Destiny." *Good Housekeeping* 109 (1939):30–31.

Anacker, H. "Ritter Ted und Teufel." *Nationalsozialistische Monatshefte* 5, no. 46.34:2.

Andernach, Andreas. *Hitler ohne Maske.* Munich: Der Antifaschist, 1932.

Arbuerster, Martin. *Adolf Hitler, Blut oder Geist.* Zurich: Reso Verlag, 1936. Kulturpolit. Schriften, no. 7.

Bade, Wilfred. *Der Weg des dritten Reichs.* 4 Bande Lubeck Coleman, 1933–1938, je 150 Seiten.

Bainville, Jacques. *Histoire de deux peuples, continuée jusqu'à Hitler.* Paris: Flammarion, 1938.

Baker, J. E. "Carlyle Rules the Reich." *Saturday Review of Literature* 10 (1933):291.

Balk, Ernst Wilhelm. *Mein Fuehrer.* Berlin: P. Schmidt, 1933.

Bavarian State Police. *Report to the Bavarian State Ministry of the Interior Re: Conditional Parole of Adolf Hitler.*

Bayles, Will D. *Caesars in Goose Step.* New York: Harper Bros., 1940.

Baynes, Helton Godwin. *Germany Possessed.* London: J. Cape, 1941.

Bedel, Maurice. *Monsieur Hitler.* Paris: Gallimard, 1937.

Belgium. *The Official Account of What Happened, 1939–40,* Belgium. New York, 1941.

Berchthold, Josef. *Hitler ueber Deutschland.* Munich: F. Eher, 1932.

Bereitschaft fuer Adolf Hitler. Vienna, 1932.

Berliner Illustrierte Zeitung. "Militarpass Adolf Hitlers," no. 32 (August 1939).

Berliner Tageblatt. "Putschprozess Hitlers Vernehmung," February 27, 1924, pp. 10–26.

————, "Hitler als Zeuge im Leipziger Reichswehrprozess," September 6, 1930.

Bertrand, Louis, M. E. . . . *Hitler.* Paris: Fayard & Cie, 1936.

Billing, R. *Rund um Hitler.* Munich: B. Funck, 1931.

Billinger, Karl (pseud.). *Hitler Is No Fool,* New York: Modern Age Books, 1939.

Binsse, H. L. "Complete Hitler." *Commonweal* 29 (1939):625–626.

————. "Hitler, German Hypnotist." *Outlook* 256 (1931):156.

Blake, Leonard. *Hitler's Last Year of Power.* London: A. Daker's Ltd., 1939.

Blank, Herbert. *Adolf Hitler, Wilhelm III.* Berlin: Rowohlt, 1931.

Bloch, E. "My Patient Hitler." *Collier's* 107 (1941):11, 69–70.

Borne, L. "27 J. Zu diesem Hitler." *Weltbuehne* (1931), p. 45.

Bouhler, Philipp. *Adolf Hitler, das Werden einer Volksbewegung.* Colemans K. Biogr., no. 11, 1935.

————. *Adolf Hitler, A Short Sketch of His Life.* Terramare Office, 1938.

Brady, Robert A. *The Spirit and Structure of German Fascism.* New York, 1937.

Braun, Otto. *Von Weimar zu Hitler.* New York: Europa Verlag, 1940.

Bredow, Klaus. *Hitler rast. Der 30. Juni.* Saarbrucken, 1934.

Brentano, Bernard. *Der Beginn der Barbarei in Deutschland.* Berlin: Rowohlt, 1930.

British War Bluebook. 1939.

Brooks, Robert Clarkson. . . . *Deliver Us from Dictators.* Philadelphia: University of Pennsylvania Press, 1935.

Buch, Walter. "Der Fuehrer." *Nationalsozialistische Monatschefte* Jehrgang 327, 4 (no. 39.33):248–251.

Buelow, Paul. *Adolf Hitler und der Bayreuther Kulturkreis.* Leipzig, 1933. Aus Deutschlands Werden, no. 9, pp. 1–16.

Caballero, G. E. "Das geheimniste Nationalsozialismus." *Nationalsozialistische Monatshefte* 3 (no. 32.32):511–513.

Cahen, Max. *Man against Hitler.* New York: Dobbs & Merrill, 1939.

Chateaubriant, Alphonse de. ... *La gerbe des forces.* Nouvelle Allemagne. 1937.

Chelius, Fritz Heinz. *Aus Hitlers Jugendland und Jugendzeit.* Leipzig: Schaufuss, 1933.

Christian Century. "Comedy Has Its Limits: Chaplinized Hitler," 57 (1940):816–817.

———. "How Seriously Must Hitler Be Taken," 53 (1936):1277.

Churchill, W. "Dictators Are Dynamite." *Collier's* 102 (1938):16–17.

Ciarlatini, Franco. *Hitler e il Fascismo.* Florence: R. Bemporad, 1933.

Citron, B. "Geldgeber der Nazis." *Weltbuehne* 2 (1931):72.

Clatchie, S. M. "Germany Awake." *Forum* 85 (1931):217–224.

Clinchy, Everett R. "I Saw Hitler, Too." *Christian Century* 49 (1932):1131–1133.

———. "The Strange Case of Herr Hitler," John Day Pamphlets, no. 24, 1933.

Collier's. "Is Hitler Crazy?" 103 (1939):82.

Commonweal. "Quandaries of Herr Hitler" 16 (1932):419.

Contemporary Review. "Adolf Hitler" 140 (1931): 726–732.

———. "The Advent of Herr Hitler" 143 (1933):366–368.

———. "Der Fuehrer Spricht" 155 (1939):357–368.

———. "Excerpt. R. of Rs." 85 (1932):56–57.

———. "Hitler's Age of Heroism" 143 (1933):532–541.

———. "Hitler's Cards. Germanicus" 154 (1938):190–196.

Crabits, P. "Masterstroke of Psychology." *Catholic World* 148 (1938):190–197.

Crabits, P. and Huddleston, S. "Hitler the Orator." *Catholic World* 149 (1939):229–230.

Crain, Maurice. *Rulers of the World*. New York, 1940.

Current History. "Ascetic Adolf; Hitler's Income" 52 (1941):27–28.

———. "Hitler's Escape" 51 (1939):12.

———. "I Was Hitler's Boss" 52 (1941):193–199.

———. "Mr. Hitler" 48 (1938):74–75.

———. "Prosecuted by Hitler, an Unbiased Account of a Real Experience" 44 (1936):83–90.

———. "Stranger in Paris" 51 (1940):54.

Czech-Jochberg, Erich. *Adolf Hitler und sein Stab*. Oldenburg: G. Stalling. 1933.

———. *Hitler, eine Deutsche Bewegung*. Oldenburg: G. Stalling, 1936.

D'Abernon, Edgar Vincent. *Diary of an Ambassador, 1920–26*. New York: Doubleday.

Denny, C. "France and the German Counter-Revolution." *Nation* 116 (1923):295–297.

Descaves, Pierre. *Hitler*. Paris: Dencl & Steele, 1936.

Deuel, Wallace R. *People under Hitler*. New York: Harcourt, 1942.

Deutsche Juristenzeitung. "Muenchener Hochverratsprozess. Graf au Dohna," vol. 330 (October 1924).

Deutsche Republik. "Das Schutzserum gegen die Hitlerei" 5:358–364.

———. "Figuren aus dem 'Dritten Reich'" 4:1476–1481.

Diebow, Hans. *Hitler, eine Biographie*. W. Kolk, 1931.

Dietrich, Otto. *Mit Hitler in die Macht*. Munich: F. Eher, 1934.

Dobert, Eitel Wolf. *Convert to Freedom*. New York: Putnam's, 1940.

Dodd, Ambassador. *Diary, 1933–38*. New York: Harcourt, 1939.

Dodd, Martha. *Through Embassy Eyes*. New York: Harcourt, 1939.

Doerr, Eugen. *Mussolini, Hitler* . . . Leipzig: S. Schnurpfeil Verlag, 1931.

Dokumente der Deutschen Politik. Berlin: Junker & Dunnhaupt Verlag, 1935–1939.

Duhamel, Georges. *Memoriel de la Guerre Blanche, 1938*. Paris, 1939.

Dutch, Oswald (pseud.). *Hitler's 12 Apostles*. London: E. Arnold & Co., 1939.

Dzelepy, E. N. *Hitler contre la France?* Paris: Editions Excelsior, 1933.

————. *Le vrai "combat" de Hitler*. Paris: L. Vogel, 1936.

Eckart, Dietrich. *Der Bolschewismus von Moses bis Lenin,* Munich, 1925.

Eichen, Carl von. "Hitler's Throat." *Time Magazine,* November 14, 1938.

Einzig, Paul. *Hitler's "New Order" in Europe,* London: MacMillan, 1941.

Emsen, Kurt von. *Adolf Hitler und die Kommenden*. Leipzig: W. R. Lindner, 1932.

Ensor, Robert Charles K. "Herr Hitler's Self Disclosure in 'Mein Kampf.' " Oxford Pamphlets no. 3 (1938).

————. "Who Hitler Is." Oxford Pamphlets no. 20 (1939).

Erckner, S. *Hitler's Conspiracy against Peace*. London: Gollanz, 1937.

Ermarth, Fritz. *The New Germany*. Washington, D.C., 1936.

Fairweather, N. "Hitler and Hitlerism." *Atlantic Monthly* 149 (1932):380–387, 509–516.

————. "A Man of Destiny." *Atlantic Monthly* 149 (1932):380–387.

Feder, Gottfried. *Was will Adolf Hitler?* Munich: F. Eher, 1931.

Fernsworth, Lawrence. *Dictators and Democrats*. New York: McBride, 1941.

Ficke, Karl. *Auf dem Wege nach Canossa*. Klausthal: Selbstverlag, 1931.

Flanner, Janet. *An American in Paris*. New York: Simon & Schuster, 1940.

Flannery, Harry W. *Assignment to Berlin*. New York, 1942.

Fodor, M. W. *Plot and Counterplot in Central Europe*. Boston: Houghton, 1937.

Francois, Jean. *L'affaire Rohm-Hitler*. Paris: Les Oeuvres Libres, 1938. 209:5–142.

Frateco (pseud.). *M. Hitler, dictateur. Trad. de l'allemand sur le manuscript, indit*. Paris: L'Eglantine, 1933.

Fried, Hans Ernest. *The Guilt of the German Army*. New York: Macmillan, 1942.

Friters, G. "Who Are the German Fascists?" *Current History* 35 (1932) :532–536.

Frommer, *Blood and Banquets*. New York: Harper Bros., 1942.

Fry, Michael. *Hitler's Wonderland*. London: Murray, 1934.

Fuchs, Martin. *Showdown in Vienna*. New York: Putnam's, 1939.

Der Fuehrer. "In 100 Buechern. Wir lesen," May 1939, pp. 1–16.

Ganzer, Karl Richard. "Vom Ringen Hitlers um das Reich, 1924-33." *Zeitgeschichte Verlag*. Berlin, 1935.

Gavit, J. P. "Much Ado about Hitler." *Survey* 68:239.

Gehl, Walter. *Der Deutsche Aufbruch*. Breslau: Hirt, 1938.

Georges-Anquetil. *Hitler conduit le bal*. Paris: Les editions de Lutece, 1939.

Gerlach, H. V. "Hitlers Vorlaufer." *Weltbuehne* (1931), pp. 814–817.

German Foreign Office. *The German White Paper*, June 23, 1940.

Gerstorff, K. L. "Illusionen ueber Hitler." *Weltbuehne* (1931), pp. 950–954.

Gillis, J. M. "Austrian Phaeton." *Catholic World* 151 (1940) :257–265.

Goebbels, Joseph. *Kampf um Berlin*. Munich: NSDAP, 1934.

————. *Vom Kaiserhof zur Reichskanzlei*. Munich: NSDAP, 1934.

Goetz, F. "Ein Offizier Hitlers erzaehlt." *Vorwaerts*, March 2, 1924.

————. "How Hitler Failed." *Living Age* 320 (1924) :595–599.

————. "Report on Putsch Prozess." *Vorwaerts*, February 26, 1924.

Golding, Louis. *Hitler through the Ages*. London: Sovereign Books Ltd., 1940.

Gollomb, Joseph. *Armies of Spies*. New York: Macmillan, 1939.

Gorel, Michael. *Hitler sans masque*.

Graach, Henrich. *Freiheitskampf . . . Saarlouis*. Hansen Verlag, 1935.

Greenwood, H. "Hitler's First Year." Spectator booklet no. 5. London, 1934.

Grimm, Alfred Max. *Horoscope Hitler*. Toelz: Selbstverlag, 1925.

Gritzbach, Erich. *Hermann Goering*. London, 1939.

Gross, Felix. *Hitler's Girls, Guns and Gangsters*. London: Hurst, 1941.

Grunsky, Karl. Warum Hitler? ... Der Aufschwung, Deutsche Reihe, 1933.

Grzesinski, Albert. *Inside Germany*. New York: Dutton, 1939.

Gumbel, Emil Julius. *Les crimes politiques en Allemagne, 1919–1929*. Paris: Gallimard, 1931.

————. *Zwei Jehre Mord (Kapp Putsch)*. Berlin: Verlag Neuess Vaterland, 1921.

Gunther, John. *The High Cost of Hitler*. London: Hamilton, 1939.

————. "Hitler." *Harper's Magazine* 172 (1936):148—159.

————. *Inside Europe*. New York: Harper Bros., 1936.

Haake, Heinz. *Das Ehrenbuch des Fuehrers*. NSDAP, 1933.

Hadamowsky, Eugen. *Hitler kaempft um den Frieden Europas*. NSDAP, 1936.

Hadeln, Hajo Freiherr von. *Vom Wesen einer Nationalsozialistischen Weltgeschichte*. Frankfurt: A. M. Osterrieth, 1935.

Haffner, S. *Germany: Jekyll and Hyde*. New York: Dutton, 1941.

Hagen, Paul. *Will Germany Crack?* New York, 1942.

Hambloch, Ernest. *Germany Rampant*. London: Duckworth, 1939.

Hanfstaengl, Ernst Franz. *Hitler in der Karrikatur der Welt*. Berlin: Verlag Braune Bucher, 1933. (Neue Folge: Tat gegen Tinte. Berlin. O. Rentsch, 1934).

————. "My Leader." *Collier's* 94 (1934):7–9.

Hanisch, Reinhold. "I Was Hitler's Buddy." *New Republic*, April 5, 1939, pp. 239–242; April 12, 1939, pp. 270–272; April 19, 1939, pp. 297–300.

Hansen, Heinrich. *Der Schlussel zum Frieden*. Berlin: Klieber, 1938.

————. *Hitler, Mussolini* ... Dresden: Raumbild Verlag, 1938.

Harsch, Joseph C. *Pattern of Conquest*. New York: Doubleday, 1941.

Hauptmann, R. "An den Pranger mit Hitler! ..." *Weltkampf* 8 (1931):154–163.

Hauser, Heinrich. *Hitler vs. Germany.* London: Jarrold, 1940.

———. *Time Was: Death of a Junker.* New York; Reynal, 1942.

Hauteoloque, Xavier de. *A l'hombre de la croix gammée.* Paris: Les éditions de France, 1933.

Heiden, Konrad. "Adolf at School." *Living Age* 351 (1936):227–229.

———. *Adolf Hitler.* Zurich: Europa Verlag, 1936.

———. *Ein Mann gegen Europa.* Zurich: Europa Verlag, 1937.

———. "Hitler klagt." *Das Tagebuch* 10 (1929):816.

———. *Les vêpres Hitleriennes.* Paris: Sorlot, 1939.

Heiner, Einar Henrik. *Adolf Hitler . . . Torekas.* Schweden: Selbstverlag, 1937.

Heinz, Heinz A. *Germany's Hitler.* London: Hurst, 1934.

Henderson, Sir Neville. *Failure of a Mission.* New York: Putnam's, 1940.

Henry, Ernst (pseud.). *Hitler over Europe.* London: Dent, 1934.

———. "The Man behind Hitler." *Living Age* 345 (1933):117.

Heuss, Theodor. *Hitlers Weg.* Union Deutsche Verlags Anstalt, 1932.

Heyst, Axel. *After Hitler.* London: Minerva Publ. Co., 1940.

High, Stanley. "Hitler and the New Germany." *Literary Digest,* October 7, 1933.

———. "The Man Who Leads Germany." *Literary Digest* 116 (1933):5.

Hinkel, Hans and Bley, Wulf. *Kabinet Hitler.* Berlin: Verlag Deutsche Kulturwacht, 1933.

Hitler, Adolf. "To Victory and Freedom, National Socialism, Labor Party." *Living Age* 342 (1932):24–25.

Hitler: Acquarelle. NSDAP, 1936.

Hitler against the World. New York: Worker's Library Publ., 1935.

Hitler Calls This Living. London, 1939.

Hitler in Hamburg. Hamburg, 1939.

Hitler: Ja, aber—was sagt Hitler selbst? Eine Auswahl v. H. Passow, 1931.

Hitler: The Man. London: Friends of Europe Publ., 1936. no. 34, pp. 1–21.

"Hitler: und die Deutsche Aufgabe." *Zeit- und Streitfragen,* no. 1 (1933).

Hoeper, Wilhelm. *Adolf Hitler, der Erzieher der Deutschen.* Breslau: Hirt Verlag, 1934.

Hoffmann, Heinrich. *Deutschlands Erwachen.* 1924.

————. *Hitler Abseits vom Alltag.* Berlin: Zeitgeschichte Verlag, 1937.

————. *Hitler baut Grossdeutschland.* 1938.

————. *Hitler befreit Sudetendeutschland.* Berlin: Zeitgeschichte Verlag, 1938.

————. *Hitler in Boehmen.* Berlin: Zeitgeschichte Verlag, 1939.

————. *Hitler in Italien.* Munich: verlag Heinrich Hoffmann, 1938.

————. *Hitler in Polen.* Berlin: Zeitgeschichte Verlag, 1939.

————. *Hitler in seinen Bergen.* Berlin: Zeitgeschichte Verlag, 1935.

————. *Hitler in seiner Heimat.* Berlin: Zeitgeschichte Verlag, 1938.

————. *Hitler, wie ihn Keiner Kennt.* Berlin, 1932.

Holbeck, K. *Kaiser, Kanzler, Kaempfer.* Leipzig: A. Hoffmann, 1933.

Holt, John G. *Under the Swastika.* Chapel Hill: University of North Carolina Press, 1936.

Honrighausen, E. G. "Hitler and German Religion." *Christian Century* 50 (1933):418–420.

Hoover, Calvin B. *Germany Enters the Third Reich.* New York, 1933.

Horle, W. H. "Ten Years of Hitler, Hundred of Goethe." *Nation* 134 (1932):307–308.

Huddleston, Sisley. *In My Time.* London: J. Cape, 1938.

Huss, Pierre J. *The Foe We Face.* New York: Doubleday, 1942.

Hutchinson, P. "Portent of Hitler." *Christian Century 50* (1933):1299–1301.

Hutton, Graham. *Survey after Munich.* Boston, 1939.

Il Popolo D'Italia. "Hitler: Un processo intentato," July 5, 1929.

————. "I diffamatori . . . condannati," May 15, 1929.

Indian Revue. "Chancellor Hitler" 34:246.

Jacob, Hans. "Hitler's Ear and Tongue." *Who* 1 (1941): 37–38.

Jastrow, J. "Dictatorial Complex: Psychologist Analyzes the Mental Pattern of Europe's Strongest Strong Men." *Current History* 49 (1938):40.

Jaszi, O. "Hitler Myth, a Forecast." *Nation* 136 (1933):553–554.

Jones, Ernest J. *Hitler, the Jews, and Communists*. Sydney, 1933.

Josephson, Matthew. "Making of a Demagogue." *Saturday Review of Literature* 10 (1933):213–214.

———. "Nazi Culture." John Day Pamphlets, 1933.

Kemp, C. D. Jr. *Adolf Hitler and the Nazis*. New York: Cook, 1933.

Kernan, Thomas. *France on Berlin Time*. New York: Lippincott, 1941.

King, Joseph. *The German Revolution*. London, 1933.

Klotz, Hermut. *The Berlin Diaries*. London, 1935.

Knickerbocker, H. R. *Is Tomorrow Hitler's?* New York: Reynal, 1941.

Koehler, Hansjurgen. *Inside Information*. London: Pallas Publ., 1940.

———. *Inside the Gestapo. Hitler's Shadows over the World*. London: Pallas Publ., 1940.

Koehler, Pauline. *The Women Who Lived in Hitler's House*. Sheridan House.

Koerber, Adolf-Victor von. *Adolf Hitler, sein Leben und seine Reden*. Munich: E. Boepple, 1923.

Korney. "The Man Who Made Hitler Rich." *Living Age* 355 (1938):337–341.

Krauss, Helene. *Des Fuehrers Jugendstatten*. Vienna: Kuhne, 1938.

Krebs, Hans. *Sudetendeutschland Marschiert*. Berlin: Osmer, 1939.

———. *Wir Sudetendeutsche*. Berlin: Runge, 1937.

Krueger, Kurt. *Inside Hitler*. New York: Avalon Press, 1941.

Ladies' Home Journal. "Story of the Two Mustaches" 57 (1940):18.

Landau, Rom. *Hitler's Paradise*. London: Faber, 1941.

Lang, T. "Hitler as Wotan ... Retreat High Bavarian Alps." *Current History* 51 (1940):50.

Lania, L. "Hitler-Prozess." *Weltbuehne* 20 (1924):298–301.

————. *Today We Are Brothers*. New York, 1942.

Laswell, H. D. "Hitler Rose to Power Because He Felt Personally Insecure." *Science News Letter* 33 (1938):195.

————. "Psychology of Hitlerism." *Political Quarterly* 4:373–384.

Laurie, Arthur Pillans. *The Case for Germany*. Berlin, 1939.

Le Bourdais, D. M. "Crackpot Chancellor." *Canadian Monthly* 91 (1939):20–22.

Lee, John Alexander. *Hitler*. Auckland Service Print., 1940.

Leers, Johann v. *Adolf Hitler*. Leipzig, 1932. (Manner und Machte.)

Lefêbvre, Henry. *Hitler au pouvoir*. Paris: Bureau d'Uditions, 1938.

LeGrix, Francois. *20 jours chez Hitler*. Paris: Grasse, 1923.

Lengyel, Emil. *Hitler*. New York, 1932.

————. "Hitler and the French Press" *Nation* 138 (1934):216–217.

Leske, Gottfried. *I Was a Nazi Flier*. New York: Dial Press, 1941.

Lewis, Wyndham. *Hitler*. London: Chatto & Windus, 1931.

————. *The Hitler Cult*. London, 1939.

Lichtenberger, Henri. *The Third Reich*. New York, 1937.

Life. "Adolf Hitler's Rise to Power" 9 (1940):61–67.

Linke. "Wie der Modies den Hitler zum Schweigen brachte." *Nationalsozialistische Monatshefte* 6, no. 55: 954–958.

Literary Digest. "Abbe Dinnet Gives His Views of Two Dictators" 118 (1934):18.

————. "Adolf Hitler States His Case" 111 (1931):15.

————. "Bewildering Magic of Fuehrer Hitler" 115 (1933):10–11.

————. "Chancellor-Reichsfuhrer. Watching His Step" 118 (1934):12.

————. "Comic Aspects of Hitler's Career" 116 (1933):13.

————. "Dangerous Days in Europe" 107 (1930):14–15.

————. "Freud's Fears of Hitler" 113 (1932):15.

————. "Gregor Strasser, Big Hitlerite Rebel" 115 (1933):13.

————. "Handsome Adolf, the Man without a Country" 107 (1930):34.

———. "Hitler, Germany's Would-be Mussolini" 107 (1930):15–16.

———. "Hitler's Astounding Outburst" 111 (1931):10.

———. "Hitler's Shattered Dream of Dictatorship" 114 (1932):13–14.

———. "Hitler's Star Still in the Ascendant" 113 (1932):12–13.

———. "Misfire of the German Mussolini" 76 (1923): 23.

———. "They Stood Out from the Crowd in 1934" 118 (1934):7.

———. "Transformation of Adolf Hitler" 112 (1932): 13–14.

———. "When Hitler Hit the Ceiling" 115 (1933):30.

Litten, Irmgard. *Beyond Tears*. New York: Alliance Book Corp., 1940.

Living Age. "From Six to Six Millions" 339 (1930):243–245.

———. "Hitler at 50" 356 (1939):451–453.

———. "Hitler and His Gang" 344 (1933):419–422.

———. "Hitler Speaks" 344 (1933):114–116.

———. "Hitler's Palace in the Clouds on the Top of the Kehlstein" 356 (1939):32–33.

———. "Hitler's Private Rabbit Warren. Reichschancellery" 360 (1941):321.

———. "Hitler's Salad Days" 345 (1933):44–48.

———. "Men Whom Hitler Obeys" 356 (1939):142– 145.

Lochner, Louis P. *What about Germany?* New York: Dodd, 1942.

Loewenstein, Hubert Prinz zu. *On Borrowed Peace*. New York, 1942.

Loewenstein, Karl. *Hitler's Germany*. New York: Macmillan, 1936.

Lorant, Stefan. *I Was Hitler's Prisoner*. London: Gollancz, 1935.

Lorimer, Emily D. *What Hitler Wants*. London: Penguin Books, 1939.

Lorre, L. "Hitler's Bid for German Power." *Current History*, May 1932.

Lucchini, Pierre (Pierre Dominic pseud.). *Deux jours chez Ludendorff*. Paris, 1924.

Ludecke, Kurt George W. *I Knew Hitler*. New York: Scribner's, 1937.

Ludwig, Emil. *The Germans*. Boston: Little, 1941.

————. *Three Portraits: Hitler, Mussolini, Stalin*. New York, 1940.

Lurker, Otto. *Hitler hinter Festungsmauern*. Berlin: Mittler, 1933.

McKelway, St. C. "Who Was Hitler?" *Saturday Evening Post* 213 (1940):12–13.

Mann, H. "A German View of Hitler." *Saturday Review* (London) 153 (1932):314–315.

Mann, K. "Cowboy Mentor of the Fuehrer, Karl May." *Living Age* 359 (1940):217–222.

Marion, Paul. *Leur combat ... Hitler*. Paris: Fayard, 1939.

Mason, John Brown. *Hitler's First Foes*. Minneapolis, 1936.

Massis, Henry. *Chefs*. Paris: Plon., 1939.

Maugham, Fred Herbert. *Lies as Allies*. New York: Oxford University Press, 1941.

Maupas, Jacques. *Le Chancellier Hitler et les élections allemandes* (Correspondent, 1933, N.S. vol. 294, pp. 836–853).

Maxwell, N. "Hitler's He-Men and the Gash." *Saturday Review* (London) 156 (1933):142.

Mehring, Walter. "Begruessung Hitlers auf literarischen Gebiet." *Weltbuehne*, p. 507.

Melville, Cecil F. *The Truth about the New Party*. London: Wishart, 1931.

Mend, Hans. *Adolf Hitler im Felde*. Dressen: Huber Verlag, 1931.

Meyer, Adolf. *Mit Hitler im Bayerischen Infanterie Regt.* Neustadt: Aupperle Verlag, 1934.

Miller, Douglas. *You Can't Do Business with Hitler!* Boston: Little, 1941.

Miltenberg, W. von. "Handsome Adolf." *Living Age* 304 (1931):14–15.

Mitteilungen des Deutschvolkischen Turnvereins Urfahr; *Adolf Hitler in Urfahr*. Felge 67:12. Jehrgang (Austria).

Moeller van den Bruck. *Das Dritte Reich*. Hamburg: Manseatisce Verlags Anstalt, 1931.

Morell, S. "Hitler's Hiding Place." *Living Age* 352 (1937):486–488.

Morus. "Hitler und Kirdirf." *Weltbuehne*. 26.J.II.245.

Morvilliers, Roger. . . . *Face à Hitler et à Mein Kampf.* *Serves en vente chez l'auteur.* 1939.

Mowrer, Edgar Ansell. *Germany Puts the Clock Back.* New York, 1933. (London: Penguin Books, 1938).

Mowrer, Lilian. *Rip Tide of Aggression.* New York: Morrow, 1942.

Muhlen, Norbert. *Hitler's Magician: Schacht.* London, 1938.

Muhsam, E. "Aktive Abwehr gegen Hitler." *Weltbuehne* (1931), p. 880.

Murphy, James Bumgardner. *Adolf Hitler, the Drama of His Career.* London: Chapman, 1934.

Naab, Ingbert. *Ist Hitler ein Christ?* Munich: Zeichenring Verlag, 1931.

Nation. "Can Hitler Be Trusted?" 140 (1935):645.

———. "Hitler Goes to Rome" 146 (1938):520.

Nationalsozialismus. Das wahre Gesicht des. Bund deutscher Kriegsteilnehmer. Magdeburg.

Nationalsozialistische Monatshefte. "Adolf Hitler, 1925 in Gera" 5, no. 54:848–849.

———. "Geschichten aus der Kampfzeit." vol. 5, no. 54.

Nazi Primer, the Official Handbook. New York: Harper, 1938.

Neumann, Franz L. *Behemoth.* New York: Oxford University Press, 1942.

New Republic. "Is Hitler Crazy?" 97 (1938):2, 3.

———. (Medicus) "A Psychiatrist Looks at Hitler" 98 1939):326–328.

Newsweek. "Adolf Hitler's Double" 13 (1939):43.

———. "Adolf Hitler's Roman Holiday" 11 (1938):15–16.

———. "Cocksure Dictator Takes Timid-Soul Precautions" 5 (1935):16.

———. "Hitler at Bavarian Retreat" 5 (1935):12–13.

———. "Hitler Enthroned" 13 (1939):21.

———. "Hitler and Mussolini Put Their Heads Together" 10 (1937):11–13.

———. "Hitler Tells How He Directed Merciless Bloodstroke" 4 (1934):10–11.

———. "Hitler's First Great Crisis" 3 (1934):3–4.

———. "Nazis Protest Use of Baby Snapshot" 3 (1934):31.

———. "Phony Fuehrer, Impersonator Dryden" 20 (1942):61–62.

———. "Reichfuehrer . . . What Hitler Is . . ." 7 (1936):27.

———. "To the Fuehrer, Hitler Is Terrific" 19 (1942):42.

———. "When Hitler Started" 13 (1939):22.

New Yorker Staatszeitung. Allerhand Merkwurdiges aus Privatleben," January 1941.

———. *Staatszeitung und Herold,* Various Articles, April 1939; December 1940.

New York Times. "Rise as Idol," November 21, 1922, p. 1.

———. "Mrs. Andre Elendt Aids Cause," December 14, 1922, p. 7.

———. "Hitler Wins Libel Suit in Munich," May 19, 1929, p. 8.

———. "Interview," October 15, 1930.

———. "Sincerity, Praised by V. F. Ridder," May 2, 1933, p. 4.

———. "Hitler Stories Told in Vienna," December 3, 1933.

———. "Gives Rides and Overcoats to Hitchhikers," December 26, 1933.

———. "Personality and Private Life," March 11, 1934. (*see* Tolischus)

———. August 12, 1934, p. 7.

———. "Interviewed by Lord Allen of Hurtwood," January 28, 1935, p. 3.

———. "Alois Hitler Opens Tea Room in Berlin," September 17, 1937, p. 4.

———. "Portrait Adolf Hitler," September 19, 1937, p. 3.

———. "Gruenscheder Says He Is Older than Record Shows," April 16, 1938, p. 3.

———. "Relatives Visit U.S.: William Patrick," March 31, 1939, p. 3.

———. "Miss Daniels Interviews on Her Dance Performance before Him," October 6, 1939, p. 4.

———. "Reports about Arrival of U. Freeman Mitford—Illness in England," January 3, 4, 7, 1940, pp. 1, 2, 6.

———. "Report to Have Sought Dr. Stekel to Interpret Dream of Undisclosed Nature," November 17, 1940, p. 4.

———. "German Official Asks Honduran Foreign Office

to Ban Book 'I Was Hitler's Waitress,'" January 16, 1941, p. 2.

————. "Reports about William Patrick and Mrs. Bridget Arrivals, Activities in Canada and U.S.," June 25, 30, 1941, pp. 3, 3.

Niekisch, Ernst. *Hitler—Ein Deutsches Verhaengnis.* Berlin: Widerstands Verlag, 1932.

Norburt, R. "Is Hitler Married?" *Saturday Evening Post* 212 (1939):14–15.

North American Revue. "Herr Hitler Comes to Bat" 234 (1932):104–109.

Oechsner, F. "Portable Lair: Fuehrerhauptquartier." *Collier's* 110 (1942):26.

————. *This is the Enemy.* Boston: Little, 1942.

Oehme, Walter. *Kommt das Dritte Reich?* Berlin: Rowohlt, 1930.

Olden, Rudolf. *Hitler.* Amsterdam: Querido, 1935.

Ossietzky, C. V. "Brutus schlaft." *Weltbuehne* (1931), pp. 157–160.

————. "Grossreinemachen bei Hitler." *Weltbuehne* (1931), p. 483.

————. "Hitler. Winterkonig." *Weltbuehne* (1931), pp. 235–237.

————. "Hitler's Horoskop." *Weltbuehne* (1931), pp. 607–611.

————. "Kommt Hitler doch?" *Weltbuehne* (1931), pp. 875–880.

Otto, Carl A. G. *Der Krieg ohne Waffen. Wird Hitler Deutschlands Mussolini.* Senitas Verlag, 1930.

Ottwalt, Ernst. *Deutschland Erwache!* Vienna: Hess & Co., 1932.

Owne, Frank. *The Three Dictators ... Hitler.* London: Allen, 1940.

Panton, S. "Hitler's New Hiding Place." *Current History* 50 (1939):71–72.

Pariser Tages Zeitung. "Das Ratsel um Hitlers, E.K.I.," April 20, 1937.

————. "Der Prozess der Brigitte Hitler," January 28, 1939.

————. Article about the Iron Cross, September 29, 1939.

————. "Vom Wahne besessen," January 23, 1940.

Pascal, Roy. *The Nazi Dictatorship.* London, 1934.

Pauli, Ernst. *Die Sendung Adolf Hitlers.* Verlag fuer Volkskunst, 1934.

Pauls, Eilhard Erich. *Ein Jahr Volkskanzler.* Aus Deutschlands Werden, no. 21–22 (1934).

Pendell, E. H. "Adolf Alias 666." *Christian Century* 50 (1933):759.

———. "Discussion," *Christian Century* 50 (1933):819, 849.

Pernot, Maurice. *L'Allemagne de Hitler.* Paris, 1933.

Peters, C. B. "In Hitler's Chalet." *New York Times Magazine,* March 16, 1941, p. 9.

Phayre, I. "Holiday with Hitler." *Current History* 44 (1936):50–58.

Phillips, Henry Albert. *Germany Today and Tomorrow.* New York: Dodd.

Plessmayr, Hermann. *Der Nationalsozialismus.* Stuttgart: Mahler, 1933.

Pollock, James Kerr. *The Government of Greater Germany.* New York: Nostrand, 1938.

Pope, Ernest R. *Munich Playground.* New York: Putnam's, 1941.

Poppelreuter, Walther. *Hitler.* Langensalza, 1934. (Heft, 1931 v. Friedr. Mann' padagog. Magazin, pp. 1–41.)

Pottmann, Karl. *Hitler—Entwicklungsmoeglichkeiten.* Oxford: Blackfriars, 1933. 14:450–454.

Price, George Ward. *I Know These Dictators.* London: Harrap, 1937.

Radek, K. "Hitler." *Nation* 134 (1932):462–464.

Radziwill, C. and Zierkursch, T.v. "Three Women Behind the Demagogue." *Pictorial Review* 34 (1933):7.

Raleigh, John McCutcheon. *Behind the Nazi Front.* New York: Dodd, 1940.

Ramsdell, E. T. "Hitler Adored and Hated." *Christian Century* 51 (1934):971.

Rauschning, Anna. *No Retreat.* New York: Bobbs Merrill, 1942.

Rauschning, Hermann. *The Beast from the Abyss.* London: Heinemann, 1941.

———. *The Conservative Revolution.* New York: Putnam's, 1941.

———. *Gesprache mit Hitler (Voice of Destruction).* New York: Europa Verlag, 1940.

———. *Hitler and the War.* American Council on Public Affairs, 1940.

————. *Men of Chaos.* New York: Putnam's, 1942.

————. *The Revolution of Nihilism.* New York: Alliance Book Corp., 1939.

Reich, Albert. *Aus Adolf Hitlers Heimat.* 1933.

Reveille, Thomas (pseud.). *The Spoil of Europe.* New York: Norton, 1941.

Reynolds, Bernard Talbot. *Prelude to Hitler.* London: J. Cape, 1933.

Ribbentrop, Manfred v. *Um den Fuehrer.* Volkische Reihe im Winterverlag, no. 1 (1933).

Riess, Curt. *The Self-Betrayed.* New York: Putnam's, 1942.

Riesse, G. "Hitler und die Armee." *Deutsche Republik,* vol. 4 (1930).

Ritter, Walther. *Adolf Hitler.* Leipzig: Verlag Nationalsoz Front, 1933.

Robert, Karl (pseud.). *Hitler's Counterfeit Reich.* New York: Alliance Book Corp., 1941.

Roberts, Stephen H. *The House That Hitler Built.* New York, 1938.

————. "Riddle of Hitler." *Harper's Magazine* 176 (1938):246–254.

Roch, Hans. "Gott segne den Kanzler." Rundfunkrede. April 20, 1933.

Roehm, Ernst. *Die Geschichte eines Hochverraters.* Munich: F. Eher, 1933.

Rogge, Heinrich. *Hitlers Friedenspolitik.* Berlin: Schlieffen, 1935.

Roper, Edith and Leiser, Clara. *Skeleton of Justice.* New York: Dutton, 1941.

Rothe, M. "Siegesallee II (A. Hitler)." *Die Tat* 21:780–784.

Santoro, Cesare. *Hitler Deutschland . . .* Berlin: inter. Nat. Verlag, 1938.

————. *Vier Jahre Hitlerdeutschland . . .* 1937.

Schacher, Gerhard. *He Wanted to Sleep in the Kremlin.* New York, 1942.

Scharping, K. "Why I Like Hitler." *Living Age* 349 (1935):303–306.

Scheffer, P. "Hitler Phenomenon and Portent." *Foreign Affairs* 10 (1932): 382–390.

Scheid, O. *Les memoires de Hitler.* Paris: Perrin, 1933.

Scher, Pet. "Hitlergesandter bei Ford." *Das Tagebuch* 7 (1928):628.

Schirach, Baldur V. *Die Pioniere des Dritten Reichs*. Essen, 1933.

Schmidt-Pauli, Edgar v. *Adolf Hitler*. Berlin: De Vo Verlag, 1934.

———. *Hitlers Kampf um die Macht*. Berlin, 1933.

———. *Die Maenner um Hitler*. Berlin: Verlag fuer Kulturpolitik, 1932 (Neue organzte Ausgabe, 1935).

Scholastic. "Hitler Crushes Foes . . ." 25 (1934):15.

Schott, Georg. *Das Volksbuch vom Hitler*. Munich: F. Eher, 1933.

Schrader, Fred Franklin. *The New Germany*. New York: Deutscher Weckruf & Beobachter, 1937.

Schroeder, Arno. *Hitler geht auf die Doerfer*. National. Soz. Verlag, 1938.

Schultze-Pfaelzer, Gerhard. *Hindenburg und Hitler*. Berlin: Stollberg, 1933.

Schulze, Kurt. *Adolf Hitler*. London: Harrap, 1935.

Schumann, Frederick Lewis. *Hitler and the Nazi Dictatorship*. London, 1936.

Schwarzschild, Leopold. "Ave Adolf." *Das Tagebuch* 12 (1931):1808.

———. *World in Trance*. New York, 1942.

Science News Letter. "Hitler's Personality Called: Paranoid, Infantile, Sadistic" 34 (1938):227–228.

Scyler, J. P. . . . *Hitler et son troisième empire*. Paris: L'Eglantine, 1933.

Seehofer, Herbert. *Mit dem Fuehrer unterwegs!* NSDAP, 1939.

Sender, Toni. *A Fighter for Peace*. New York: Vanguard, 1939.

Shirer, William L. *Berlin Diary*. New York: Knopf, 1941.

Shuster, George N. *Strong Man Rules*. New York, 1934.

Siebart, Werner. *Hitler's Wollen*. NSDAP, 1935.

Simone, Andre. *Men of Europe*. New York: Modern Age, 1941.

Smith, Howard K. *Last Train from Berlin*. New York, 1942.

Snyder, Louis (Nordicus, pseud.). *Hitlerism*. New York: Mohawk Press, 1932.

Sondern, F. Jr. "Schuschnigg's Terrible Two Hours." *Saturday Evening Post* 211 (1938):23.

Spencer, Franz. *Battles of a Bystander*. New York: Liveright, 1941.

Spiwak, J. L. "Hitler's Racketeers." *Reader's Digest* 28

(1936):52–54.

Starhemberg, Ernst and Rudiger, Prinz. *Between Hitler and Mussolini.* London: Hodder, 1942.

Stark, Johannes. *Adolf Hitler Ziele....* Deutscher Volksverlag, 1930.

Statist. "Hitler's Day" 123 (1934):161.

Steed, Henry Wickham. *Hitler Whence and Whither?* London: Nisbet, 1934.

Steel, Johannes. *Hitler als Frankenstein.* London, 1933.

Stern-Rubarth, E. "Heinrich Himmler, Hitler's Fouche, Head of Gestapo." *Contemporary Review* 158 (1940):641–645.

Steyrer Zeitung. "Adolf Hitler als Schueler in Steyr, April 17, 1938.

Stoddard, Lothrop. *Into the Darkness.* New York: Duell, 1940.

Strasser, Otto. *Aufbau des deutschen Sozialismus.* Prag. i., Heinrich Grunow, 1936.

———. *Die deutsche Bartholomausnacht.* Zurich: Reso Verlag, 1935.

———. *Flight from Terror.*

———. *Free Germany against Hitler.* Brooklyn, N.Y., 1941.

———. *Hitler and I.* Boston: Houghton, 1940.

Stresemann, Gustav. *Letters and Diaries.* London: MacMillan, 1935–1940.

Tacitus Redivivus (pseud.). *Die Grosse Trommel.*

Taylor, Edmond. *The Strategy of Terror.* Boston: Houghton, 1940. rev. ed., 1942.

Teeling, William. *Know Thy Enemy!* London: Nicholson, 1939.

Tennant, E. W. D. "Herr Hitler and His Policy." *English Review* 56 (1933):362–375.

Tesson, Francois de. *Voici Adolf Hitler.* Paris: Flammarion, 1936.

Thompson, Dorothy. "Good bye to Germany." *Harper's Magazine,* December 1934.

Thyssen, F. "I Made a Mistake When I Backed Hitler." *American Magazine* 130 (1940):16–17.

———. *I Paid Hitler.* New York: Farrar, 1941.

———. *I Saw Hitler.* New York, 1932.

Time. "Aggrandizer's Anniversary" 33 (1939):23–24.

———. "Critic Hitler" 30 (1937):32–A2.

———. "Dictator's Hour" 37 (1941):26–28.

———. "Eleven Minutes: Hitler's Narrow Escape" 34 (1939):21–22.

———. "Fuehrer's Next" 33 (1939):22.

———. "Happy Birthday" 37 (1941):22–23.

———. "Happy Hitler" 36 (1940):18.

———. "Hitler Comes Home" 31 (1938):18–22.

———. "Hitler's Throat" 32 (1938):55.

———. "Hitler Takes a Trip" 36 (1940):28.

———. "Hitler vs. Hitler" 33 (1939):20.

———. "Inside Hitler" 39 (1942):43.

———. "Let's Be Friends" 27 (1936):21–22.

———. "Man of the Year" 33 (1939):11–14.

———. "Mississippi Frontier, K. H. v. Wiegand's Interview" 35 (1940):37–38.

———. "Office and Official Residence" 33 (1939):17–18.

———. "Orator Hitler" 37 (1941):19.

———. "Two Diagnoses" 33 (1939):22.

Tolischus, Otto D. "Portrait of a Revolutionary." *New York Times Magazine*. May 19, 1940, p. 3.

———. *They Wanted War*. New York: Reynolds, 1940.

Toller, E. "Reichskanzler Hitler." *Weltbuehne*, p. 537.

Tourley, Robert and Lvovsky, Z. *Hitler*. Paris: Editions du siècle, 1932.

Trossman, Karl. *Hitler und Rom*. Nuremberg: Sebaldus Verlag, 1931.

Trotzky, Leon. "How Long Can Hitler Stay?" *American Mercury* 31 (1934):1–17.

———. *What Hitler Wants*. New York: John Day Co., 1933.

Tschuppik, Karl. "Hitler spricht." *Das Tagebuch*, vol. 498 (1927).

Turner, James. *Hitler and the Empire*. London, 1937.

Ullstein, H. "We Blundered Hitler into Power." *Saturday Evening Post* 213 (1940):12–13.

Umbell, H. D. "Dept of Brief Biography. Reply to Emil Ludwig." *Forum* 98 (suppl., 1937):10–11.

Unruh, Fritz v. "Hitler in Action." *Living Age*, August 1931, p. 551.

Verges, Ferni. *El Pangermanisme abans de Hitler*. Revista de Catalunya, 1938. juny 15, pp. 213–225.

Vie des Peuples. *Adolf Hitler*. Année 4. Paris, 1923. Pp. 536–544.

Villard, O. G. "Folly of Adolf Hitler." *Nation* 136 (1933):392.

——. "Hitler's Me and Gott." *Nation* 139 (1934):119.

——. "Issues and Men." *Nation* 143 (1936):395.

——. "Nazi Child-Mind." *Nation* 137 (1933):614.

Voight, F. A. *Unto Caesar*. New York: Putnam's, 1938.

Wagner, Ludwig. *Hitler, Man of Strife*. New York: Norton, 1942.

Waldeck, Countess. "Girls Did Well under Hitler." *Saturday Evening Post* 215 (1942):18.

Wallach, Sidney. *Hitler, Menace to Mankind*. Emerson Books, 1933.

Weltbuehne. "Hitler und die Japaner" 22 (1926):672.

——. "Mit Gott fuer Hitler und Vaterland" 21 (1925):720.

Wendel, Friedrich. *Der Gendarm von Hildburghausen*. Berlin: Dietz, 1932.

What Hitler Did Not Want the English Speaking Countries to Know. Paris: Centre d'Information documentaire. Pamphlets 5.

Wheeler-Bennett, John. *The Wooden Titan*. 1936.

White, W. C. "Hail Hitler: M." *Scribner* 9 (1932):229–231.

Whittlesey, Derwent. *German Strategy of World Conquest*. New York, 1942.

Wiegand, Karl von. "Hitlers Fliegerei." *Weltbuehne* (1931), pp. 918–920.

——. "Hitler Foresees His End." *Cosmopolitan*, April 1939, pp. 28 ff.; May 1939, pp. 48 ff.

Wild, Alfons. *Hitler und das Christentum*. Augsburg: Hass., 1931.

Wilson, Sir Arnold. *Nineteenth Century*, October 1936, pp. 503–512.

Wir fliegen mit Hitler. Berlin: Deutsche Kulturwacht, 1934.

Wistinghausen, R. von. "Handsome Adolf, Reply." *Living Age* 341 (1931):185–186.

Wolf, John. *Nazi Germany*. London, 1934.

Wyl, Hans von. *Ein Schweizer erlebt Deutschland*. Zurich: Europa Verlag, 1938.

Ybarra, T. R. "Hitler." *Collier's* 94 (1934):50.

——. "Hitler Changes His Clothes." *Collier's* 95 (1935):12–13.

——. "Hitler on High." *Collier's* 100 (1937):21–22.

————. "Says Hitler, Interview." *Colliers* 29 (1933):17.

Yeats-Brown, F. "A Tory Looks at Hitler." *Living Age* 354 (1938):512–514.

Young, William Russel. *Berlin Embassy*. 1941.

Ziemer, Gregor. *Education for Death*. New York: Oxford University Press, 1941.

Ziemer, Patsy. *2010 Days of Hitler*. New York: Harper, 1940.

INDEX

Academy of Art, Vienna, 121, 185

Amann, Max, 128

anti-Semitism, 44, 54, 124, 125, 161, 187–189, 194, 197–199, 201, 207, 225–227, 228, 235–237, 239

Antonescu, Ion, 236

Aristotle, 73

Austin Riggs Center, Massachusetts, 223

Barzun, Jacques, 223

Bayles, Will D., 85

Bechstein, Frau Helena, 91, 94

Bechstein, Lottie, 94

Becker, Carl, 223

Beer Hall Putsch, 43, 47, 51, 87, 171, 201–202

Berchtesgaden, 37, 47, 58, 61, 81, 95, 97, 98, 102, 115, 116, 170, 216

Billing, R., 78

Bloch, Eduard, 111, 112, 116, 118, 120, 121, 124, 183–184, 236

Blood-Purge, 87, 99, 128

Bockelsson, Jan, 215

Bracher, Karl Dietrich, 226–227, 233

Braddick, Henderson B., 33

Braun, Eva, see Hitler, Eva Braun

Bromberg, Norbert, 223, 235

Brown House, Munich, 170

Bullock, Alan, 225, 233

Castro, F., 32

Catholic Church, 74, 76

Chamberlain, Neville, 94, 187

Churchill, Winston, 154, 236

Communists, 76, 96, 130, 200, 207

Coordinator of Information, 13, 17

Czechoslovakia, 60

Danzig, 102

Diem, Ngo Dinh, 32

Dirksen, Frau Victoria von, 94

Dollfuss, Engelbert, 107, 108

Donovan, William J., vii–viii, 13, 14, 15, 16, 17, 19–20, 21, 22–23, 29, 30, 234

Dowling, Bridget, 113

Eckart, Dietrich, 44

Einstein, A., 233

Erikson, Erik, 223, 229, 235

Federal Bureau of Investigation (FBI), 22, 23

Flanner, Janet, 55

Flannery, Harry W., 89

Foerster (gauleiter), 178

Francois-Poncet (Ambassador), 174, 200, 204

Frank, Hans, 136, 237

Freud, S., 26, 148, 233

Fromm, Bella, 88–89, 90

Fry, Michael, 91, 137

Fuchs, Martin, 37

gauleiters, 100, 101, 178

Geli, see Raubal, Geli

Gestapo, 136, 234, 237

Goebbels, Joseph, 77, 91, 93

Goebbels, Mrs. J., 95

Goering, Hermann, W., 76, 91, 93, 115, 201

Gruber, Max von, 52

Gunther, John, 112

Strasser, Otto, 23, 38, 40, 54,
82, 83, 84, 86, 91–92, 94,
128, 176, 179, 204–205,
208, 229, 232
Streicher, Julius, 86, 91
Stuck, Franz von, 222

Taylor, A. J. P., 224
Teeling, William, 64
Thompson, Dorothy, 52, 65
Thyssen, F., 75, 107, 136
Tischgespraeche, 234
Trevelyan, G. M., 227
Trevor-Roper, Hugh, 224
Tschuppik, Karl, 53–54

U.S. Department of State, 23
Upper Austrian Archives,
Linz, 234, 236

Vienna, 77, 87, 92, 120–126,
130, 131, 145–146, 152,
157, 164, 165, 170, 184–
186, 192, 195, 198, 234,
236, 237
Voigt, F. A., 84, 133

Wagner, Friedelinde, 47, 83,
93, 94, 95, 101, 127, 229
Wagner (gauleiter), 100
Wagner, Ludwig, 45
Wagner, Richard, 43, 57–58,
62, 95, 100, 174
Wagner, Siegfried, 95
Wagner, Winifred, 91, 95
Waite, Robert G. L., 221–241
White, W. C., 45
Wiedemann (Captain), 127
Wiegand, Karl von, 40, 42, 45,
58, 84, 93, 137
Wilhelm II, 213
Wolf (dog), 221–222, 240
Wolf, Frau, *see* Hitler, Paula
Wolf, Johanna, 222
Wolf (nickname), 91, 94, 95,
116, 221
Wolf's Gulch, 222
Wolf's Lair, 222
Woollcott, Alexander, 221

Yeates-Brown, F., 55

Zeissler, A., 136, 175
Ziemer, Patsy, 64

Related Titles from MERIDIAN

(0452)

☐ **THE GERMANS by Gordon A. Craig.** Written by one of the most distinguished historians of modern Germany, this provocative study traces the evolution of the postwar German character by carefully looking at the past and offering a fascinating perspective on Germany today.
(006228—$8.95)

☐ **THE WEIMAR CHRONICLE: Prelude to Hitler by Alex deJonge.** This living portrait of the ill-fated Weimar Republic begins with the abdication of Kaiser Wilhelm II and culminates with Hitler's assumption of office. Eyewitness accounts, diary extracts, newspaper reports and personal reminiscences give a vivid portrayal of those fascinating years.
(005159—$5.95)

☐ **VOICES FROM THE HOLOCAUST edited by Sylvia Rothchild.** Introduction by Eli Wiesel. A vivid, moving, and totally honest re-creation of the lives of 30 ordinary people caught in the tragic cataclysm of the war against the Jews, this unique oral history tells what it was like to grow up Jewish in Europe, to survive Hitler's "final solution," and to rebuild a new life in America. The stories told here taken from tapes held in the William E. Weiner Oral History Library. (006910—$8.95)

☐ **SOLDIERS OF THE NIGHT: The Story of the French Resistance by David Schoenbrun.** Schoenbrun, a journalist who saw the Resistance up close as an American intelligence agent and war correspondent, vividly details isolated acts of defiance which changed the course of the war. Photos. "A prodigious work. . . ."—*The Saturday Review*
(006120—$9.95)

☐ **THE MAKING OF EUROPE by Christopher Dawson.** An introduction to the history of European unity. One of the major historical works of the 20th century. Illustrated. "Admirable . . . The Dark Ages lose their darkness, take on form and significance."—Aldous Huxley.
(004020—$3.95)

All prices higher in Canada.

To order, use the convenient coupon on the next page.

Ⓟ